P9-CAL-949

Microsoft® Word® 2002

fast&easy®

Check the Web for Updates:

To check for updates or corrections relevant to this book and/or CD-ROM visit our updates page on the Web at **http://www.prima-tech.com/support**.

Send Us Your Comments:

To comment on this book or any other PRIMA TECH title, visit our reader response page on the Web at **http://www.prima-tech.com/comments**.

How to Order:

For information on quantity discounts, contact the publisher: Prima Publishing, P.O. Box 1260BK, Rocklin, CA 95677-1260; (916) 787-7000. On your letterhead, include information concerning the intended use of the books and the number of books you want to purchase. For individual orders, turn to the back of this book for more information.

Microsoft® Word® 2002

fast&easy®

Diane Koers

PRIMA
TECH

A Division of Prima Publishing

© 2001 by Prima Publishing. All rights reserved. No part of this book may be reproduced or transmitted in any form or by any means, electronic or mechanical, including photocopying, recording, or by any information storage or retrieval system without written permission from Prima Publishing, except for the inclusion of brief quotations in a review.

A Division of Prima Publishing

Prima Publishing and colophon and Fast & Easy are registered trademarks of Prima Communications, Inc. PRIMA TECH is a trademark of Prima Communications, Inc., Roseville, California 95661.

Publisher: Stacy L. Hiquet

Associate Marketing Manager: Heather Buzzingham

Managing Editor: Sandy Doell

Acquisitions Editor: Debbie Abshier

Technical Reviewer: Randall Clark

Editorial and Production: Argosy

Copy Editor: Howard Jones

Cover Design: Prima Design Team

Microsoft, Windows, and Word are either registered trademarks or trademarks of Microsoft Corporation in the United States and/or other countries.

Important: Prima Publishing cannot provide software support. Please contact the appropriate software manufacturer's technical support line or Web site for assistance.

Prima Publishing and the author have attempted throughout this book to distinguish proprietary trademarks from descriptive terms by following the capitalization style used by the manufacturer.

Information contained in this book has been obtained by Prima Publishing from sources believed to be reliable. However, because of the possibility of human or mechanical error by our sources, Prima Publishing, or others, the Publisher does not guarantee the accuracy, adequacy, or completeness of any information and is not responsible for any errors or omissions or the results obtained from use of such information. Readers should be particularly aware of the fact that the Internet is an ever-changing entity. Some facts may have changed since this book went to press.

ISBN: 0-7615-3393-1

Library of Congress Catalog Card Number: 200186692

Printed in the United States of America

01 02 03 04 05 DD 10 9 8 7 6 5 4 3 2 1

To: My grandsons – I love you!

Contents at a Glance

Introduction xxiii

PART I
CREATING YOUR FIRST DOCUMENT 1

Chapter 1   Getting Started with Word 3
Chapter 2   Getting Help 21
Chapter 3   Saving, Opening, Closing, and Printing. 31
Chapter 4   Working with Multiple Windows 49
Chapter 5   Editing Text 55

PART II
MAKING YOUR DOCUMENTS LOOK GOOD 75

Chapter 6   Working with Pages. 77
Chapter 7   Arranging Text on a Page 91
Chapter 8   Using Fonts Effectively 99
Chapter 9   Inserting Special Characters 115
Chapter 10   Working with Lists 123

PART III
ADDING VISUAL INTEREST 135

Chapter 11   Communicating Ideas with Art 137
Chapter 12   Creating WordArt 149
Chapter 13   Using the Drawing Toolbar 159

PART IV
USING TABLES, CHARTS, AND COLUMNS 167

Chapter 14	Working with Tables 169
Chapter 15	Creating Charts 195
Chapter 16	Using Newspaper Columns 215

PART V
USING THE WORD TOOLS 225

Chapter 17	Discovering Tools for Speed 227
Chapter 18	Discovering Tools for Quality 243
Chapter 19	Using Mail Merge to Create Form Letters 253
Chapter 20	Creating Envelopes and Labels 267

PART VI
WORKING WITH LONG DOCUMENTS 287

Chapter 21	Working with Paragraph Styles 289
Chapter 22	Discovering Templates 301
Chapter 23	Adding Headers and Footers 313
Chapter 24	Working with Footnotes or Endnotes 319

PART VII
USING WORD TECHNOLOGY 333

| Chapter 25 | Using Word to Create Web Pages . . . . 335 |
| Chapter 26 | Speaking with Word . . . . 357 |

PART VIII
APPENDIXES 379

| Appendix A | Installing Microsoft Office XP . . . . 381 |
| Appendix B | Using Keyboard Shortcuts . . . . 397 |

| Glossary | . . . . 403 |
| Index | . . . . 409 |

Contents

Introduction xxiii

PART I
CREATING YOUR FIRST DOCUMENT 1

Chapter 1   **Getting Started with Word**. 3

Starting Word 4

Discovering the Word Screen 5

Using Personalized Menus 6

Using Toolbars 8

    Moving a Toolbar 9

    Viewing Additional Toolbars 10

Working with the Task Pane 10

    Changing Task Panes 11

    Closing the Task Pane 11

    Redisplaying the Task Pane 12

Entering Text 13

Moving Around the Screen 14

    Using Click and Type 14

    Using the Scroll Bars 16

    Using the Keyboard to Move Around 18

    Using the Go To Command 18

Chapter 2   **Getting Help**. **21**

Using the Office Assistant 22

    Asking the Assistant for Help 22

    Having Fun with Office Assistant 24

    Choosing a Different Assistant 25

    Hiding the Assistant 26

    Turning Off the Assistant 27

Using What's This? 28

Searching the Web for Help 30

Chapter 3   **Saving, Opening, Closing, and Printing** **31**

Saving Your Document 32

    Saving a Document the First Time 32

    Resaving a Document 34

Enabling AutoRecover 34

Creating a New Document 36

    Creating a New Document Using the Toolbar 36

    Creating a New Document Using the Task Pane 36

Closing a Document 37

Opening an Existing Document 38

    Displaying the Open Dialog Box 38

    Opening A Recently Used Document 40

E-mailing a Document 40

Printing a Document 41

    Using Print Preview 41

    Printing with the Print Button 44

    Printing from the Menu 45

    Scaling Your Document for Printing 46

Exiting Word 48

Chapter 4   **Working with Multiple Windows** **49**

Arranging Windows 50

Splitting a Window 50

Removing the Split 51

Moving Between Documents 52

Viewing Multiple Documents Together 52

Restoring a Window to Maximized Size 53

Chapter 5   **Editing Text** **55**

Inserting, Selecting, and Deleting Text 56

Inserting Text 56

Selecting Text 57

Deleting Text 58

Changing Text Case 59

Using Undo and Redo 60

Undoing the Previous Step 60

Redoing the Previous Step 61

Undoing a Series of Actions 61

Moving and Copying Text 62

Moving Text 62

Copying Text 64

Using Drag and Drop 66

Using the Office Clipboard 67

Discovering Smart Tags 69

Using Smart Tags with the Clipboard 69

Adding Contact Information from a Smart Tag 71

Displaying Nonprinting Symbols 72

PART II
MAKING YOUR DOCUMENTS LOOK GOOD 75

Chapter 6   **Working with Pages** **77**

Setting Margins 78

Setting Margins for the Entire Document 78

Adjusting Margins for Part of a Document 79

Changing Document Orientation 81

Setting the Paper Size 82

Working with Page Breaks 83

    Inserting a Page Break 83

    Deleting a Page Break 85

Viewing a Document 86

    Viewing in Print Layout View 86

    Viewing in Normal View 87

    Using the Zoom Feature 88

Chapter 7   **Arranging Text on a Page**. **91**

Working with Tabs 92

    Setting Tabs 92

    Moving a Tab 94

    Deleting a Tab 94

Changing Line Spacing 95

Aligning Text 96

Chapter 8   **Using Fonts Effectively**. **99**

Selecting a Font and Font Size 100

    Choosing a Font 100

    Choosing a Font Size 101

    Applying Bold, Italic, or Underline 102

    Applying Color 103

Highlighting Text 104

Using Special Effects and Animation 105

    Applying a Font Special Effect 105

    Adding Animation to Text 106

Copying Formatting to Another Selection 108

Using the Styles and Formatting Task Pane 110

    Identifying Text Characteristics 111

    Applying Formatting 111

Clearing Formatting 112

Changing the Default Font 113

Chapter 9   Inserting Special Characters 115

Using Drop Caps 116

Creating a Drop Cap 116

Removing a Drop Cap 119

Inserting Special Characters and Symbols 120

Chapter 10   Working with Lists 123

Using AutoFormat As You Type 124

Using AutoFormat to Create a List 124

Turning Off AutoFormat 126

Working with Bulleted or Numbered Lists 127

Switching Between Bulleted and Numbered Lists 128

Changing a List Style 129

Creating Multilevel Numbered Lists 130

Removing Bullet or Number Formatting 133

PART III
ADDING VISUAL INTEREST 135

Chapter 11   Communicating Ideas with Art 137

Inserting Clip Art 138

Inserting Personal Images 140

Customizing Art 141

Resizing Art 141

Moving Art 142

Adjusting the Brightness or Contrast 143

Cropping the Picture 145

Wrapping Text Around Art 146

Deleting Art 148

Chapter 12   Creating WordArt **149**

Adding WordArt 150

Making Adjustments to the WordArt 152

Editing WordArt 152

Reshaping an Object 154

Moving Objects on a Page 155

Rotating WordArt 157

Chapter 13   Using the Drawing Toolbar **159**

Displaying the Drawing Toolbar 160

Working with AutoShapes 160

Drawing AutoShapes 160

Adding Text to Objects 162

Creating Shadows 163

Making Shapes 3-Dimensional 164

PART IV
USING TABLES, CHARTS, AND COLUMNS 167

Chapter 14   Working with Tables **169**

Creating a Simple Table 170

Inserting a Table Using the Menu 170

Creating a Table using the Toolbar 172

Using the Draw Table Feature 172

Entering Text 175

Moving Around in a Table 176

Adjusting Column Width 176

Changing Column Width Using the Mouse 177

Using AutoFit 178

Formatting Cell Contents 178

Aligning Cell Contents 178

Formatting Text in Cells 180

Using AutoFormat 181

Using AutoSum 182

Totaling Cells with AutoSum 182

Updating AutoSum Totals 183

Adding and Deleting
Rows and Columns 184

Adding a Row to the End of a Table 184

Inserting a Row between Existing Rows 185

Inserting a Column 186

Deleting Rows or Columns 187

Erasing Cell Partitions 188

Changing the Direction of Your Text 189

Modifying Table Cell Borders 190

Adding a Table Heading Row 191

Moving a Table 192

Chapter 15   Creating Charts **195**

Creating a Chart from a Table 196

Resizing a Chart 199

Editing a Chart 201

Hiding the Datasheet 201

Adding a Chart Title 202

Formatting Chart Text 203

Modifying Chart Colors and Patterns 204

Selecting Bar Shapes 206

Changing the Chart Type 207

Editing Chart Data 209

Deleting a Chart 210

Creating a Chart from Scratch 210

Chapter 16   Using Newspaper Columns **215**

Creating Newspaper Columns 216

Changing the Number of Columns 217

Changing Column Width 218

   Changing the Width of Columns 218

   Changing the Width of Space Between Columns 219

Creating Vertical Lines Between Columns 220

Removing Newspaper Columns 222

PART V
USING THE WORD TOOLS 225

Chapter 17   Discovering Tools for Speed. 227

Working with AutoCorrect 228

   Turning AutoCorrect Features On and Off 228

   Adding AutoCorrect Entries 229

   Deleting AutoCorrect Entries 230

   Exploring AutoFormat as You Type 231

Using AutoText 232

   Working with AutoComplete 232

   Creating Your Own AutoText Entry 233

   Inserting AutoText Using the Menu 235

   Deleting AutoText Entries 236

Using Find and Replace 237

   Using Find 237

   Using Replace 239

Finding Document Statistics 242

Chapter 18   Discovering Tools for Quality 243

Correcting Spelling and Grammatical Errors 244

   Checking Spelling as You Go 244

   Checking Grammar as You Go 245

   Running a Spelling and Grammar Check 246

   Disabling Grammar Check 249

Finding that Elusive Word with the Thesaurus 250

Chapter 19   Using Mail Merge to Create Form Letters **253**

Creating the Main Document 254

Specifying Data for Your Mail Merge 255

    Creating the Data Source 255

    Adding Additional Data Fields 257

    Selecting Recipients 259

    Inserting Merge Fields 260

Previewing the Mail Merge 263

Chapter 20   Creating Envelopes and Labels **267**

Generating a Single Envelope 268

Creating Merged Envelopes 270

    Opening a Data File 272

    Arranging Data on the Envelope 274

    Completing the Merge 275

Creating Merged Mailing Labels 277

PART VI
WORKING WITH LONG DOCUMENTS 287

Chapter 21   Working with Paragraph Styles **289**

Displaying the Style Area 290

Working with Word Styles 292

Creating New Styles 293

    Using an Example to Create a New Style 293

    Creating a New Style from Scratch 295

Deleting a Style 297

Revealing Formatting 298

Chapter 22   Discovering Templates **301**

Using a Word Template 302

Saving a File as a Template 304

Applying a Template 306

Editing a Template 308

Deleting a Template 311

Chapter 23 Adding Headers and Footers **313**

Inserting a Header or Footer 314

Adding Date, Time, or Page Number 315

Arranging Headers and Footers on Different Pages 317

Chapter 24 Working with Footnotes or Endnotes **319**

Creating a Footnote or Endnote 320

Copying Notes 324

Moving Notes 326

Deleting a Footnote or Endnote 327

Converting a Footnote to an Endnote 328

PART VII
USING WORD TECHNOLOGY **333**

Chapter 25 Using Word to Create Web Pages **335**

Saving a Word Document as a Web Document 336

Creating a New Web Page 338

Using the Web Page Wizard 338

Using Word Themes 343

Editing a Web Page 346

Typing Text 346

Adding Scrolling Text 347

Including a Background Sound 350

Inserting Links 351

Inserting a Picture 352

Saving Your Web Pages 352

Viewing the Document in Internet Explorer 354

Publishing Web Documents 355

Chapter 26 **Speaking with Word** **357**

Installing Speech 358

    Setting up Your Microphone 359

    Training Speech Recognition 361

Understanding the Language Bar 365

    Moving the Language Bar 365

    Hiding the Language Bar 366

Speaking Into Word 367

    Making Corrections 370

    Creating Special Words 372

    Dictating Menu Commands 374

Working with the Keyboard Commands 376

Handwriting 376

PART VIII
APPENDIXES **379**

Appendix A **Installing Microsoft Office XP** **381**

Understanding System Requirements 382

Installing Office XP 383

    Installing with Default Settings 384

    Installing Office Components 386

Working in Maintenance Mode 390

    Repairing or Reinstalling Office 391

    Adding or Removing Components 393

    Uninstalling Microsoft Office 394

Appendix B **Using Keyboard Shortcuts** **397**

Learning the Basic Shortcuts 398

    Getting Help 398

    Working with Documents 398

Working with Text 399

Selecting Text 399

Editing Text 400

Formatting Text 401

Speech Commands 402

Glossary **403**

Index **409**

Acknowledgments

I am deeply grateful to the many people at Prima Publishing who worked on this book. Thank you for all the time you gave and for your assistance.

Editors:
While I can't name everyone involved, I'd like to especially thank Debbie Abshier for the opportunity to write this book and her confidence in me; Howard Jones for his assistance in making this book grammatically correct; Randall Clark for his wonderful technical advice; and Caroline Roop for all her patience and guidance in pulling the project together. It takes a lot of both to work with me!

Lastly, a big hug and kiss to my husband, Vern, for his never-ending support and big shoulders for me to cry on.

About the Author

Diane **Koers** owns and operates All Business Service, a software training and consulting business formed in 1988 that services the central Indiana area. Her area of expertise has long been in the word processing, spreadsheet, and graphics area of computing as well as providing training and support for Peachtree Accounting Software. Diane's authoring experience includes 14 other Prima Publishing Fast & Easy books including *Windows Millennium Fast & Easy, WordPerfect 9 Fast & Easy, Paint Shop Pro 7 Fast & Easy, Office 2000 Fast & Easy, Office XP Fast & Easy,* and she has co-authored Prima's *Essential Windows 98.* She has also developed and written software training manuals for her clients' use.

Active in her church and civic activities, Diane enjoys spending her free time traveling and playing with her grandson and her three Yorkshire Terriers.

Introduction

Welcome to the world of Microsoft Word.

This new Fast & Easy book from Prima Publishing will help you use the many and varied features of one of Microsoft's most popular products—Microsoft Word.

Microsoft Word is a powerful word processing program that will take your documents far beyond what you can produce with a typewriter. Whether you want to create a simple letter to a friend, produce a newsletter for a professional organization, or even write a complicated, multiple page report containing graphics and tables with numerical data, you will find the information that you need to quickly and easily get the job done in the *Word 2002 Fast & Easy* guide.

This book uses a step-by-step approach with illustrations of what you will see on your screen, linked with instructions for the next mouse movements or keyboard operations to complete your task. Computer terms and phrases are clearly explained in non-technical language, and expert tips and shortcuts help you produce professional-quality documents.

Word 2002 Fast & Easy provides the tools you need to successfully tackle the potentially overwhelming challenge of learning to use Microsoft Word. Whether you are a novice user or an experienced professional, you will be able to quickly tap into the program's user-friendly integrated design and feature-rich environment.

Through this book you learn *how* to create documents, however, *what* you create is totally up to you—your imagination is the only limit! This book cannot begin to teach you everything you can do with Microsoft Word, nor does it give you all the different ways to accomplish a task. What I *have* tried to do is give you the fastest and easiest way to get started with this fun and exciting program.

This book is divided into seven parts and two appendices. In Part I, I show you how to create a basic document. While it's not the most exciting section of the book, it's certainly the most practical. Look out after that—things start to be lots of fun! In Parts II, III, and IV, you learn how to enhance the appearance of your documents with fonts, tables, and graphics. Parts V and VI illustrate ways to improve the quality of your document content. Part VII teaches you how Word's newest technological features enable you to create Web documents and even talk to your computer—allowing your voice to do the work instead of your fingers!

Two helpful appendixes show you how to install Microsoft Word and how to save your valuable time with keyboard shortcuts.

WHO SHOULD READ THIS BOOK?

This book can be used as a learning tool or as a step-by-step task reference. The easy-to-follow, highly visual nature of this book makes it the perfect learning tool for a beginning computer user as well as those seasoned computer users who are new to Microsoft Word. No prerequisites are required from you, the reader, except that you know how to turn your computer on and how to use your mouse.

In addition, anyone using a software application always needs an occasional reminder about the steps required to perform a particular task. By using the *Word 2002 Fast & Easy* guide, any level of user can look up steps for a task quickly without having to plow through pages of descriptions.

ADDED ADVICE TO MAKE YOU A PRO

You'll notice that this book uses steps and keeps explanations to a minimum to help you learn faster. Included in the book are a few elements that provide some additional comments to help you master the program, without encumbering your progress through the steps:

- **Tips** often offer shortcuts when performing an action, or a hint about a feature that might make your work in Word quicker and easier.
- **Notes** give you a bit of background or additional information about a feature, or advice about how to use the feature in your day-to-day activities.

Read and enjoy this Fast & Easy book. It certainly is the *fastest and easiest* way to learn Microsoft Word 2002.

—Diane Koers

PART I

Creating Your First Document

Chapter 1
Getting Started with Word 3

Chapter 2
Getting Help. 21

Chapter 3
Saving, Opening, Closing, and
Printing 31

Chapter 4
Working with Multiple Windows 49

Chapter 5
Editing Text. 55

1

Getting Started with Word

If this is your first opportunity to use Word, you may be a little intimidated by the vast array of buttons and icons on the opening screen. Just remember that although Word is a powerful program, it's also easy to use, which is why many businesses have adopted it. Don't worry! You'll be creating your first document after just a couple of mouse clicks. In this chapter, you'll learn how to:

- Start Word
- Use toolbars, menus and task panes
- Make selections in dialog boxes
- Enter text and move around the screen

Starting Word

Microsoft Word appears as an icon on the Programs menu of the Start button.

1. Click on the **Start button**. A pop-up menu will appear.

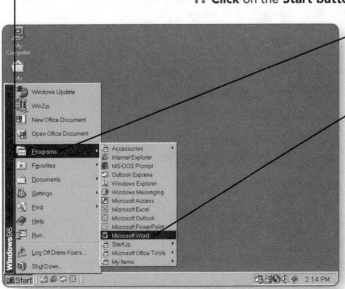

2. Move your **mouse** arrow up to **Programs**. Another pop-up menu will appear.

3. Click on **Microsoft Word**. The Welcome to Word screen will appear briefly before the main Word window appears.

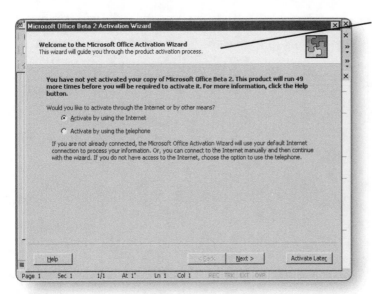

If this is the first time you have accessed Microsoft Word, the Activation Wizard will appear. You can only access Microsoft Office a total of 50 times without using the Activation Wizard. After the 50 uses, you will not be able to access Office until you register your product with the Activation Wizard.

Discovering the Word Screen

The Word screen includes a variety of items:

- **Title bar**. A bar displayed at the top of a document that displays the name of the current document.

- **Menu bar**. A grouping of all available features in the Microsoft Word program.

- **Toolbar**. A selection of commonly used features. A single click on a toolbar item activates the feature.

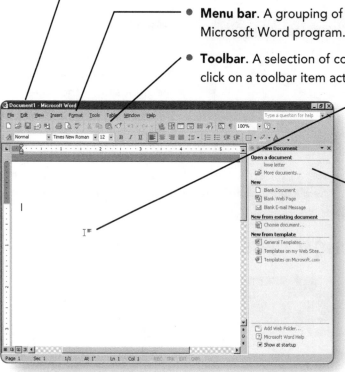

- **Mouse pointer**. The mouse pointer, which will change as it moves to different locations on the screen.

- **Task pane**. Small windows that assist you in working with Word. Task panes store collections of important features and present them in ways that are much easier to find and use. There are several different task panes.

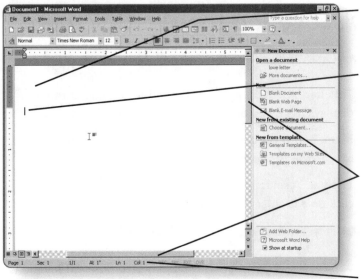

- **Document screen**. The white area of the screen where the actual text will appear.

- **Insertion point**. The blinking vertical line in the document screen that indicates where text will appear when you begin typing.

- **Scroll bars**. Horizontal and vertical bars on the bottom and right side of the screen that allow you to see more of a document.

- **Status bar**. A bar at the bottom of the screen indicating document information such as the current page or the location of the insertion point.

Using Personalized Menus

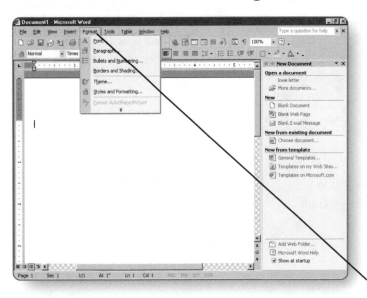

All Windows programs use menus to list items that you can select from, but Word has added personalized menus. When the menu is first accessed, only the most common features are displayed. If you pause the mouse over the top item on the menu bar or move it down to the double arrows at the bottom of a menu, the menu will expand to include all available features for that menu.

1. Click on **Format**. The Format menu will appear with seven options.

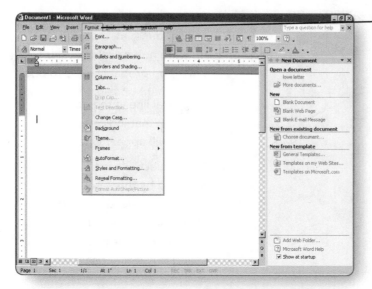

2. Pause the **mouse pointer** over the Format menu. The Format menu will expand to include 16 items.

TIP

Click on the top item of the menu bar to close a menu without making any selection.

When you see a right-pointing arrowhead in a menu, it means another menu is available.

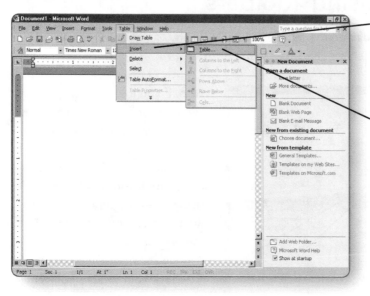

3. Move the **mouse arrow** down a menu until the item with the arrow is highlighted. A second menu will appear.

4. Move the **mouse arrow** to the right of your selection. The selection will be highlighted.

5. Click on a **selection**. The feature associated with that menu item will be activated.

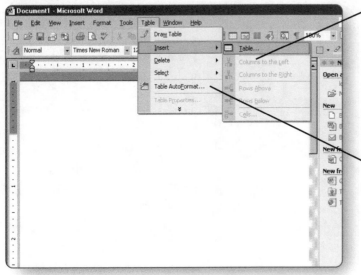

Some options in the menu may appear dimmed, meaning that they are not available at this time. You probably need to open a document or select text before you can use items that are dimmed.

Many selections in the menu are followed by three periods, called an *ellipsis*. Selections followed by ellipses indicate that, if you select one of these items, a dialog box will appear with more options.

Using Toolbars

Position the mouse pointer over any toolbar item to see a description of that feature.

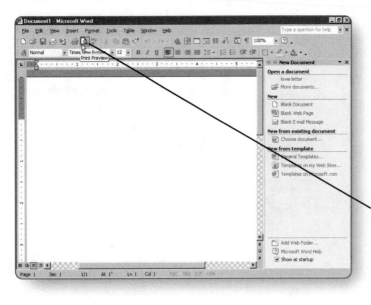

Also, if you look closely, you can see that the buttons have been grouped into related activities, so that, for example, the Alignment buttons (left, center, right, and justify) are together. Using these alignment buttons will be discussed in Chapter 7, "Arranging Text on a Page."

1. Place your **mouse pointer** over a button. The name of the button will appear.

2. Click on the **button**. The requested action will occur.

Moving a Toolbar

If a toolbar is not located in a favorable position for you to access, move it!

1. **Position** the **mouse pointer** at the far-left side of any toolbar. The mouse changes to a black cross with four arrowheads on it.

2. **Hold** down the mouse **button** and **drag** the **mouse** into the document area. The toolbar may change shape.

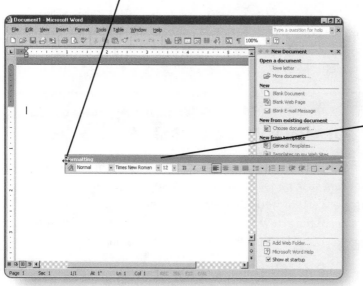

3. **Release** the **mouse button**. The toolbar will be moved.

TIP

To put a toolbar back in its original position, press and hold the mouse button over the toolbar title bar and drag it back up to the top of the screen.

Viewing Additional Toolbars

Word includes 19 different toolbars, and each has tools designed for specific tasks. You can display as many toolbars on your screen as you would like.

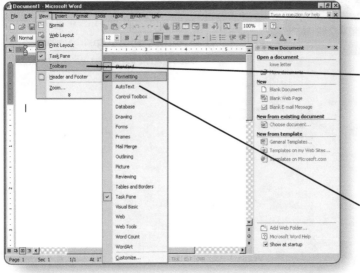

1. **Click** on **View**. The View menu will appear.

2. **Click** on **Toolbars**. The Toolbars submenu will appear, displaying a list of available toolbars. Toolbars that are currently displayed have a check mark beside them.

3. **Click** on a **toolbar** with no check mark beside it. The display of the toolbar will be turned on.

TIP

If you find you don't use the toolbars and they are taking up valuable screen space, click View, Toolbars and click on any checked toolbar to turn off the display of that toolbar.

Working with the Task Pane

The task pane is new to Word 2002. Actually, there are several different task panes, each of which appears when various Word tasks are attempted. One feature of the task pane will assist you in creating new documents, while another function will enable you to format your document more quickly.

Changing Task Panes

By default, Word displays the New Document task pane. The New Document task pane lists common features associated with creating a new document. As you select various functions of Word, the task pane changes automatically.

1. **Click** on the **task pane drop-down arrow**. A list of other task panes will appear.

2. **Click** on a **task pane name**. The selected task pane will appear.

Closing the Task Pane

You can choose to close the task pane during your current session of Word. The task pane will redisplay the next time you start Word.

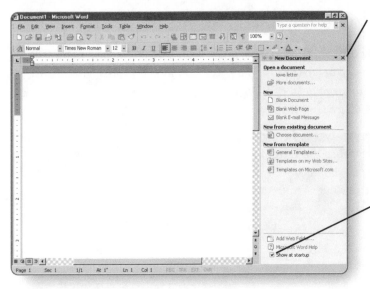

1. **Click** on the **Close button**. The task pane will close.

If you choose a Word feature (such as mail merge) that uses the task pane, the task pane will reappear.

TIP

Click on Show at Startup to remove the check mark, then click on the close button. The task pane will close. The next time you launch Word, the task pane will not automatically appear.

Redisplaying the Task Pane

As mentioned previously, if you choose a Word feature that used the task pane, it automatically reappears. You can, however, redisplay the task pane whenever you want it.

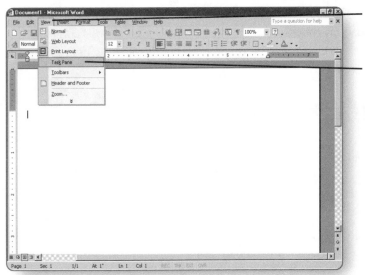

1. **Click** on **View**. The View menu will appear.

2. **Click** on **Task Pane**. The task pane reopens.

NOTE

For the purposes of this book, most screens will appear without the task pane, unless a feature that uses the task pane is being shown.

Entering Text

Notice that there is a flashing vertical bar on your screen. This is called the *insertion point*. It marks the location where text will appear when you type.

If you type a few lines of text, you'll notice that you don't need to press the Enter key at the end of each line. The program automatically moves down (or wraps) to the next line for you. This feature is called *word wrap*. You only press the Enter key to start a new paragraph.

1. Type a small amount of **text** such as today's date. The text will display on the screen.

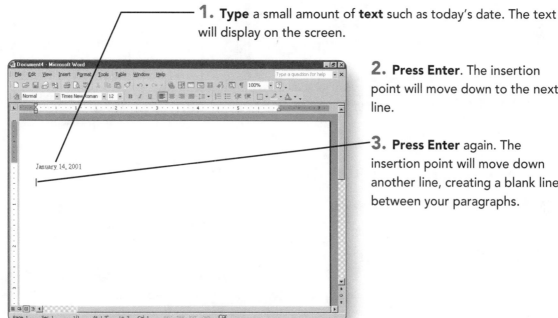

2. Press Enter. The insertion point will move down to the next line.

3. Press Enter again. The insertion point will move down another line, creating a blank line between your paragraphs.

4. **Type** a **paragraph** of **text**. Don't press Enter; just keep typing until you have several lines of text.

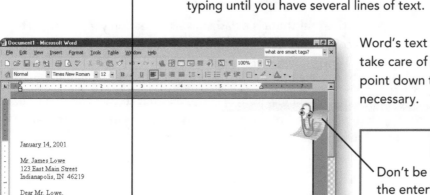

Word's text wrap feature will take care of moving the insertion point down to the next line when necessary.

NOTE

Don't be concerned about the entertaining paper clip that may appear on your screen. That's the Office Assistant, which we'll discuss in Chapter 2, "Getting Help."

Moving Around the Screen

To work with your document, you'll need to place the insertion point. You can use several methods to move around the Word screen, and Word includes a feature called Click and Type.

Using Click and Type

You can position the insertion point with the mouse and double-click where you would like to enter text.

The Click and Type feature does not work if you are using Word's Outline view or Normal view. Learn about Word's different views in Chapter 6, "Working with Pages."

Before double-clicking the mouse, pay close attention to the position of the lines surrounding the pointer. If the lines are to the right of the I-beam, the text you type will flow to the right of the insertion point. If the lines are to the left, the text will flow to the left of the insertion point. If the lines are under the I-beam, the text will be centered at the insertion point.

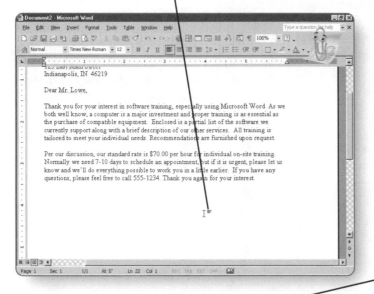

NOTE

If your mouse pointer doesn't appear with the little lines next to or below the mouse (make sure it's in the same position), the Click and Type feature may not be enabled. Click on Options from the Tools menu. On the Edit tab check the Enable click and type box.

1. Double-click the **mouse pointer** anywhere on the white text area of the screen. A blinking insertion point will appear.

NOTE

Word is actually placing a tab stop at the position of the double-click. Tabs are covered in Chapter 7, "Arranging Text on a Page."

2. Type some **text**. The text will appear at the insertion point you clicked.

Using the Scroll Bars

Two scroll bars are in the document window: a vertical scroll bar and a horizontal scroll bar. Displaying text by using the scroll bars does not move the insertion point. You'll need to click the mouse wherever you'd like the insertion point to be located.

1a. Click on the **arrow** at either end of the vertical scroll bar to move the document up or down in the window.

OR

1b. Click on the **arrow** at either end of the horizontal scroll bar to move the document left or right.

To move the document more quickly, use the scroll box.

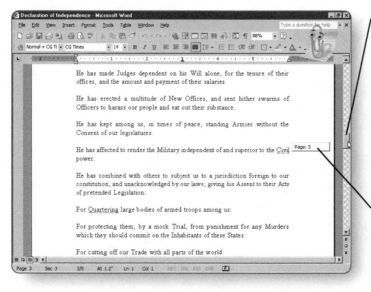

2. **Place** the mouse **pointer** on the **box** in the vertical or horizontal scroll bar.

3. **Press** and **hold** the left mouse button and **drag** the box up or down in the vertical scroll bar, or left or right in the horizontal scroll bar.

Notice that when you move the scroll box in the vertical scroll bar, if you have more than one page, an indicator box will appear telling you which page you're on.

4. **Release** the **mouse button** at the desired location. The screen will move to that location.

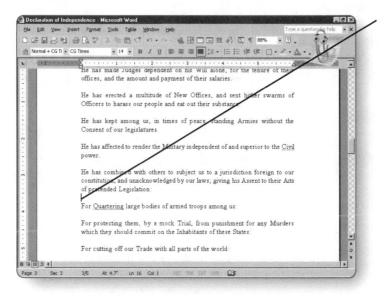

5. **Click** the **mouse pointer** in the body of the document. The insertion point will be moved.

Using the Keyboard to Move Around

As you've seen, you can work on any part of the document that shows on your screen by clicking the mouse pointer where you want to be. You also can move around in a Word document by pressing the Up, Down, Right, or Left Arrow keys on the keyboard.

There are several shortcut keys designed to speed up the process of moving around in a Word document. The following table illustrates these shortcut keys.

To Move	Do This
A word at a time	Press Ctrl+Right Arrow or Ctrl+Left Arrow
A paragraph at a time	Press Ctrl+Up Arrow or Ctrl+Down Arrow
A full screen up at a time	Press the PageUp key
A full screen down at a time	Press the PageDown key
To the beginning of a line	Press the Home key
To the end of a line	Press the End key
To the top of the document	Press Ctrl+Home
To the bottom of the document	Press Ctrl+End
To a specified page number	Press Ctrl+G; then enter the page number

Using the Go To Command

If you have a rather lengthy document, use the Go To command to jump to a specific location in the document.

1. **Click** on **Edit**. The Edit menu will appear.

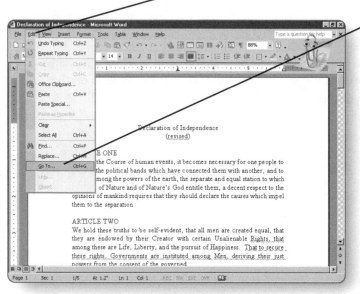

2. **Click** on **Go To**. The Go To page of the Find and Replace dialog box will appear.

NOTE

The Go To command is one of those commands that may not display immediately upon choosing the Edit menu. Hold the mouse over the Edit menu for a few seconds to display the full Edit menu.

TIP

Press Ctrl+G to quickly display the Go To page of the Find and Replace dialog box.

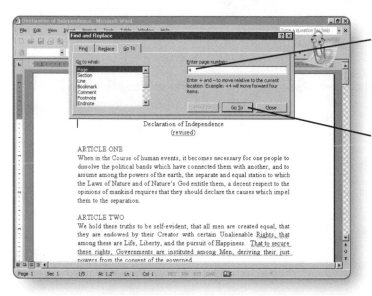

3. **Type** the **page number** you'd like to display. The number will appear in the Enter Page Number text box.

4. **Click** on **Go To**. The specified page will be displayed. The insertion point will be located at the beginning of the specified page.

2

Getting Help

Although you'll find many answers to your questions in this book, sometimes you need additional information. Microsoft supplies you with several types of assistance. In this chapter, you'll learn how to:

- Work with the Office Assistant
- Use the Help menu
- Get help on the Web

Using the Office Assistant

When you opened Word for the first time, you probably noticed that little paper clip trying to get your attention. That's Clippit, the Office Assistant, Word's Help feature.

Asking the Assistant for Help

What sets Office Assistant apart from other Word help is that you can use simple, everyday language to ask for help.

1. **Click** anywhere on the **Office Assistant**. A balloon will appear, asking, "What would you like to do?"

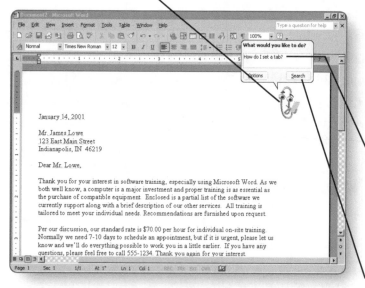

<table>
<tr><td>

TIP

Pressing F1 also brings up the Assistant query window.

</td></tr>
</table>

2. **Type** in a **question** or a word or two of what you're needing assistance with. An example might be "How do I set a tab?" The text will appear in the white text box.

3. **Click** on **Search**. A new window will appear with more choices related to your topic.

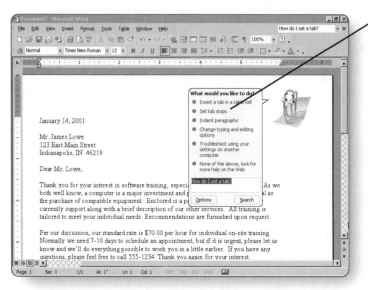

4. Click on the **topic** with which you need help. The help information window will appear on your screen.

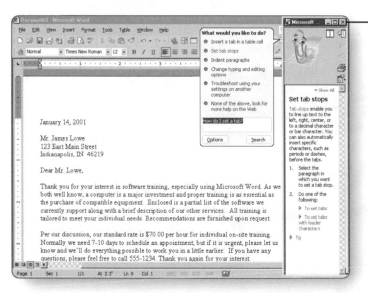

5. Click on the help **Close button** when you are finished reading the help topic. The help window will close and the Word window will return to full size.

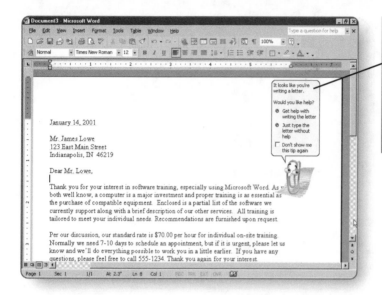

NOTE

Sometimes the Assistant will try to guess what you are doing and offer assistance. Click on an option for help or no help.

Having Fun with Office Assistant

Want to see Clippit do some tricks? He may not sit or roll over on command, but he can be quite entertaining!

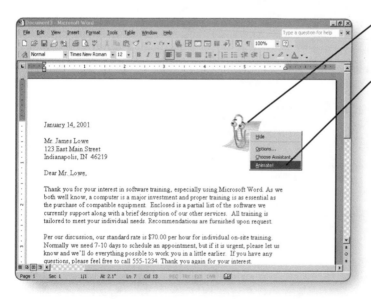

1. **Right-click** on the Assistant. A shortcut menu will appear.

2. **Click** on **Animate**. Clippit will perform some small trick on your screen.

Each time you choose Animate, Clippit picks a trick from its library.

Choosing a Different Assistant

Is Clippit, the helpful little piece of metal, getting a little dull or just not your style? You may be able to select a different icon for Office Assistant.

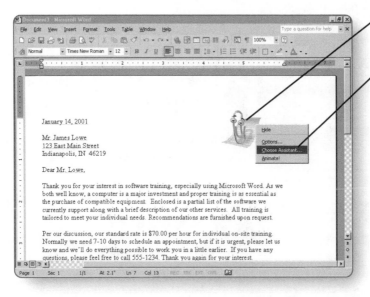

1. Right-click on the Assistant. A shortcut menu will appear.

2. Click on **Choose Assistant**. The Office Assistant dialog box will open with the Gallery tab on the top.

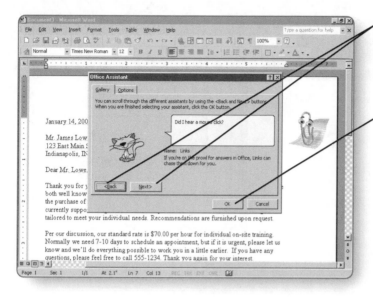

3. Click on **Back** or **Next** to view other Assistants. A picture and description of the available assistants will appear.

4. Click on **OK** when you see the one you want. The Office Assistant dialog box will close and you'll have a new helper!

NOTE

Depending upon the options selected when Word was installed, you may be prompted to insert your Word or Office CD.

Hiding the Assistant

The Office Assistant is cute, but sometimes it's just in your way. You can hide the Assistant and recall it whenever you need it.

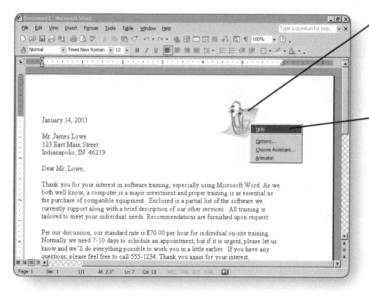

1. Right-click while the mouse pointer is positioned on top of the Office Assistant. A shortcut menu will appear.

2. Click on **Hide**. The Office Assistant will disappear.

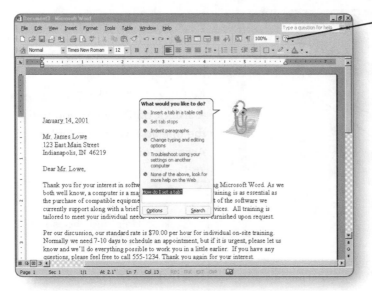

3. **Click** on the **Microsoft Word Help button**. The Office Assistant will reappear ready to answer your next query.

NOTE

If the Office Assistant is in the way when you are typing text in your document, it will automatically move as your insertion point gets close to it. You can also move it manually by clicking on top of it and dragging it to a new location.

Turning Off the Assistant

If you find you don't use the Office Assistant and don't want to see it, you can choose not to display it at all.

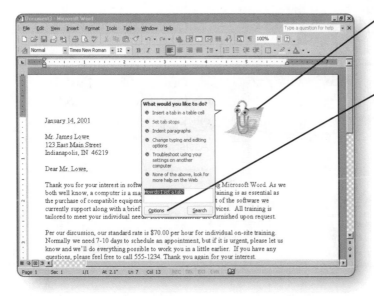

1. **Click** anywhere on the **Office Assistant**. The "What would you like to do?" balloon will appear.

2. **Click** on **Options**. The Office Assistant dialog box will open.

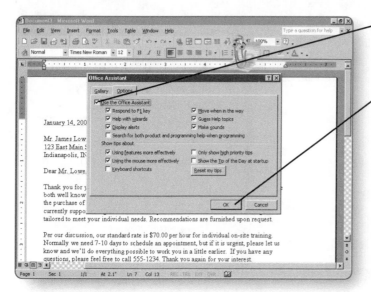

3. Click on **Use the Office Assistant**. The check mark will be removed from the box.

4. Click on **OK**. The Office Assistant will be turned off until you manually choose to use it again.

TIP

Click on Help and choose Show the Office Assistant to return the Assistant to an active status.

Using What's This?

There are so many items on a Word screen that it's hard to remember what each item is or does. Use the What's This? feature to identify the various buttons and components.

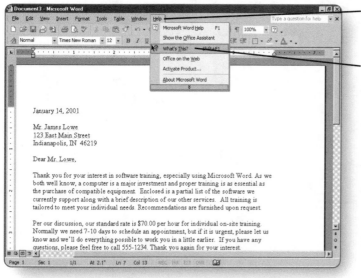

1. Click on **Help**. The Help menu will appear.

2. Click on **What's This?** The mouse pointer will change to a black pointer with a question mark.

TIP

Pressing Shift+F1 is another way to access the What's This? feature.

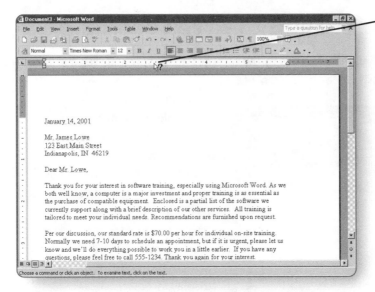

3. **Click** the **mouse pointer** over any button or item on the screen. A detailed information screen tip will appear explaining the function of the item you clicked on.

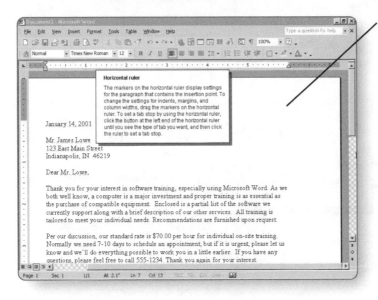

4. **Click** anywhere on the **Word window**. The What's This? screen tip will close.

Searching the Web for Help

If you have access to the Internet, Microsoft includes some assistance on its Web site.

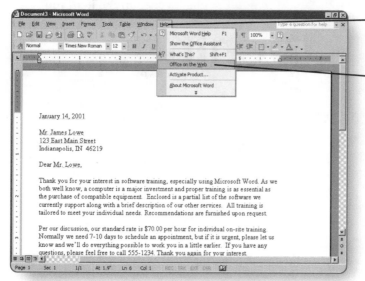

1. **Click** on **Help**. The Help menu will appear.

2. **Click** on **Office on the Web**. If you are not already connected to the Internet, you will be prompted to connect. Your Web browser program will launch and a Microsoft Office Web page will display.

3. **Follow** the **instructions** on the screen. You'll have access to various help topics.

NOTE

Web pages change frequently. The Web page you see may not be the same one displayed in this book.

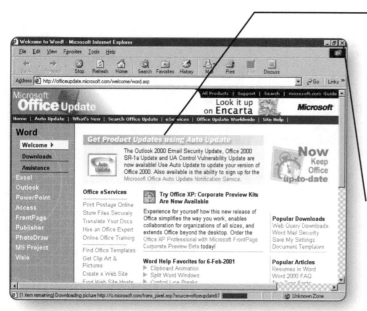

When you have completed accessing the Web help, you'll want to close the Internet Explorer.

4. **Click** on the **Close button**. The Internet Explorer window will close.

You may be prompted to disconnect from your Internet Service Provider (ISP).

3

Saving, Opening, Closing, and Printing

With the adoption of e-mail within corporations and extensive use of the Internet, many documents today might never be printed on paper; they might only exist electronically. However, before you can send these documents into cyberspace, you need to save them. There will always be times when you need a paper copy. In this chapter, you'll learn how to:

- Save a document
- Print or e-mail a document
- Create a new document and open an existing one
- Work with windows and close Word

Saving Your Document

Anyone who uses a computer has probably lost data at one time or another. If you haven't been saving to disk regularly, it only takes a few seconds to lose hours of work. Word has built-in features to help protect you against this eventuality. However, you still need to save.

Saving a Document the First Time

When you first create a document, it has no name. If you want to use that document later, it must have a name so Word can find it. Word asks for a name the first time you save the document, and after that, the name you give it will appear in the title bar at the top of the screen.

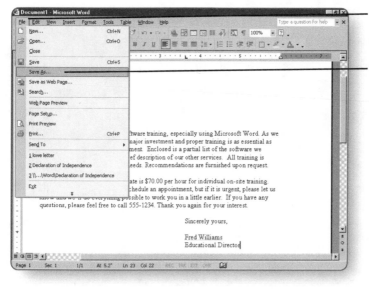

1. **Click** on **File**. The File menu will appear.

2. **Click** on **Save As**. The Save As dialog box will open.

3. **Type** a **name** for your file in the File name text box. File names can contain spaces, dashes, and some other special characters, but cannot include the asterisk (*), slash (/), backslash (\), or question mark (?) characters. The file name will be displayed.

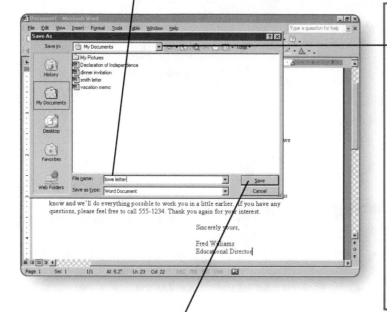

NOTE

The Save in drop-down list box lists folder options where you can save the document. The default folder that appears is "My Documents." If you don't want to save it to this folder, or if you want to save your document to another disk, you can select another one. Click on the down arrow to browse, or look, for the folder where you wish to store the document.

4. **Click** on **Save**. Your document will be saved and the name you specified will appear in the title bar.

Resaving a Document

As you work on your document, you should resave it every ten minutes or so to help ensure that you do not lose any changes.

1. Click on the **Save button**. The document will be resaved with any changes. No dialog box will open because the document is resaved with the same name and in the same folder as previously specified.

TIP

If you want to save the document with a different name or in a different folder, click on File, then choose Save As. The Save As dialog box will prompt you for the new name or folder. The original document will remain as well as the new one.

Enabling AutoRecover

Word has a feature called AutoRecover, which periodically saves a temporary version of your document for you. After a crash, when you boot up and reopen Word, the program opens a recovery version of the files you were working on at the time of the crash. You can then save them.

Word will allow you to specify the time intervals for the AutoRecover to save your work.

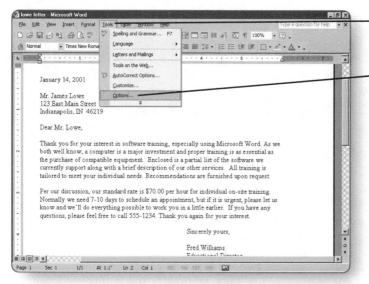

1. Click on **Tools**. The Tools menu will appear.

2. Click on **Options**. The Options dialog box will open.

3. Click on the **Save** tab. The Save tab will come to the front of the stack.

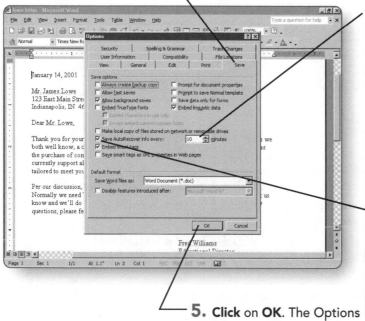

4. Set the **Save AutoRecover info every** interval. Click on the down arrow to decrease the time or click on the up arrow to increase the time between AutoRecover saves. The number of minutes you select will appear in the box.

TIP

If the AutoRecover text box is dimmed, click in the Save Options check box to activate the feature. A check mark in the box indicates the feature is activated.

5. Click on **OK**. The Options dialog box will close.

Creating a New Document

When a Word session is first started a blank document appears ready for you to use. However, during the course of using Word, you may need another blank document. Word includes several methods to access a new document.

Creating a New Document Using the Toolbar

Creating a new document using the standard Word settings is only a mouse click away!

1. **Click** on the **New Blank Document** button. A new screen will appear with the title Document 2, 3, 4, and so on, depending on how many documents you've created during this session.

Creating a New Document Using the Task Pane

If you choose to create a new document from the task pane you can select a standard blank document or choose from a variety of templates. Templates are discussed in Chapter 22, "Discovering Templates."

TIP

Click on View, Task Pane if your task pane is not already displayed.

1. **Click** on **Blank Document**. A standard blank document will appear on the screen.

Closing a Document

When you are finished working on a document, you should close it. Closing is the equivalent of putting the document away for later use. When you close a document, you are only putting the document away—not the program. Word is still active and ready to work for you.

1a. **Click** on **File**. The File menu will appear.

2a. **Click** on **Close**. The document will be put away.

OR

1b. **Click** on the **Close Button**. The document will be closed. By choosing this method, you combine Steps 1 and 2.

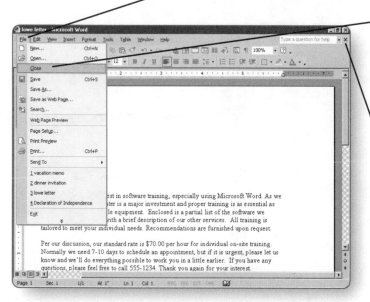

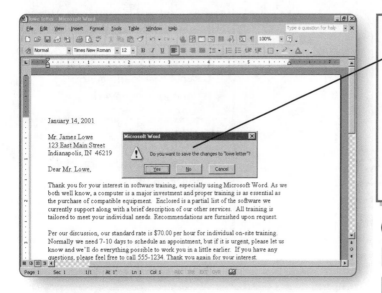

NOTE

If you close a document with changes that have not been saved, Word will prompt you with a dialog box. Choose Yes to save the changes or No to close the file without saving the changes.

Opening an Existing Document

Opening a document is putting a copy of that file into the computer's memory and onto your screen so that you can work on it. If you make any changes, be sure to save the file again. Word provides several different ways to open a document.

Displaying the Open Dialog Box

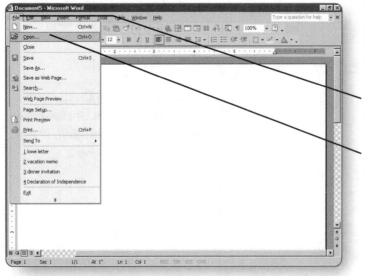

Word's Open dialog box lists all previously saved Word documents located in a particular folder.

1. Click on **File**. The File menu will appear.

2. Click on **Open**. The Open dialog box will open.

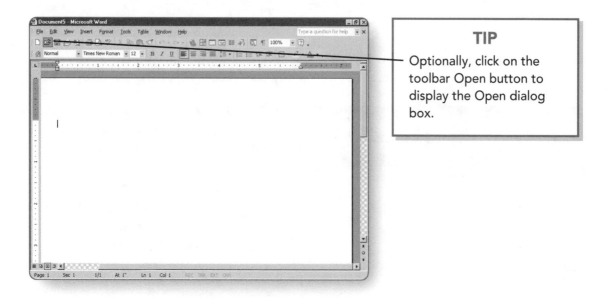

TIP

Optionally, click on the toolbar Open button to display the Open dialog box.

3. Click on the **file name** you want to open. The file name will be highlighted.

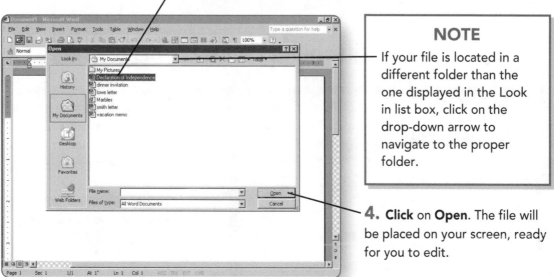

NOTE

If your file is located in a different folder than the one displayed in the Look in list box, click on the drop-down arrow to navigate to the proper folder.

4. Click on **Open**. The file will be placed on your screen, ready for you to edit.

Opening A Recently Used Document

The task pane lists several of the documents you've recently used. You can quickly open a document using the task pane.

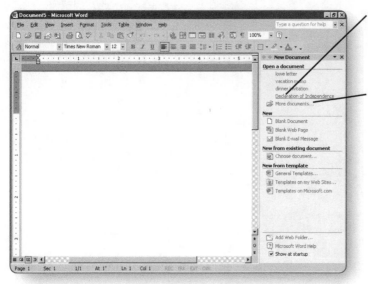

1. **Click** on the **document name** you want to open. The document will appear on your screen.

If the document you want isn't listed, click on More Documents to display the Open dialog box, from which you can select additional files.

E-mailing a Document

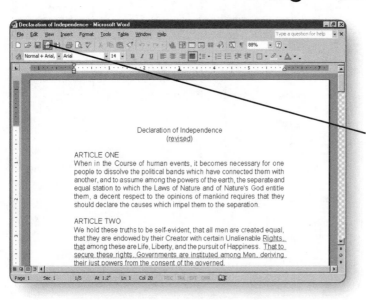

If you have e-mail access, you can send a document directly to another person. Word copies the content of the document into a blank e-mail message.

1. **Click** on the **e-mail button**. The e-mail header box will open.

2. Type the **recipient's e-mail address**. The e-mail address will appear in the To box.

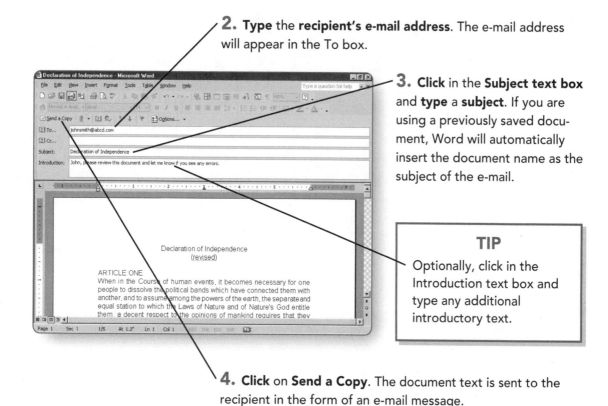

3. Click in the **Subject text box** and **type** a **subject**. If you are using a previously saved document, Word will automatically insert the document name as the subject of the e-mail.

TIP

Optionally, click in the Introduction text box and type any additional introductory text.

4. Click on **Send a Copy**. The document text is sent to the recipient in the form of an e-mail message.

Printing a Document

When your document is complete, it is time to print it. You can print it to your printer for a hard copy of the document.

Using Print Preview

Before you print your document, you should preview it full-screen. Previewing a document lets you see how document layout settings, such as margins, will look in the printed document.

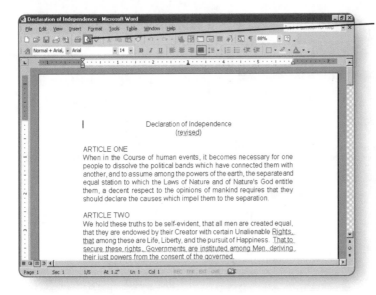

1. **Click** on the **Print Preview button**. The document will be sized so that an entire page is visible on the screen. The mouse pointer will become a magnifying glass with a plus sign in it.

NOTE

You won't be able to edit the document from the Print Preview screen.

---

2. **Press** the **Page Down key (on your keyboard)**. The next page of the document will be displayed.

3. **Press** the **Page Up key (on your keyboard)**. The previous page of the document will be displayed.

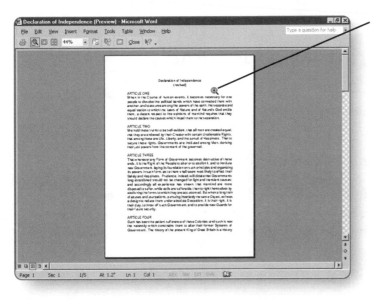

4. **Click** anywhere on the **body** of the document. The text will become larger on the screen and the mouse pointer will become a magnifying glass with a minus sign in it.

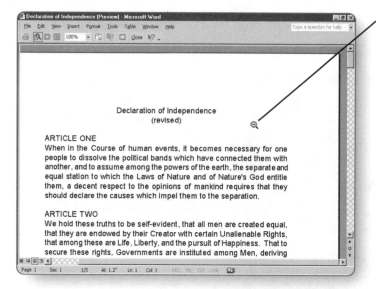

5. **Click** anywhere on the **body** of the document. The text will become smaller on the screen.

6. **Click** on the **Multiple Pages button**. A selection of available views will appear.

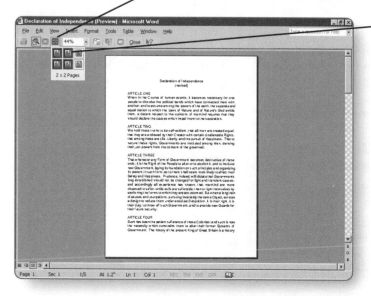

7. **Click** on the **number of pages** you'd like to display at the same time. The number of pages you selected will display on the screen.

8. Click on the **One Page button**. The view will return to a single page.

9. Optionally, **click** on the **Print button**. The document will automatically print with standard options.

10. Click on **Close**. The document will be returned to the normal editing view.

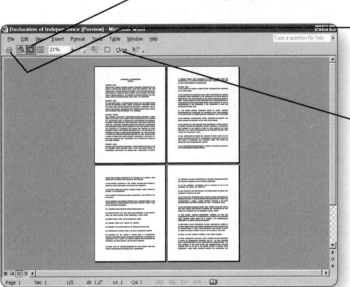

Printing with the Print Button

The fastest and easiest way to print is to use the Print button included on the Word toolbar.

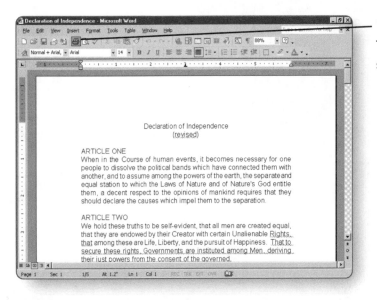

1. Click on the **Print button**. The document will print with standard options.

Printing from the Menu

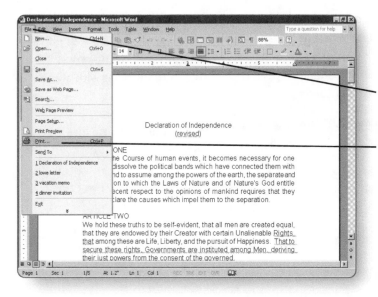

If you'd like more control over the printing of your document, use the Print dialog box.

1. Click on **File**. The File menu will appear.

2. Click on **Print**. The Print dialog box will open.

Many options are available from the Print dialog box, including the following:

- **Name**. If you are connected to more than one printer, you can choose which one to use for this print job. Click on the down arrow in the Name drop-down list box and make a selection.

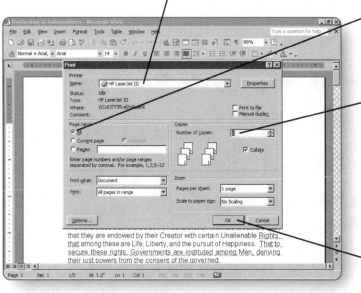

- **Page range**. You can choose which pages of your document to print with the Page range options.

- **Number of copies**. Choose the number of copies to be printed by clicking on the up or down arrows at the right of the Number of copies list box.

3. Click on any desired **option**. The option will be activated.

4. Click on **OK** after you have made your selections. The document will be sent to the printer.

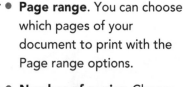

Scaling Your Document for Printing

Word has the ability to scale your documents. For example, if your document is just a little over two pages long, and it needs to be exactly two pages, the scaling feature will reduce the font size and line spacing just enough to make the document fit on two pages.

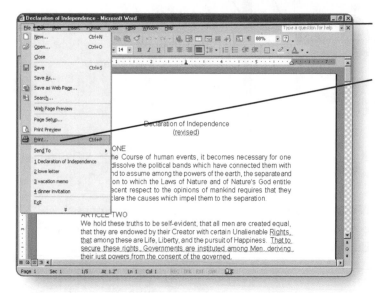

1. Click on **File**. The File menu will appear.

2. Click on **Print**. The Print dialog box will open.

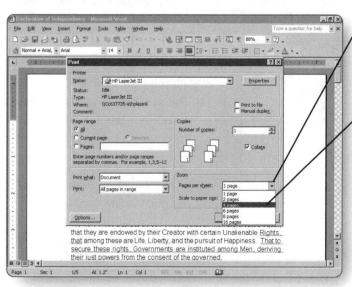

3. Click the **down arrow** in the Pages per sheet drop-down list box. A list of numbers will appear.

4. Click the **number of pages** you want your document to be. The number will appear in the box. In this example, a five-page document is being scaled down to a four-page document.

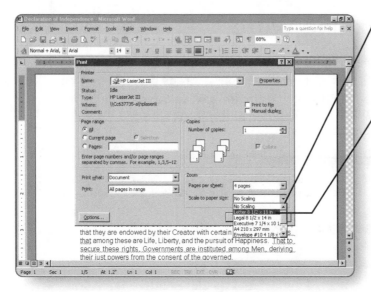

5. Click on the **down arrow** in the Scale to paper size drop-down list box. A list of paper sizes will appear.

6. Click on the **paper size** you'll use for your document. The paper size will appear in the box.

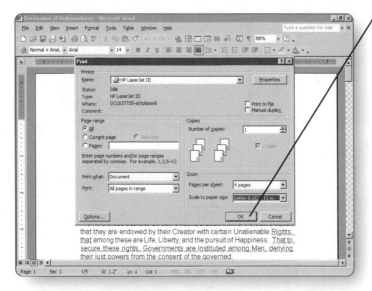

7. Click on **OK**. The document will print to the number of pages you specified.

Exiting Word

When you are finished working with Word, exit the program. This procedure protects your data and prevents possible program damage. It also frees up valuable computer memory that can be used for other programs.

1a. **Click** on **File**. The File menu will appear.

2. **Click** on **Exit**. The Word program will be closed.

OR

1b. **Click** on the **Application Close** button. The Word program will close.

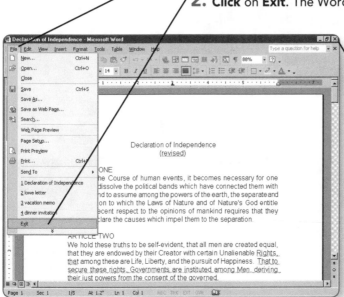

NOTE

If any documents are open that you haven't saved, Word will ask you whether you want to save changes to those files. Choose Yes to save the file or No to discard any changes.

4

Working with Multiple Windows

Word gives you the ability to work with multiple documents at the same time. When multiple windows are active, you'll need a way to manage them. In this chapter, you'll learn how to:

- Split a document window
- Move between open documents
- Display multiple document windows
- Maximize a document window

Arranging Windows

Word allows multiple documents to be open simultaneously.

Splitting a Window

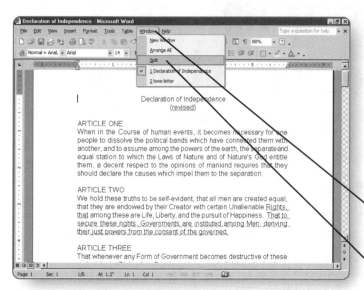

If you want to see two parts of a document but you can't get them to fit on the screen at the same time, you can split a window. This enables you to view the opening paragraph of a long document in one window while you view the closing paragraph in the lower window.

1. **Click** on **Window**. The Window menu will appear.

2. **Click** on **Split**. A gray horizontal line with a double-headed arrow will appear.

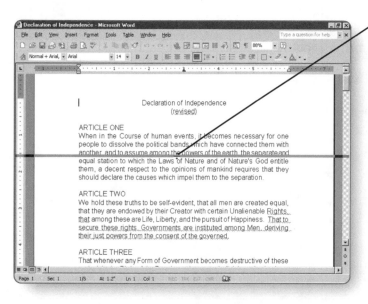

3. **Click** the **mouse** where you want the window to be divided. The gray horizontal line will remain at the location you clicked.

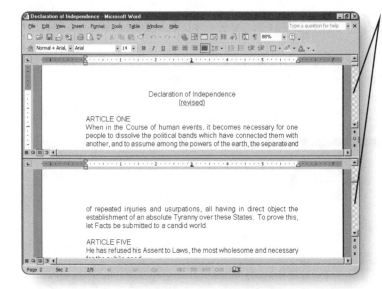

The window will be divided in two—each section having its own scroll bar.

Removing the Split

When you close the split, your document will appear all on a single screen.

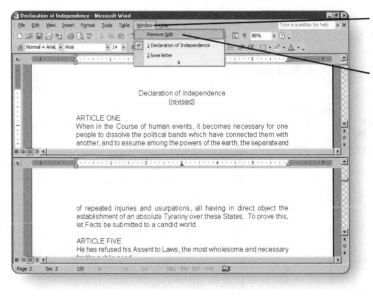

1. **Click** on **Window**. The Window menu will appear.

2. **Click** on **Remove Split**. The split between the windows will disappear.

Moving Between Documents

Windows includes the ability to work on a number of different documents at the same time. They are likely to be Word documents, but can just as easily be documents from other applications, such as Excel. A button for each open document will be displayed on the Windows taskbar. All Word documents are indicated by a blue "W" on the document's icon.

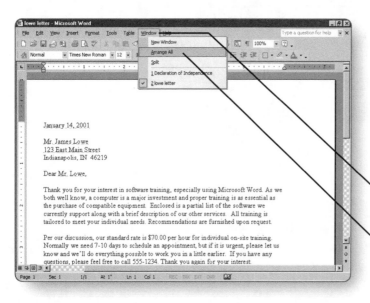

1. Click on any Word **document button** on the taskbar. The selected document will become the active document.

Viewing Multiple Documents Together

Occasionally, you may need to view more than one document at a time. You can use the Arrange All feature to accomplish this. Arrange All will divide the screen space among the open documents. It is not recommended for more than three documents at a time.

1. Click on **Window**. The Window menu will appear.

2. Click on **Arrange All**. The entire work area will be divided (tiled) between the open documents.

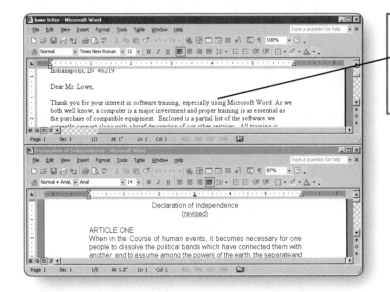

TIP

To edit a document, click anywhere on the window for that document.

Restoring a Window to Maximized Size

After a window has been resized, Word tends to leave the window at the smaller size. Use the Windows Maximize feature to fill your screen size.

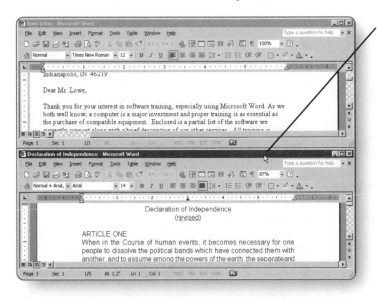

1. Double-click on the **title bar** of the current document. The window will be maximized.

5

Editing Text

Unless you're a perfect typist, you probably have a few mistakes in your document, or perhaps you've changed your mind about some of the text in the document. In a word processing program, corrections and changes are easy to make. In this chapter, you'll learn how to:

- Insert and delete text
- Select text
- Change the case of text
- Use the Undo and Redo commands
- Move and copy text
- Discover Word's Smart Tags
- Display symbols in a document

Inserting, Selecting, and Deleting Text

Editing text with Word is a breeze. Need extra words? Just type them in. Need to delete words? Just highlight them and press the Delete key.

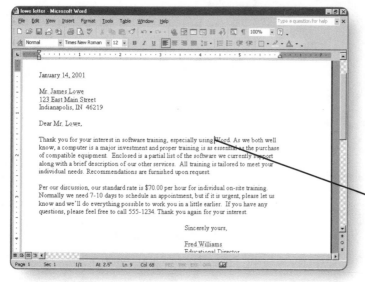

Inserting Text

Word begins in *insert* mode. This means that when you want to add new text to a document, simply place the insertion point where you want the new text to be and start typing.

1. Click the **mouse pointer** directly in front of the word in the body of the document where you want new text to appear. The blinking insertion point will appear.

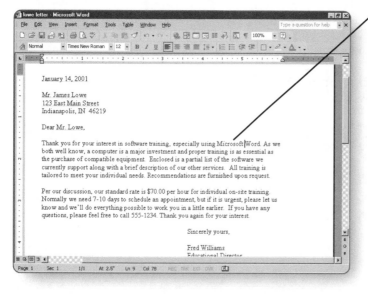

2. Type any new **word or phrase**, adding a space before or after as necessary. The new text is inserted into the document.

Word will push the existing text to the right and keep moving it over or down to make room for the new text.

Selecting Text

To move, copy, delete, or change the formatting of text, select the text you want to edit. When text is selected, it will appear as light type on a dark background on your screen, the reverse of unselected text. In previous versions of Microsoft Word, you could only select a sequential block of text at a time, not bits of text in different places. New to Word 2002 is the ability to select nonsequential blocks of text.

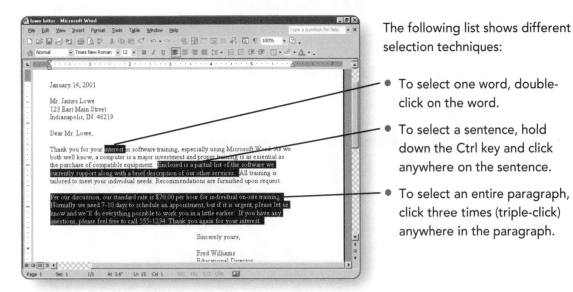

The following list shows different selection techniques:

- To select one word, double-click on the word.

- To select a sentence, hold down the Ctrl key and click anywhere on the sentence.

- To select an entire paragraph, click three times (triple-click) anywhere in the paragraph.

TIP
To select the entire document, press Ctrl+A or choose Edit, Select All.

- To select a single line of text, click once in the left margin with the mouse arrow next to the line to be selected.

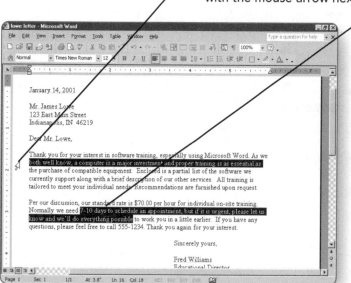

- To select a block of text, click at the beginning of the text, hold the mouse button down, and drag across the balance of the text to be selected.

- To select a nonsequential block of text, hold down the Ctrl key and use the preceding selection techniques for each additional text block you want to include.

TIP

To deselect text, click anywhere in the document where the text is not highlighted.

Deleting Text

You can delete unwanted text one character, one word, one paragraph at a time, or any combination of the above.

Two common keys used to delete text are the Backspace and the Delete key. Pressing the Backspace key will delete one character at a time to the left of the insertion point; pressing the Delete key will delete one character at a time to the right of the insertion point.

TIP

An easy way to remember which direction the Backspace key will delete is to look at the arrow printed on the Backspace key (most keyboards). The arrow points to the left, indicating this is the direction the characters will be deleted.

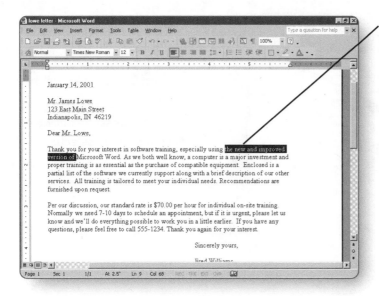

1. **Select** the **text** to be deleted. The text will be highlighted.

2. **Press** the **Delete key**. The text will be deleted.

Changing Text Case

When you need to change the capitalization case of text, Word provides an easy way to change it without retyping.

1. **Select** the **text** to be changed. The text will be highlighted.

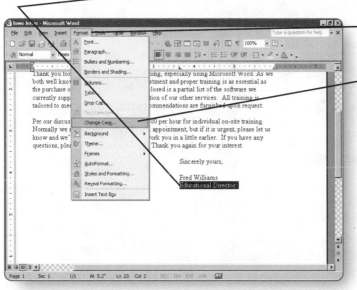

2. **Click** on **Format**. The Format menu will appear.

3. **Click** on **Change Case**. The Change Case dialog box will open.

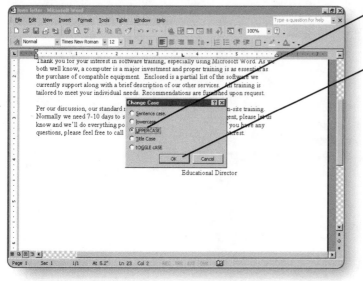

4. **Click** on a **case option**. The option will be selected.

5. **Click** on **OK**. The text will be modified.

Using Undo and Redo

If you want to restore text you deleted, or reverse an action recently taken, use the Undo feature of Word.

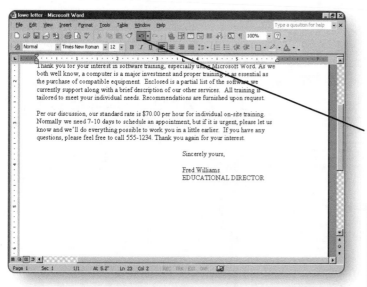

Undoing the Previous Step

You're one click away from reversing your previous action.

1. **Click** on the **Undo button**. The last action taken will be reversed.

TIP

Optionally, choose Undo from the Edit menu.

Redoing the Previous Step

If you undo an action and then decide you liked it better the way you had it, choose the Redo feature.

1. **Click** on the **Redo button**. The Undo action will be reversed.

TIP

Optionally, choose Redo from the Edit menu.

Undoing a Series of Actions

Word keeps track of several steps you have recently taken. When you Undo a previous step, you'll also Undo any actions taken after that step.

For example, imagine you changed the case of some text, then bolded the text, and then underlined the text. If you choose to Undo the case change, the bolding and underlining will also be reversed.

1. **Click** on the **arrow** next to the Undo button. A list of the most recent actions will be displayed.

2. **Click** on the **action** you want to undo. The action will be undone as well as all actions above it on the list.

Moving and Copying Text

Windows includes a feature called the *Clipboard*, which lets you hold information temporarily. Microsoft Word uses the Clipboard feature to move or copy text from one place to another.

Moving Text

The features used to move text from one place to another are called *Cut and Paste*. With Cut and Paste, the original text is deleted and placed in the new location.

1. Select the **text** to be moved. The text will become highlighted.

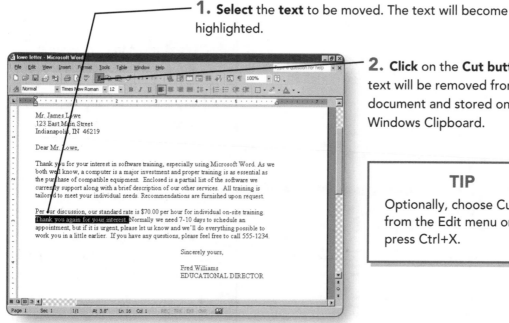

2. Click on the **Cut button**. The text will be removed from the document and stored on the Windows Clipboard.

TIP

Optionally, choose Cut from the Edit menu or press Ctrl+X.

3. Click the **mouse** where you want the text to be located. The blinking insertion point will appear.

4. Click on the **Paste button**. The text will be placed at the new location.

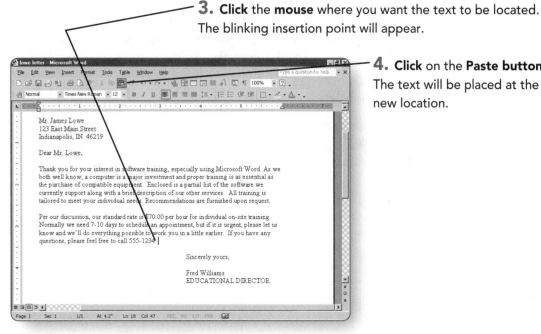

Notice the small icon that appears when you pasted the text. The icon, new to Word 2002, is one of Word's Smart Tags. You'll learn about Smart Tags later in this chapter.

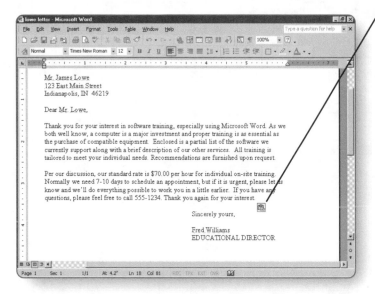

Copying Text

Copying text will leave the text in its original location while a copy of it is placed on the Windows Clipboard.

1. **Select** the **text** to be copied. The text will be highlighted.

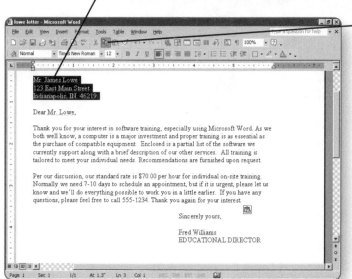

2. **Click** on the **Copy button**. The text will be stored on the Windows Clipboard.

NOTE

Depending on how many times you've copied (or cut) text, the Clipboard task pane may appear. You'll learn more about the Clipboard task pane later in this chapter.

TIP

Optionally, choose Copy from the Edit menu or press Ctrl+C.

3. Click the **mouse** where you want the text to be located. The blinking insertion point will appear.

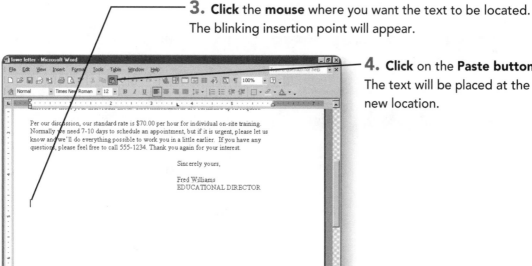

4. Click on the **Paste button**. The text will be placed at the new location.

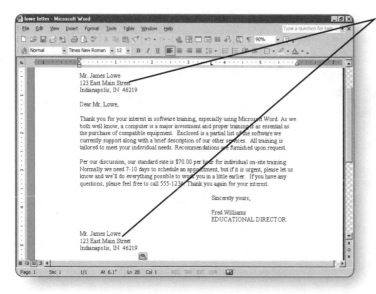

Notice that both the original text and the copy of the text are in the document.

TIP

A very quick way to use Cut, Copy, and Paste is to right-click on top of your selection. Choices from a shortcut menu can be made using the left or right mouse button.

Using Drag and Drop

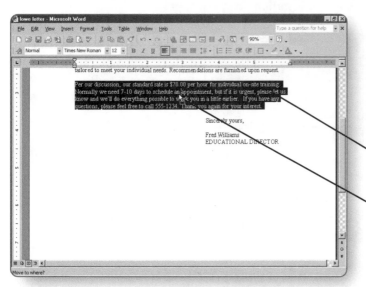

Another method of moving text from one location to another is to use Drag and Drop. The Drag and Drop method works best for moving a small amount of text a short distance.

1. Select the **text** to be moved. The text will be highlighted.

2. Position the **mouse pointer** on top of the highlighted text. The white mouse arrow will point to the left.

3. Hold the **mouse button** down and **drag** the text to the desired location. A small box will appear at the bottom of the mouse arrowhead and a gray line will indicate the position of the text.

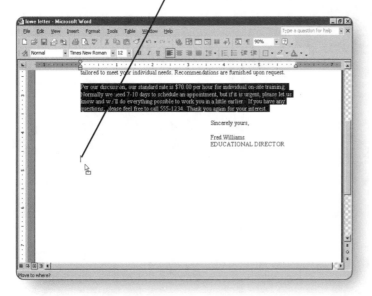

> ### TIP
> To copy text with Drag and Drop, hold down the Ctrl key before dragging the selected text. Release the mouse button before releasing the Ctrl key.

4. Release the **mouse button**. The text will be moved.

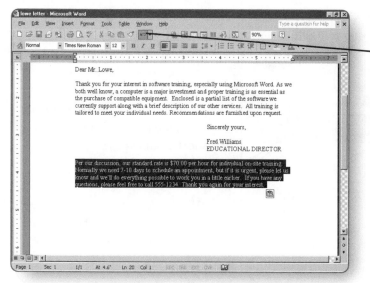

TIP

If you accidentally move text, click on the Undo button to reverse the move.

Using the Office Clipboard

If you have copied or cut multiple items, even if from other Office or Windows applications, the Office clipboard stores those items together. Each item is appended to the clipboard contents and then inserted as individuals or as a group in a new location or document.

1. Click on **Edit**. The Edit menu will appear.

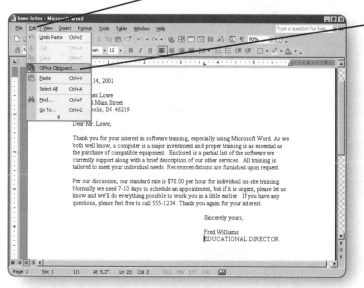

2. Click on **Office Clipboard**. The Clipboard task pane will appear.

The Office Clipboard stores up to 24 items you copied or cut. It doesn't matter whether you used the Edit menu, the cut or copy icons on the toolbar, the shortcut menu, or the shortcut keys.

You can insert any desired item from the clipboard or you can insert all items.

3. **Click** the **mouse** where you want to insert the Clipboard contents. The blinking insertion point will appear.

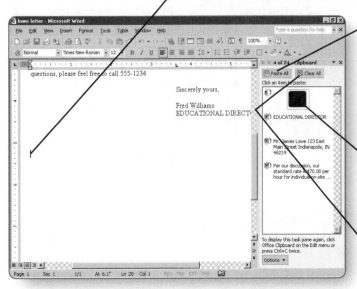

4a. **Click** on the **Paste All button**. The contents of the Clipboard will be placed in the document.

OR

4b. Click on the individual item you want to insert. The item will be inserted into the document.

TIP

To clear the Clipboard contents, click on the Clear All button.

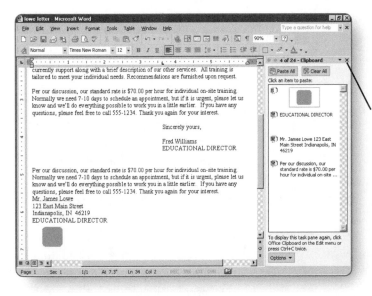

If you are finished with the Clipboard task pane, you may find it helpful to put the task pane away.

5. **Click** on the **Close Button**. The Clipboard toolbar will disappear.

Discovering Smart Tags

Smart tags are new to Word 2002. *Smart tags* are small icons that appear throughout your document as you perform various tasks or enter certain types of text. Smart tags perform actions in Word that would normally require you to open other programs.

Smart Tag functions range from quickly adding a name or address from your document to an Outlook contact folder to offering options when pasting data from the Clipboard.

Using Smart Tags with the Clipboard

By default, when data is pasted from the clipboard, formatting is included. This means that if the original text is underlined, the pasted text will be underlined as well. One Smart Tag provides the option to paste text with or without formatting. (You'll learn how to add formatting in Chapter 8, "Using Fonts Effectively.")

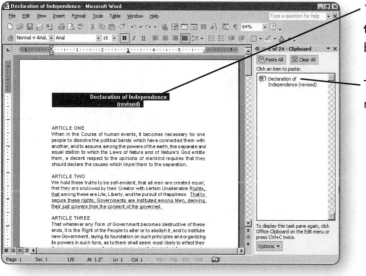

1. Select and cut or copy some **text**. The text and formatting will be placed on the clipboard.

The Clipboard Task Pane does not show formatting.

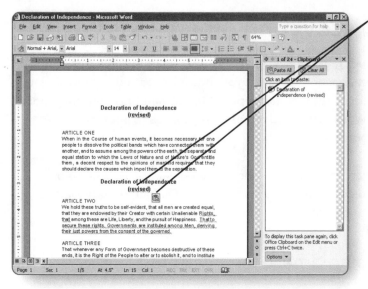

2. Paste the **text** into a different location. The text appears, including formatting, and a Smart Tag icon appears nearby.

3. Click on the **down arrow** next to the Smart Tag. A list of options appears.

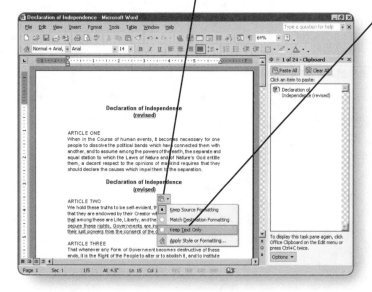

4. Click on an **option**. The resulting action will depend on the option you select.

- **Keep Source Formatting**. Leaves the pasted text formatted the same as the original text

- **Match Destination Formatting**. Modifies the pasted text to match the text closest to the pasted text

- **Keep Text Only**. Modifies the pasted text to be the default font

Adding Contact Information from a Smart Tag

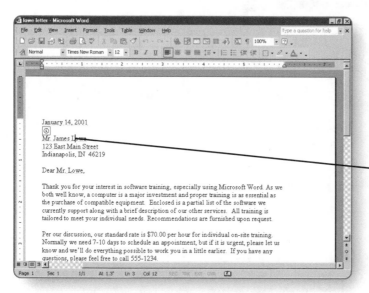

If you see text with purple dotted lines under it, Word recognizes that text as Smart Tag text. If you move your mouse over the text, an indicator in the form of an icon will appear.

1. Position the **mouse** over text such as a name or address. A Smart Tag icon will appear.

2. Click on the **Smart Tag icon**. A menu of options will appear.

3. Click on **Add to Contacts**. A contact card from Microsoft Outlook appears with the name and possibly the address already entered.

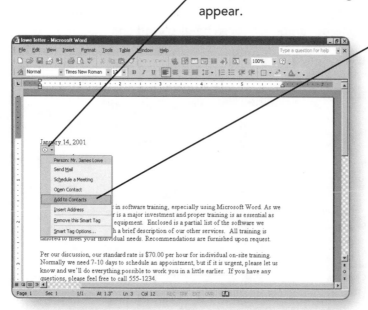

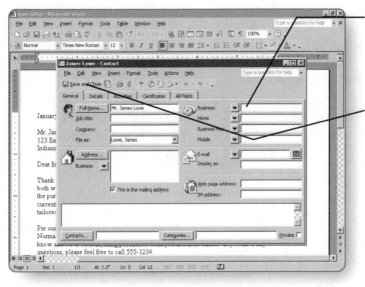

4. If desired, **complete** the rest of the **contact data**. Refer to your Microsoft Outlook reference for instructions.

5. Click on **Save and Close**. The contact window will close and you will again see your Word document.

Displaying Nonprinting Symbols

To assist you in editing a document, Word can display hidden symbols it uses to indicate spaces, tabs, and hard returns, which are created when you press the Enter key. These symbols do not print but can be displayed on your screen.

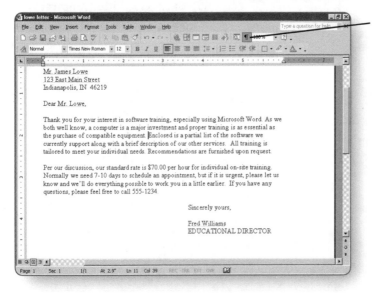

1. Click on the **Show/Hide¶ button**. The hidden characters will be displayed.

Spaces are indicated with a dot: paragraph hard returns are displayed with the paragraph symbol—¶.

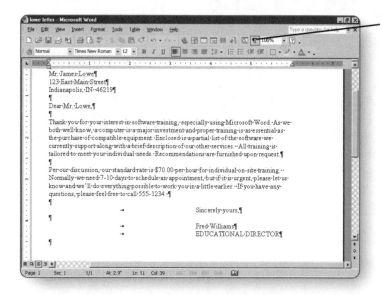

2. Click on the **Show/Hide¶ button**. The displayed special characters will be hidden.

Part I—Creating Your First Document (1–5)

1. How can you turn a toolbar on or off? *See "Viewing Additional Toolbars" in Chapter 1*

2. When do task panes appear? *See "Working with the Task Pane" in Chapter 1*

3. What is Click and Type? *See "Using Click and Type" in Chapter 1*

4. In what language do you type questions to the Office Assistant? *See "Asking the Assistant for Help" in Chapter 2*

5. What is AutoRecover? *See "Enabling AutoRecover" in Chapter 3*

6. What is one reason you might want to scale your document before printing? *See "Scaling Your Document for Printing" in Chapter 3*

7. How can you view more than one document at a time? *See "Viewing Multiple Documents Together" in Chapter 4*

8. What's a quick way to select an entire sentence? *See "Selecting Text" in Chapter 5*

9. What type of information do the nonprinting symbols represent? *See "Displaying Nonprinting Symbols" in Chapter 5*

10. What can you do if you discover you just made a mistake? *See "Undoing the Previous Step" in Chapter 5*

PART II

Making Your Documents Look Good

Chapter 6
    Working with Pages. **77**

Chapter 7
    Arranging Text on a Page **91**

Chapter 8
    Using Fonts Effectively **99**

Chapter 9
    Inserting Special Characters **115**

Chapter 10
    Working with Lists. **123**

6

Working with Pages

Balancing *white space*—the amount of blank space compared to print on a page—is an important aspect of designing professional-looking pages. You can tune white space by adjusting margins and the amount of text you place on a page. In this chapter, you'll learn how to:

- Set and adjust margins
- Change the document orientation
- Select a document paper size
- Insert and remove a page break
- View a document from different perspectives

Setting Margins

Margins are the space between the edges of the paper and where the text actually begins to appear. Word will allow you to set margins for any of the four sides of the document and will also allow you to mix and match margins for different pages.

The default margins are 1 inch on the top and bottom and 1.25 inches for the left and right margins.

Setting Margins for the Entire Document

You can set the document margins before you begin entering text into a document, after you've completed the entire document, or at any time in between.

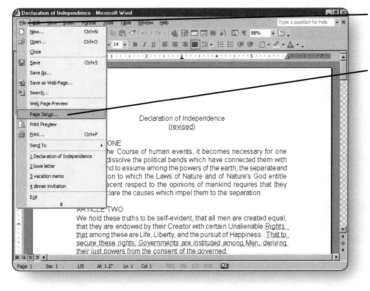

1. **Click** on **File**. The File menu will appear.

2. **Click** on **Page Setup**. The Page Setup dialog box will open.

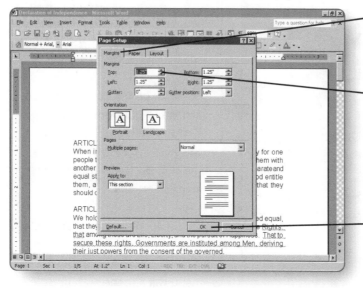

3. If necessary, **click** on the **Margins tab**. The Margins tab will be displayed.

4. Click on the **up or down arrows** to the right of the Top, Bottom, Left, and Right text boxes to increase or decrease the top, bottom, left, or right margin settings.

5. Click on **OK**. The new settings will be applied to the entire document.

Adjusting Margins for Part of a Document

Word can apply different margin settings to selected sections of a document.

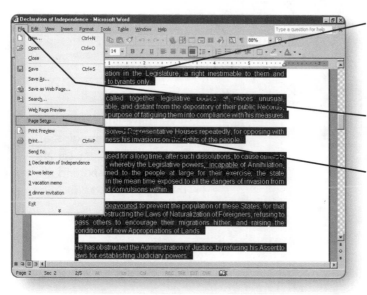

1. Select the **text** in the document that you want to adjust. The text will be highlighted.

2. Click on **File**. The File menu will appear.

3. Click on **Page Setup**. The Page Setup dialog box will open.

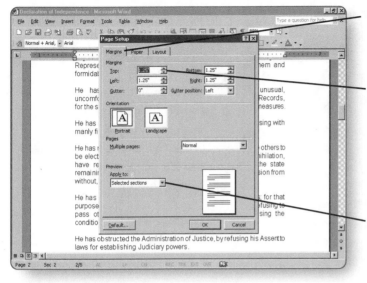

4. If necessary, **click** on the **Margins tab**. The Margins tab will be displayed.

5. Click on the **up or down arrows** to the right of the Top, Bottom, Left, and Right text boxes to increase or decrease the top, bottom, left, or right margin settings.

6. Click on the **down arrow** to the right of the Apply to drop-down list box. A drop-down menu will appear.

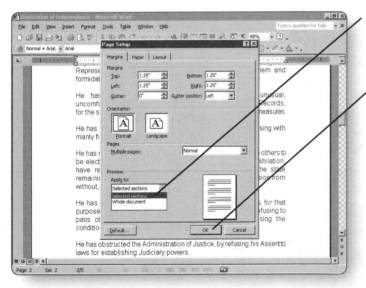

7. Click on **Selected sections**. The option will appear in the Apply to drop-down list box.

8. Click on **OK**. The new margin settings will be applied.

NOTE

If you have changed the top or bottom margins, a page break will appear at the beginning and end of the selected text.

Changing Document Orientation

Use the Page Setup dialog box to change your document to be printed in landscape (along the long edge of the paper).

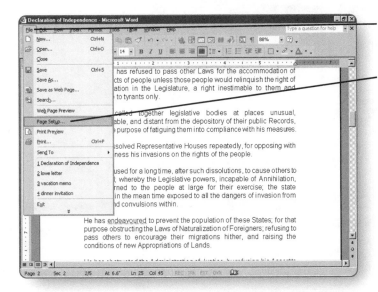

1. **Click** on **File**. The File menu will appear.

2. **Click** on **Page Setup**. The Page Setup dialog box will open.

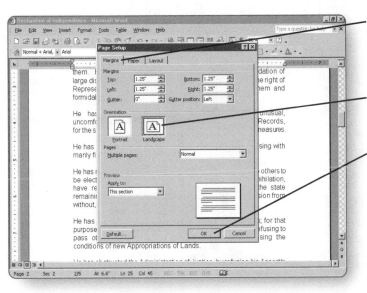

3. If necessary, **click** on the **Margins tab**. The Margins tab will come to the top.

4. **Click** on **Landscape**. The option will be selected.

5. **Click** on **OK**. The document will be switched to landscape.

Setting the Paper Size

Although Word can work with many different sizes of paper, the available selections will depend on the type of printer you are using.

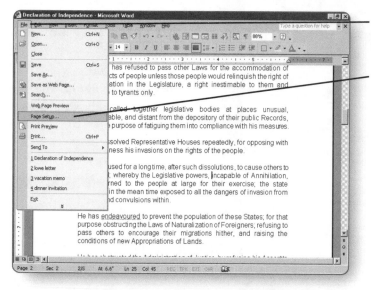

1. **Click** on **File**. The File menu will appear.

2. **Click** on **Page Setup**. The Page Setup dialog box will open.

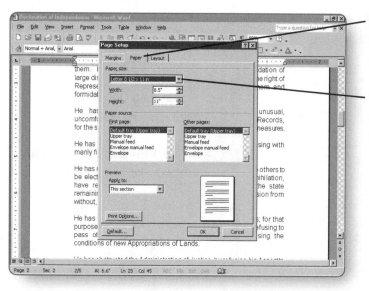

3. **Click** on the **Paper tab**. The Paper Size tab will come to the top.

4. **Click** on the **Paper size down arrow**. A list of available paper sizes will appear.

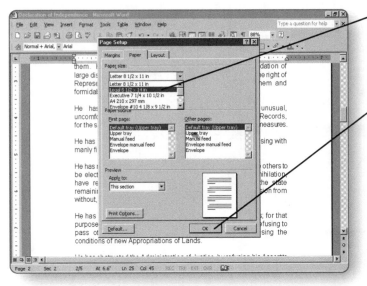

5. Click on a **paper size**. The selected paper size will appear in the Paper size drop-down list box.

6. Click on **OK**. The Page Setup dialog box will close.

Working with Page Breaks

Word automatically inserts a page break when text fills the page. Sometimes page breaks don't fall where you want them. You can override Word's automatic page break by creating your own page break.

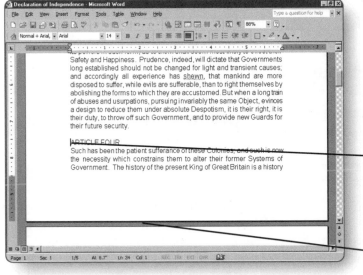

Inserting a Page Break

You can break the page at a shorter position than Word chooses, but you cannot make a page longer.

1. Click the **mouse** in front of the text where you want the new page to begin. The blinking insertion point will appear.

Notice the normal page break location Word would be applying.

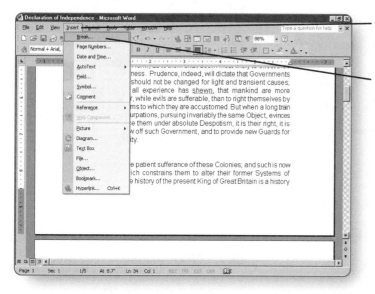

2. Click on **Insert**. The Insert menu will appear.

3. Click on **Break**. The Break dialog box will open.

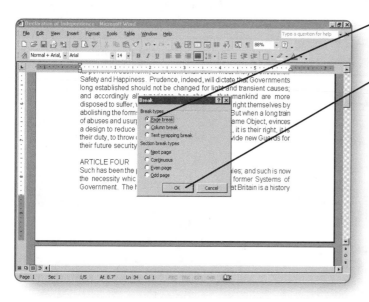

4. Click on **Page break**. The option will be selected.

5. Click on **OK**. The page break will be inserted.

TIP

A faster way to insert a page break is to follow Step 1 and then press Ctrl+Enter.

Depending on which document view you are using, you may see the words "Page Break" along with a dotted line where the new page begins. Document views are discussed later in this chapter.

NOTE

This page break is called a *hard page break* because unlike the page breaks that Word inserts, this one will not move if you delete text above it, adjust the margins, or otherwise change the amount of text on the page.

Deleting a Page Break

Word's automatic page breaks cannot be deleted, but the hard page breaks that you have inserted manually can be deleted at any time.

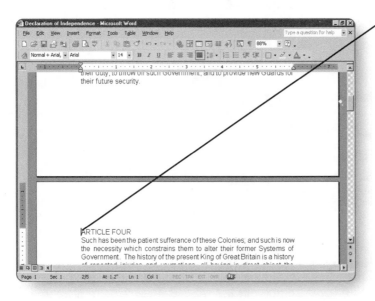

1. Click the **mouse pointer** at the beginning of the text after the page break indication. The blinking insertion point will appear.

2. Press the **Backspace key**. The page break will be deleted.

The document text will readjust to fit on the pages correctly.

Viewing a Document

Word gives you several different views to use when displaying a document. Each view has its own advantage; for example, in Chapter 3, "Saving, Opening, Closing, and Printing," you used the Print Preview view when you were printing your document.

Viewing in Print Layout View

Use Print Layout view to see how text, graphics, and other elements will be positioned on the printed page. This view is especially helpful if you are working with text columns. Columns are discussed in Chapter 16, *"Using Newspaper Columns."* In the default Print Layout view, you'll see the document top and bottom margins as well as headers and footers.

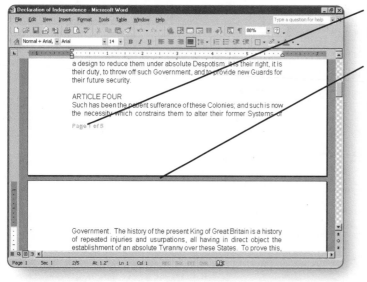

The footer is displayed in a light gray type.

Breaks between pages are indicated by a thick dark gray area.

Viewing in Normal View

Normal view is the default view for Word and is used for typing, editing, and formatting text. It simplifies the layout of the page so you can type and edit quickly. Headers, footers, page margins, backgrounds, and some other objects do not appear in Normal view.

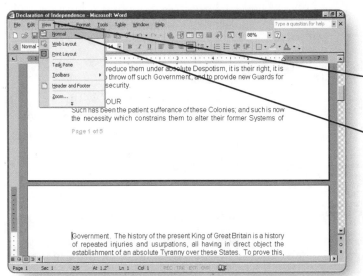

1. **Click** on **View**. The View menu will appear.

2. **Click** on **Normal**. The document view will change to normal.

Page breaks are indicated by a dotted line.

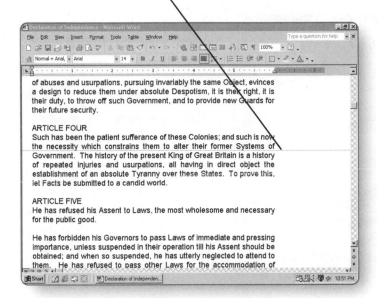

Footers and top and bottom margins are not displayed.

NOTE

Another view, Web Layout view, will be used when creating a Web page. You'll be able to see backgrounds and objects as they might be seen in a Web browser. Chapter 25, *"Using Word to Create Web Pages,"* will show you how to create a Web page using Microsoft Word.

Using the Zoom Feature

Using Word's ability to zoom in allows you to get a close-up view of your text. You also can zoom out to see more of the page at a reduced rate.

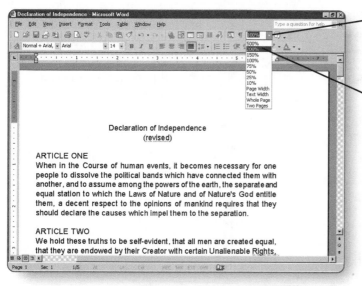

1. **Click** on the **Zoom drop-down list arrow**. A list of zoom percentages will display.

2. **Click** on **200%**. The document display will enlarge. The text will look larger, but less of the overall page will appear on the screen.

NOTE

Using the Zoom feature does not alter the size the document will print.

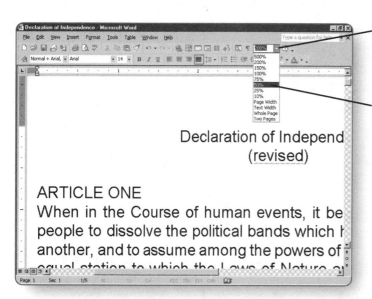

3. **Click** on the **Zoom drop-down list arrow**. A list of zoom percentages will display.

4. **Click** on **50%**. The document display will shrink and more of the page will be displayed on the screen.

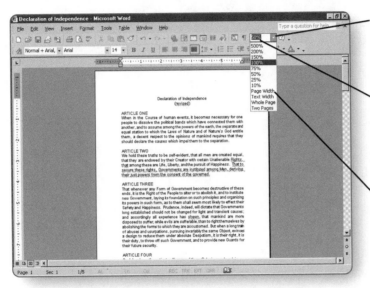

5. Click on the **Zoom drop-down list arrow**. A list of zoom percentages will display.

6. Click on **100%**. The document display will return to normal.

TIP

Setting the Zoom to Page Width can be very helpful if your document page is set to landscape.

7

Arranging Text on a Page

Word includes several features to assist you in placing text on the page just the way you want it. You can align text left to right with tabs or alignment options or you can adjust your text vertically using the line spacing options. In this chapter, you'll learn how to:

- Set, move, and delete tabs
- Select line spacing
- Center, justify, left-align, and right-align text

Working with Tabs

If you press the Tab key to move across the page, you'll notice that Word has default stops set every 1/2 inch.

Setting Tabs

You can set tabs at particular points along the ruler so that when you press the Tab key, the cursor moves to that point automatically, instead of stopping every 1/2 inch.

1. **Click** the **mouse pointer** at the location where you want to create a tabbed paragraph. The blinking insertion point will appear.

TIP

If you want to set tabs for multiple previously typed paragraphs, select the paragraphs before proceeding to Step 2.

---

2. **Click** the **mouse pointer** on the Tab button at the left end of the ruler to select from the following alignments:

- **Left**. The Tab button is already set to the left tab symbol, an "L." Text will appear with the left edge of the text at the tab.

- **Center**. Click one time to display the center tab symbol. An upside-down "T" will appear. Text will center around a center tab.

- **Right**. Click two times to display the right tab symbol. A backward "L" will appear. Text will appear with the right edge of the text at the tab.

- **Decimal**. Click three times to display the decimal tab symbol. An upside-down "T" with a dot on the right will appear. Decimal points, such as dollars and cents, align to the tab. The decimal tab is selected in this example.

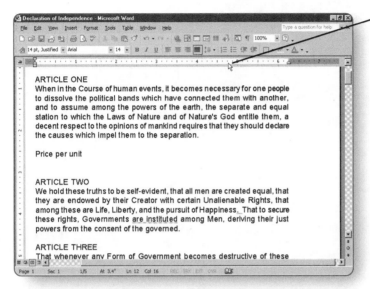

3. Click on the **ruler** to set the tab for the current paragraph or any currently selected text. A left, right, center, or decimal tab symbol will appear in the ruler at the spot you selected.

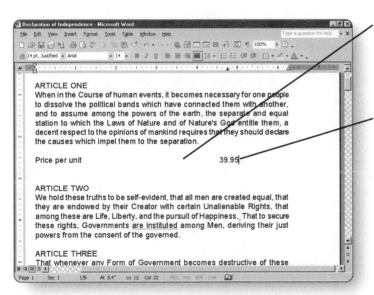

4. Click in the paragraph and **press** the **Tab key**. The insertion point will move to the tab where you want the text to appear.

5. Type some **text**. Text will appear on the page. This example shows the decimal tab alignment.

Moving a Tab

If you don't like the position where you placed the tab stop, you can easily move it!

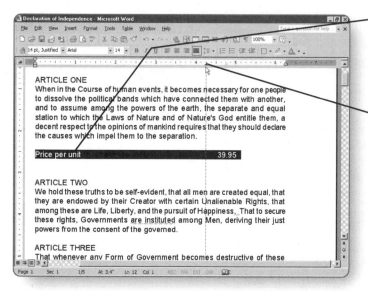

1. Select the **paragraphs** that have a tab that needs to be moved. The text will be highlighted.

2. Drag the **current tab setting** to the new desired location on the ruler bar. A vertical dotted line will indicate the new tab position.

3. Release the **mouse button**. The tab will be reset and any text will move to the new tab position.

Deleting a Tab

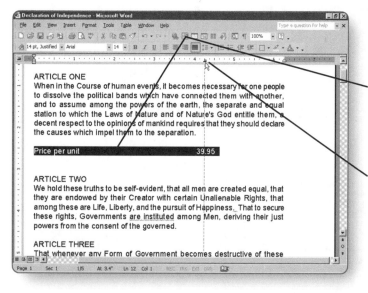

Deleting an unwanted tab stop is an easy process when you use Word's ruler.

1. Select the **paragraphs** that have a tab that needs to be deleted. The text will be highlighted.

2. Drag the **current tab setting** off the ruler, into the body of the document. A vertical dotted line will appear.

3. Release the **mouse button**. The tab will be deleted.

Changing Line Spacing

Line spacing is the amount of vertical space between each line of text. You might want to change line spacing when you want to make a document easier to read, for example, or for a draft so that the reader has room to make changes.

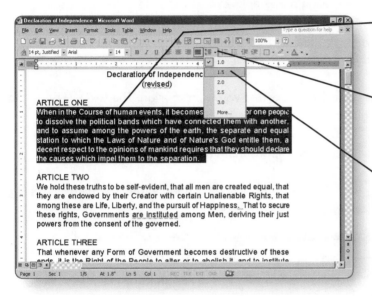

1. **Select** the **text** in which you want to change the line spacing. The text will be highlighted.

2. **Click** on the **Line Spacing button down arrow**. Line spacing options will appear.

3. **Click** on an **option**. The new spacing selection is applied to the highlighted text.

TIP

Shortcut keys to set line spacing are: Ctrl+1 for single-spacing, Ctrl+2 for double-spacing, and Ctrl+5 for 1.5 line spacing.

Aligning Text

Alignment arranges the text to line up at one or both margins, or centers it across the page. Like line spacing, alignment is usually applied to an entire paragraph or document.

You can align paragraphs of text to the left, right, or center. You also can justify your text, which means that the text will be evenly spaced across the page from the left edge to the right edge.

1. Select the **text** that you want to align. The text will be highlighted.

2. Click on the appropriate **alignment button**:

- **Align Left**. The text will be aligned at the left margin. This is the default choice in Word.

- **Center**. The text will be centered.

- **Align Right**. The text will be aligned at the right margin.

- **Justify**. The text will be evenly spaced across the page.

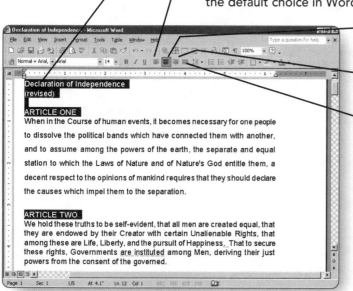

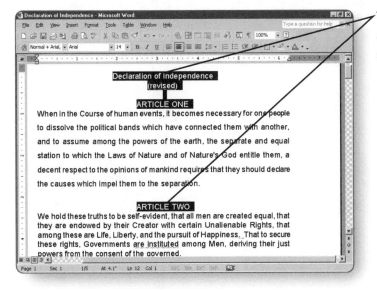

The selected text will realign according to the option you selected.

8

Using Fonts Effectively

When you speak, the tone of your voice conveys how you feel about what you're saying. You can convey your enthusiasm (or lack of it), be friendly, or be sarcastic. In a similar way, fonts, which are families of design styles for the numbers, letters, and symbols that make up text, can provide additional information to the reader. Fonts can, for example, make a document appear mature and businesslike or young and casual. In this chapter, you'll learn how to:

- Choose and apply an appropriate font
- Add Bold, Underline, and Italic
- Use special effects, such as outlining, embossing, subscripts, or animation
- Copy formatting from one selection to another
- Change the default font

Selecting a Font and Font Size

In addition to the fonts you already have on your machine, Word comes with extra fonts. The name of the currently selected font and font size for selected text are displayed on the Font and Font Size drop-down lists on the toolbar.

Choosing a Font

Choose a font such as Times New Roman if you want the text to be modern and businesslike, or choose a font like Monotype Corsiva for a handwritten style!

1. Select the **text** to be formatted. The text will be highlighted.

2. Click on the **down arrow** to the right of the Font drop-down list. A list of fonts will appear.

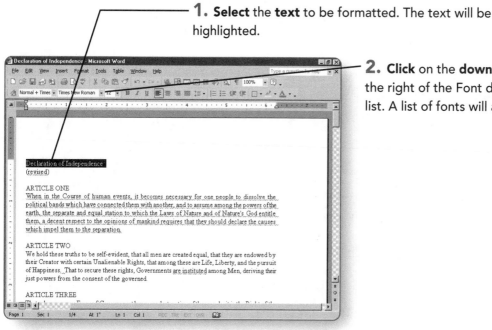

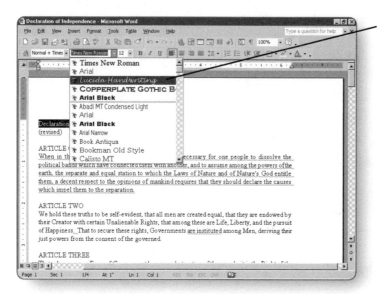

3. **Click** on a **font**. The new font will be applied to the selected text.

Choosing a Font Size

Each font can be used in different sizes. Font sizes are measured in *points*, and a point is approximately 1/72 of an inch. A 72-point font, therefore, is approximately 1 inch tall.

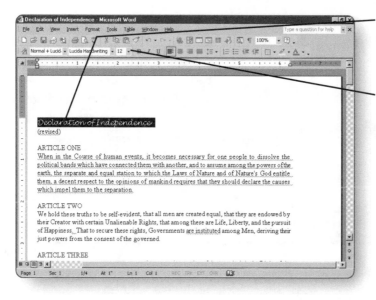

1. **Select** the **text** to be formatted. The text will be highlighted.

2. **Click** on the **down arrow** to the right of the Font Size drop-down box. A list of available sizes will appear.

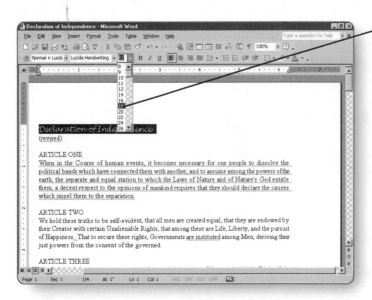

3. Click on a **size**. The new size will be applied to your text.

Applying Bold, Italic, or Underline

Applying formatting attributes like **bold**, *italic,* or <u>underline</u> will call attention to particular parts of your text. You can easily access these choices with the Word toolbar.

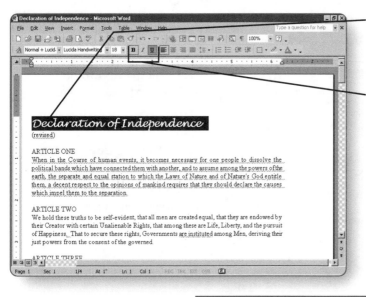

1. Select the **text** to be formatted. The text will be highlighted.

2. Click on the appropriate **toolbar button**: either **B** for bold, *I* for italic, or <u>U</u> for underline, or any combination of the three. The formatting will be applied.

You can repeat the previous steps to remove the attribute.

TIP

Shortcut keys include Ctrl+B for bold, Ctrl+I for italic, and Ctrl+U for underline.

Applying Color

If you have a color printer or are going to share the document electronically, add impact by adding some color.

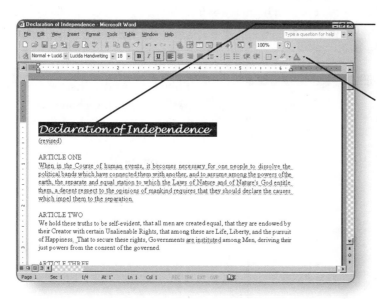

1. **Select** the **text** to be formatted. The text will be highlighted.

2. **Click** on the **down arrow** to the right of the Font Color button. A list of available colors will appear.

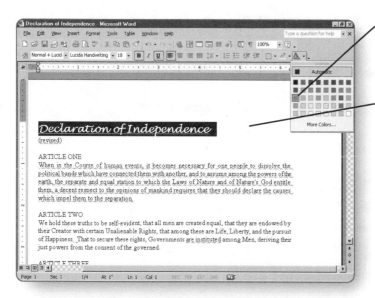

3. **Click** on a **color** in the palette. The Color Palette box will close.

4. **Click** anywhere **in the document** to deselect the text. The text will appear in the selected color.

Highlighting Text

You can highlight text in your document in the same manner that you highlight text in a book with a marker. You can even choose the color of highlighter your want to use. On a black-and-white printer, highlighting appears with gray shading over the text.

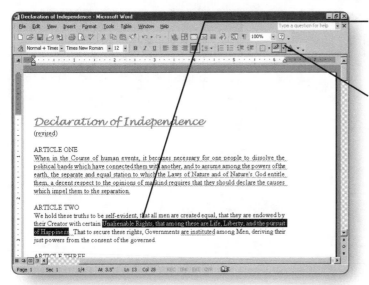

1. **Select** the **text** to be formatted with highlighting. The text will be highlighted.

2. **Click** on the **down arrow** to the right of the Highlight button. A list of available colors will appear. The default color is yellow.

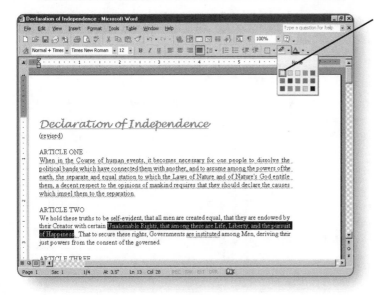

3. **Click** on a **color**. The text will become deselected and the highlighting color will be applied.

Using Special Effects and Animation

Word has other special effects you can apply to your text. Some are great for printed documents, whereas others are designed for documents being shared electronically.

Applying a Font Special Effect

Font effects can include shadowing, embossing, engraving, and others.

1. **Select** the **text** to be formatted. The text will be highlighted.

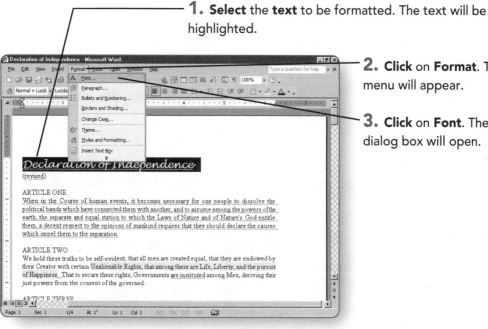

2. **Click** on **Format**. The Format menu will appear.

3. **Click** on **Font**. The Font dialog box will open.

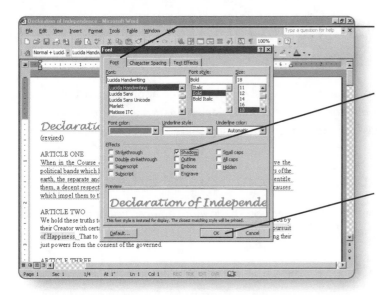

4. If necessary, **click** on the **Font tab**. The Font tab will be on top.

5. Click on any desired **options** in the Effects boxes. A check mark will appear in any selected effect.

6. Click on **OK**. The dialog box will close and the effect will be applied to your text.

Adding Animation to Text

Word includes six animation effects that can be added to a document. These effects will only display on a document being viewed electronically.

1. Select the **text** to be formatted. The text will be highlighted.

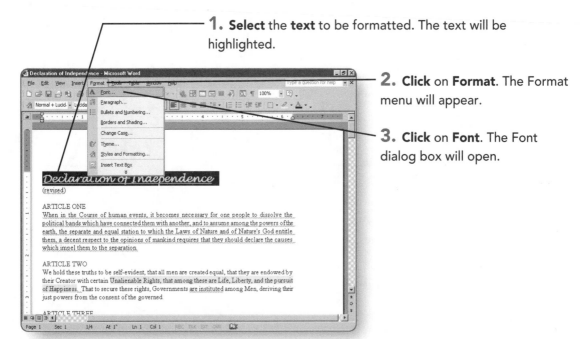

2. Click on **Format**. The Format menu will appear.

3. Click on **Font**. The Font dialog box will open.

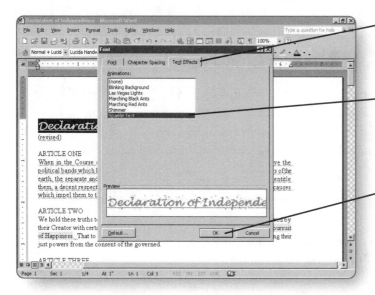

4. If necessary, **click** on the **Text Effects tab**. The Text Effects tab will be on top.

5. **Click** on the desired **animation** in the Animations list box. A sample of the effect will display in the preview box.

6. **Click** on **OK**. The dialog box will close and the effect will be applied to your text.

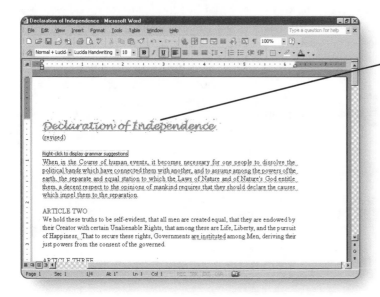

NOTE

Word is quirky sometimes with special effects. If the effect does not display on your screen, try pressing the Page Down and Page Up keys a few times and then returning to the text with the special effect. The effect should be activated.

Copying Formatting to Another Selection

If you spend several minutes setting up just the right formatting for a heading that will appear multiple times in a long document, you don't want to have to try and remember your selections and repeat them. Instead, you can use the Format Painter tool.

> **TIP**
> You also can copy formatting by using the Styles and Formatting Task Pane, as you'll learn in the next section.

1. Select some of the **text** that has the formatting you want to use elsewhere. The text will be highlighted.

2. Click on the **Format Painter button**. The mouse pointer will change to a paintbrush.

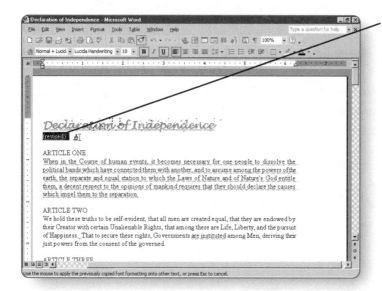

3. **Press and hold** the mouse button and **drag** over the text to be formatted. The new text becomes highlighted.

4. **Release** the **mouse button**. The new text will have the attributes of the original text.

TIP

To keep the Format Painter function on for repeated use, click twice on the Format Painter button. When finished using the Format Painter function, click on the button again to turn it off.

Using the Styles and Formatting Task Pane

In Chapter 1, "Getting Started with Word," you learned about Word's new task panes. One of the task panes, the Styles and Formatting task pane, assists you with formatting.

TIP

If you don't already have the task pane displayed, click on View, task pane.

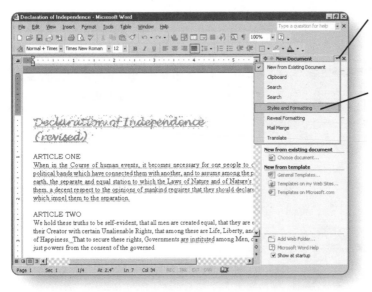

1. **Click** on the **task pane drop-down arrow**. A list of other task panes will appear.

2. **Click** on **Styles and Formatting**. The Styles and Formatting task pane will appear.

Identifying Text Characteristics

The Styles and Formatting task pane shows you the different character styles you've used in your current document.

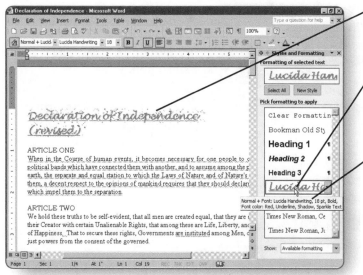

1. Click in the **text** you want to identify. A black box surrounds the style description of the text.

2. Pause the **mouse pointer** over the black style box. A yellow tip will appear.

The yellow tip lists all style characteristics.

Applying Formatting

Earlier in this chapter you learned how to use the Format Painter tool to copy formatting from one block of text to another. You also can use the Styles and Formatting Task Pane to apply formatting.

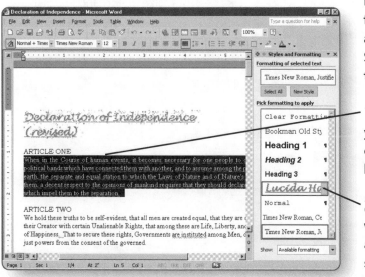

1. Select the **text** to which you want to apply the text characteristics. The text will be highlighted.

2. Click in the **style box** you want to use. The new text attributes will be applied to the selected text.

Clearing Formatting

You also can quickly clear all formatting from selected text by
using the Styles and Formatting Task Pane.

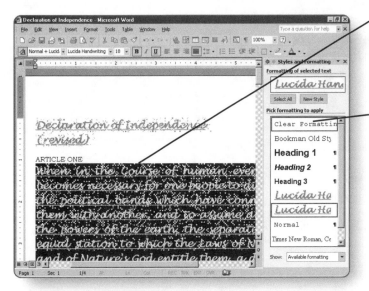

1. Highlight the **text** from
which you want to remove
formatting. The text will be
highlighted.

2. Click on **Clear Formatting**.
All formatting will be removed
from the selected text.

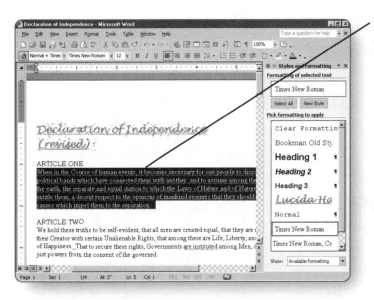

The text appears in the default
font, size, color, and so forth.

Changing the Default Font

The default font, the font used by Word unless you change it, is 12-point Times New Roman. If you use a different font for most of your documents, change the default.

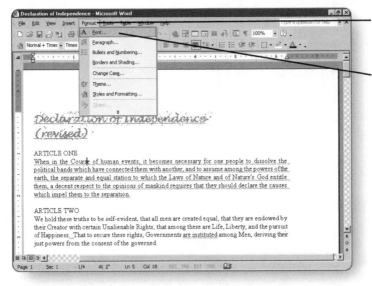

1. Click on **Format**. The Format menu will appear.

2. Click on **Font**. The Font dialog box will open.

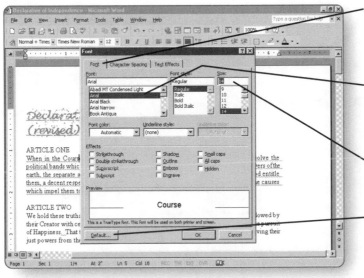

3. If necessary, **click** on the **Font tab**. The Font tab will come to the front.

4. Click on a **font** from the Font box. The font name will be selected.

5. Click on a **size** from the Size box. The size will be selected.

6. Click on **Default**. A dialog box will open.

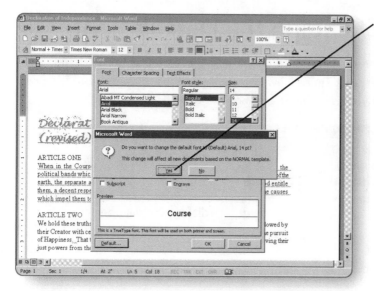

7. Click on **Yes**. The dialog box will close and the next time you create a new document, the font you selected will be the current font.

9

Inserting Special Characters

When you look at all of the keys on the computer keyboard, you may think that you have every character you'd ever need at your fingertips. Occasionally, however, you'll need a special character that isn't on the keyboard. When that happens, Word has several features that can help. In this chapter, you'll learn how to:

- Use drop caps
- Insert special characters and symbols

Using Drop Caps

If you're writing a newsletter, preparing a special report, or creating a letterhead, you may want to use a *drop cap*, an enlarged first letter.

Creating a Drop Cap

Only the first letter of a paragraph can be formatted as a drop cap.

1. Click anywhere in the **paragraph** you want to have a drop cap. The blinking insertion point will appear in the paragraph.

2. Click on **Format**. The Format menu will appear.

3. Click on **Drop Cap**. The Drop Cap dialog box will open.

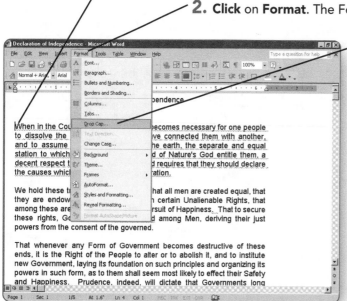

TIP

If Drop Cap does not immediately appear on your Format menu, hold the mouse over the word Format for a couple of seconds. The menu will expand and the Drop Cap option will be displayed.

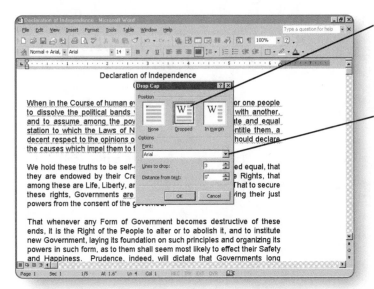

4. Click on a **position** for the Drop Cap character. The selected option will have a box around it.

5. Optionally, **click** on the **Font drop-down arrow**. A list of font choices will appear.

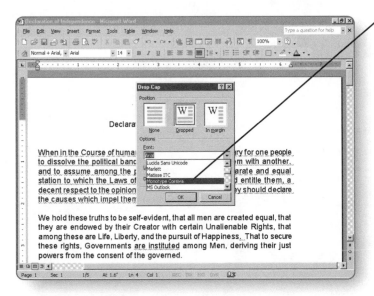

6. Click on a **font name**. The selection will appear in the Font drop-down list box.

NOTE

Your font choices may vary from the ones displayed here.

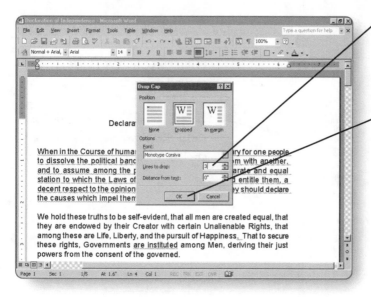

7. **Click** on the **up or down arrows** in the Lines to drop list box. A higher number indicates a larger drop cap.

8. **Click** on **OK**. The first character of the paragraph will be changed to a drop cap character.

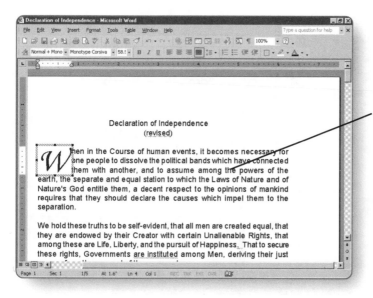

A drop cap character actually appears in a graphic box. You'll learn about graphic images in Part III, "Adding Visual Interest."

9. **Click** in the **body** of the paragraph. The box surrounding the drop cap will disappear.

Removing a Drop Cap

If you later decide you don't want the first letter of the paragraph to be a drop cap, you can remove it.

1. Click anywhere in the **paragraph** from which you want to remove the drop cap. The blinking insertion point will appear in the paragraph.

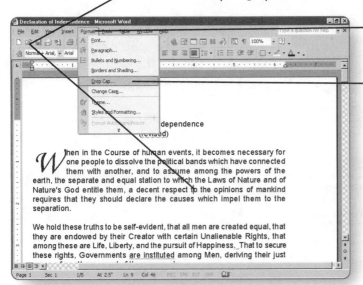

2. Click on **Format**. The Format menu will appear.

3. Click on **Drop Cap**. The Drop Cap dialog box will open.

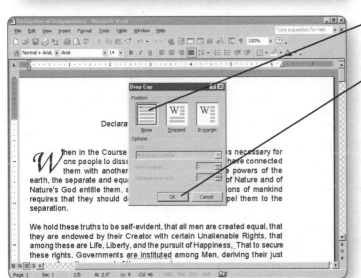

4. Click on **None**. The option will have a box around it.

5. Click on **OK**. The first character of the paragraph will return to normal.

Inserting Special Characters and Symbols

Word provides hundreds of special characters and symbols for you to use in your document. Symbols include things like copyright or trademark symbols, stars, check marks, or airplanes.

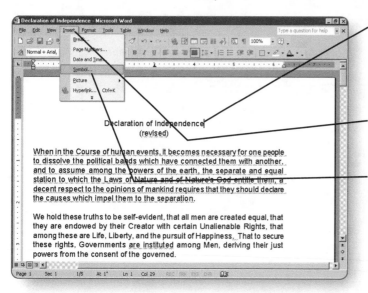

1. **Click** the **mouse** where you want the special character to appear. The blinking insertion point will appear.

2. **Click** on **Insert**. The Insert menu will appear.

3. **Click** on **Symbol**. The Symbol dialog box will open.

NOTE

If you don't see the symbol you want, it may be available in a different font.

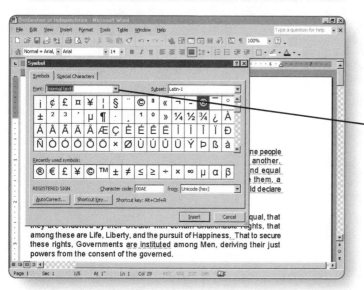

4. **Click** on the **Font drop-down arrow**. A list of fonts will appear.

NOTE
Your font choices may vary from the ones displayed here.

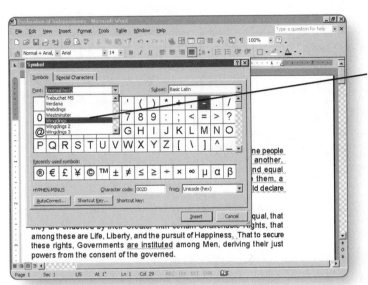

5. Click on a **font**. The symbols available for that font will display.

TIP
For a large variety of unusual characters, look at the Monotype Sorts or the Wingdings fonts.

6. Click on a **character**. The character will appear selected.

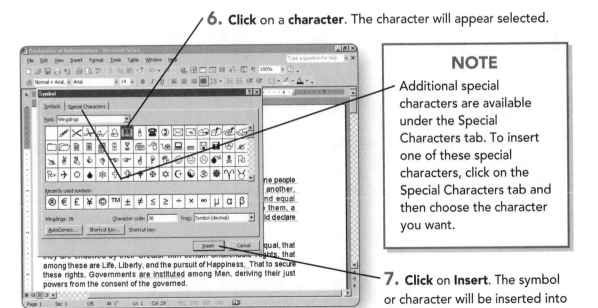

NOTE
Additional special characters are available under the Special Characters tab. To insert one of these special characters, click on the Special Characters tab and then choose the character you want.

7. Click on **Insert**. The symbol or character will be inserted into your document.

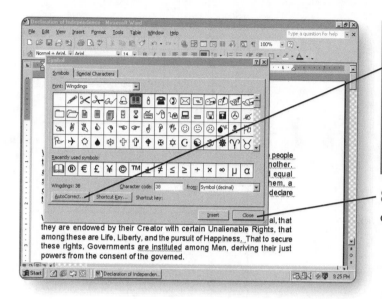

TIP

Click on AutoCorrect to add the selected symbol to your AutoCorrect list. Chapter 17, "Discovering Tools for Speed," shows you about AutoCorrect.

8. Click on **Close**. The symbol dialog box will close.

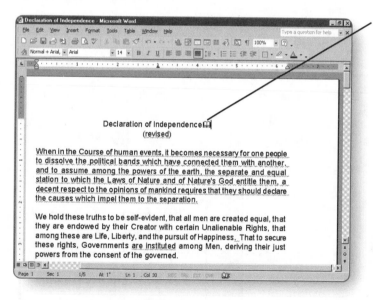

A special character inserted into a document.

10

Working with Lists

Everyone uses lists—from shopping lists and checklists to meeting agendas and outlines. Word can help you format lists in your documents automatically. In this chapter, you'll learn how to:

- Use AutoFormat
- Create a bulleted or numbered list
- Modify the bullet style
- Create a multilevel numbered list
- Remove bullets or numbering

Using AutoFormat As You Type

Word includes a feature called *AutoFormat As You Type*, which guesses what you're trying to do from what you type. This can be a substantial time-saver when you're creating lists.

Using AutoFormat to Create a List

If you type the first list item, preceding it with a bullet character or a number, Word continues the list using the same format.

1. **Type** a **number** then a **closing parenthesis**, a **period**, or a **hyphen.** The number will display in your document.

2. **Press** the **spacebar or Tab key.** The insertion point will move accordingly.

3. **Type** the **text** for the first item on your list. The text will display in the document.

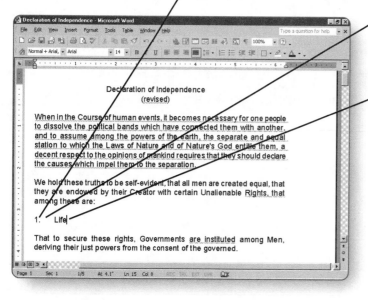

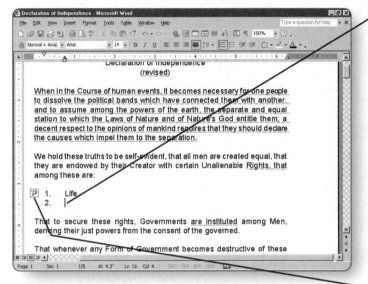

4. Press the **Enter key**. Word will assume you are trying to create a numbered list and will begin the next line with the next item number. Numbered items are also indented.

For example, if you typed a 1 in the first step, then the next line will be a 2; however, if you typed a 6 in the first step, the next line will be a 7.

TIP

A Smart Tag appears from which you can select not to use the automatic numbering, or to discontinue automatic numbering.

5. Type the **text** for the second item on your list. The text will display in the document.

6. Repeat Steps 4 and 5 for each item on your list. The items will be automatically numbered.

NOTE

If you delete a line that has an automatic number, all steps under that line will be renumbered correspondingly.

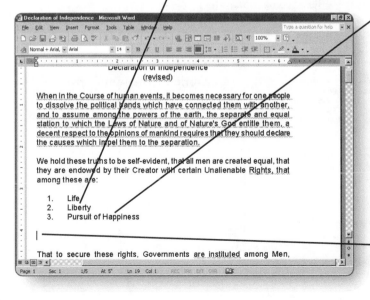

7. Press the **Enter key twice** after the last item in your list. Word will stop automatically entering numbers.

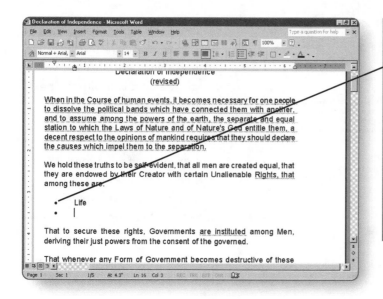

TIP

To begin a bulleted list, instead of typing a number at the first item, type an asterisk, hyphen, or dash. Word will continue the list with the same character. Note that when you use the asterisk key, Word will convert it to a round filled-in bullet.

Turning Off AutoFormat

If the AutoFormat As You Type feature is adding numbers or bullets when you don't want numbers or bullets, you can easily turn off the feature.

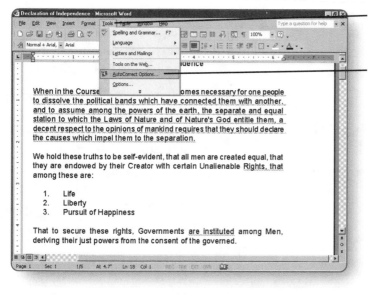

1. **Click** on **Tools**. The Tools menu will appear.

2. **Click** on **AutoCorrect Options**. The AutoCorrect Options dialog box will open.

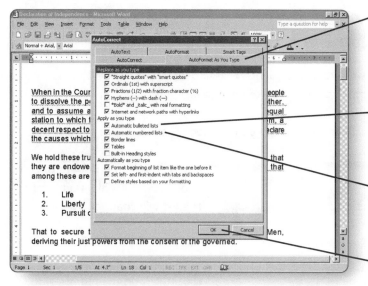

3. **Click** on the **AutoFormat As You Type tab**. The AutoFormat As You Type tab will come to the front.

4. **Click** in the **Automatic bulleted lists check box**. The check mark will be removed.

5. **Click** in the **Automatic numbered lists check box**. The check mark will be removed.

6. **Click** on **OK**. Word will no longer automatically create bulleted and numbered lists.

Working with Bulleted or Numbered Lists

If you've typed text without bullets or numbering, you can use the toolbar to quickly apply them to your list.

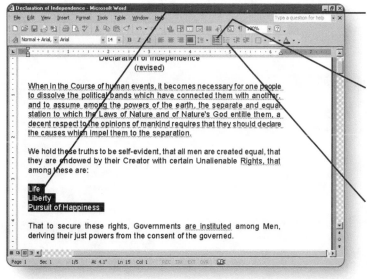

1. **Select** the **list** to be bulleted or numbered. The text will be highlighted.

2a. **Click** on the **Numbering button** on the toolbar. The list will have numbers applied to it.

OR

2b. **Click** on the **Bullets button** on the toolbar. The list will have bullets applied to it.

Switching Between Bulleted and Numbered Lists

If you created a bulleted list and would prefer it to be numbered, it's easy to change it.

1. **Select** the **list** to be changed. The list will be highlighted.

2a. **Click** on the **Bullets button** if the list is currently numbered. The list will change to bulleted.

OR

2b. **Click** on the **Numbering button** if the list is currently bulleted. The list will change to numbered.

Changing a List Style

By default, Word places a round bullet at the beginning of each item in a bulleted list and uses Arabic numbers for numbered lists. There are many other styles of bullets and numbers from which you can choose.

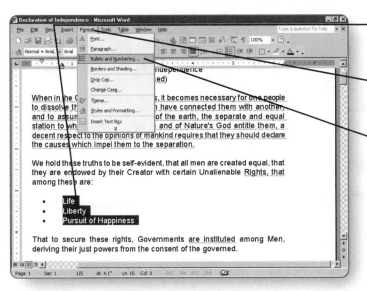

1. Select the **list**. The list will be highlighted.

2. Click on **Format**. The Format menu will appear.

3. Click on **Bullets and Numbering**. The Bullets and Numbering dialog box will open.

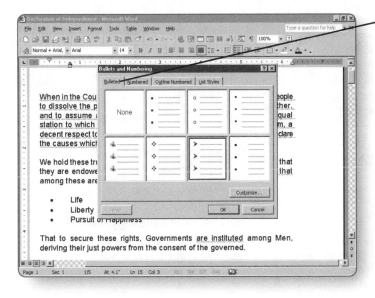

4a. Click on the **Bulleted tab** if you want to change the style of bullet. The Bulleted tab will come to the front.

OR

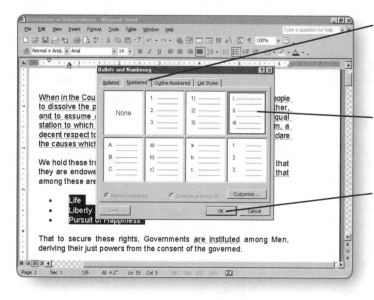

4b. **Click** on the **Numbered tab** if you want to change the numbering style. The Numbered tab will come to the front.

5. **Click** on a **style**. A frame will appear around the selected style.

6. **Click** on **OK**. The dialog box will close.

Word will apply the new style to the existing list and any new lists will be formatted the same way.

Creating Multilevel Numbered Lists

Often you will want to have a list within a list. You can tell Word to create different levels within your lists and to choose the style of those levels. Word calls these multilevel lists *Outline Numbered Lists*.

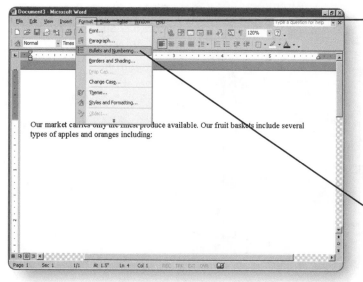

1. **Click** on **Format**. The Format menu will appear.

> ### TIP
> For an Outline Numbered list it's easier if you set the formatting before you actually type the list.

2. **Click** on **Bullets and Numbering**. The Bullets and Numbering dialog box will open.

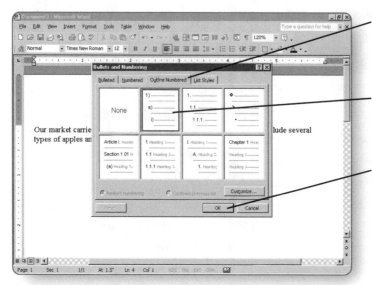

3. Click on the **Outline Numbered tab**. The Outline Numbered tab will be on top.

4. Click on a **Style**. A frame will appear around the selected style.

5. Click on **OK**. The dialog box will close and Word will insert a first-level character in your document.

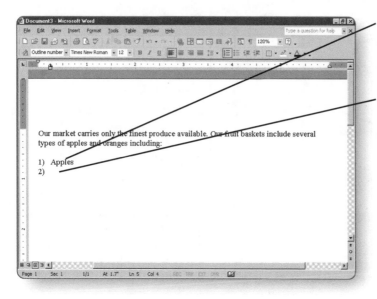

6. Type the **text** of the first-level item. The text will appear in the document.

7. Press the **Enter key**. Word will move to the next line and insert another first-level character.

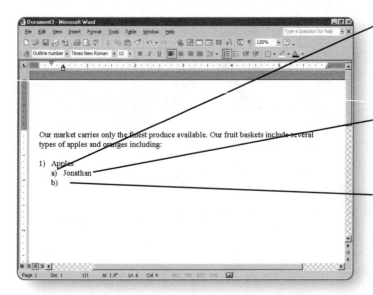

8. Press the **Tab key**. Word will indent the line to the next level and insert the second-level character.

9. Type the **text** for the second-level item. The text will appear in the document.

10. Press the **Enter key**. Word will move to the next line and insert the next second-level character.

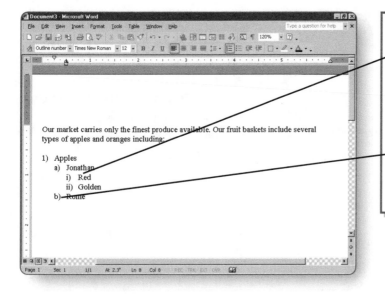

TIP

Each time you want to move another level inward, press the Tab key. Word will shift to the next-level character.

To revert to a higher level, press the Shift and Tab keys.

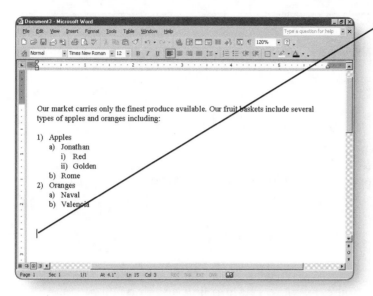

11. **Press** the **Enter key twice** after the last item in the list has been added. The Outline Numbered list will stop.

Removing Bullet or Number Formatting

If you no longer want the bullet or numbering style applied to your list, it only takes a click to remove it.

1. **Select** the **list** to be cleared of bullets or numbers. The text will be highlighted.

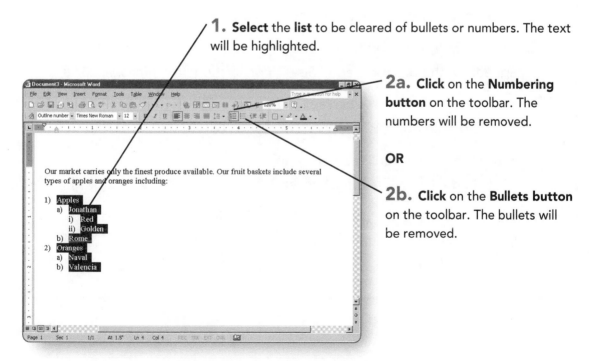

2a. **Click** on the **Numbering button** on the toolbar. The numbers will be removed.

OR

2b. **Click** on the **Bullets button** on the toolbar. The bullets will be removed.

Part II—Making Your Documents Look Good (6–10)

1. What are the default margin settings in a standard Word document? *See "Setting Margins" in Chapter 6*

2. What is Page Orientation? *See "Changing Document Orientation" in Chapter 6*

3. What types of items are displayed in Print Layout View but not in Normal View? *See "Viewing in Print Layout View" in Chapter 6*

4. What are the keyboard shortcuts to change line spacing? *See "Changing Line Spacing" in Chapter 7*

5. What happens to justified text? *See "Aligning Text" in Chapter 7*

6. How large is a font point? *See "Choosing a Font Size" in Chapter 8*

7. When printing to a black-and-white printer, how does highlighting appear on the printed page? *See "Highlighting Text" in Chapter 8*

8. How must a document display to see text animation effects? *See "Adding Animation to Text" in Chapter 8*

9. How many characters in a paragraph can have a Drop Cap? *See "Creating a Drop Cap" in Chapter 9*

10. What happens to the remaining numbered items when you delete a line with automatic numbering? *See "Using AutoFormat to Create a List" in Chapter 10*

PART III

Adding Visual Interest

Chapter 11
  Communicating Ideas with Art **137**

Chapter 12
  Creating WordArt **149**

Chapter 13
  Using the Drawing Toolbar **159**

11

Communicating Ideas with Art

In a world where everyone is frantically busy, you need to communicate your ideas quickly. Pictures help you do this. No time to draw? That's not a problem. Word comes with a wide variety of clip art. *Clip art* is simply a collection of computer pictures or graphics that are ready to use. You just select an appropriate picture and insert it in your document. In this chapter, you'll learn how to:

- Insert clip art and other images
- Move and size the art object
- Adjust the contrast and brightness
- Wrap text around the art

Inserting Clip Art

Clip art pictures can be inserted into a document in any Word view, although to view these visual elements you'll need to be in Print Layout or Web Layout view. If you're not already using one of these views, Word will automatically switch you into Print Layout view so you can see your image.

1. Click the **mouse pointer** approximately where you want to insert your image. The blinking insertion point will appear.

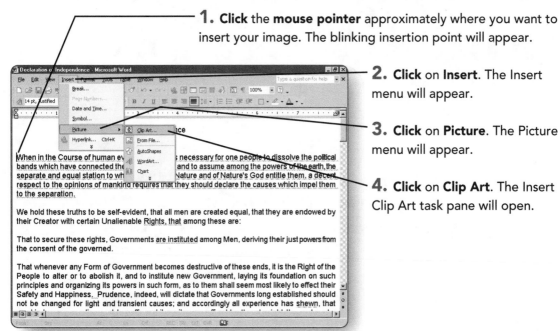

2. Click on **Insert**. The Insert menu will appear.

3. Click on **Picture**. The Picture menu will appear.

4. Click on **Clip Art**. The Insert Clip Art task pane will open.

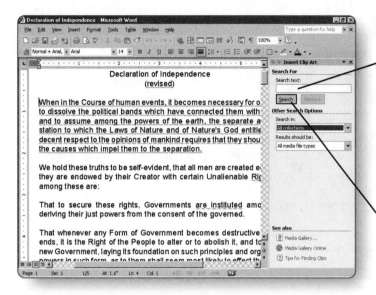

TIP

If you know the specific name of the clip art you want, type it in the search box; otherwise, leave the search box empty and Word will display samples of all clip art.

5. **Click** on **Search**. Word searches for clip art located on your hard drive.

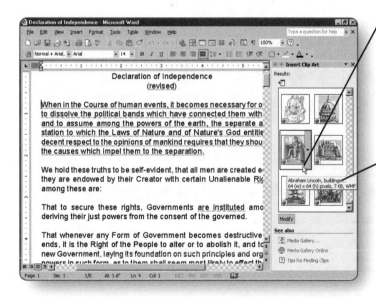

6. **Pause** the **mouse** over a picture. The selected picture will have a frame around it and an arrow on the right side.

NOTE

A tip box describes the selected image.

7. **Click** on the **arrow**. A menu will appear.

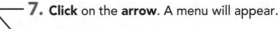

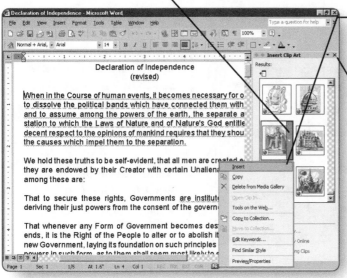

8. **Click** on **Insert**. The clip art will be inserted into your document.

9. **Click** on the **Close button**. The Clip Art task pane will close.

Inserting Personal Images

You can easily insert your own artwork into a Word document, whether it's a photograph, drawing, or other type of artwork.

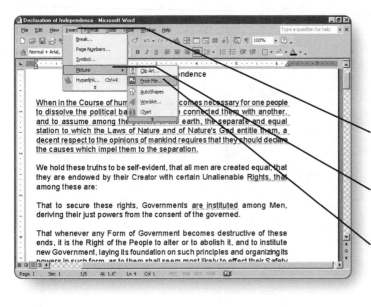

1. **Click** the **mouse pointer** approximately where you want to insert your image. The blinking insertion point will appear.

2. **Click** on **Insert**. The Insert menu will appear.

3. **Click** on **Picture**. The Picture menu will appear.

4. **Click** on **From File**. The Insert Picture dialog box will open.

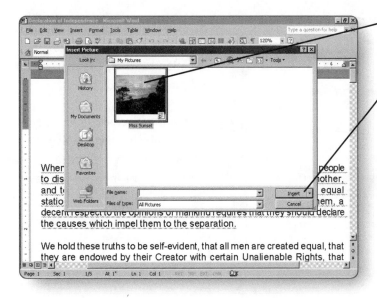

5. Locate and click on the **image** you want to insert. The image will be selected.

6. Click on **Insert**. The image will be inserted into your current document.

You'll learn in the next section how to move, resize, and adjust any image you insert into your document.

Customizing Art

After the image is in your document, you can make adjustments to it so that it works with your document. You can move it, change its size, adjust the brightness and contrast, and wrap text around it or over it.

Resizing Art

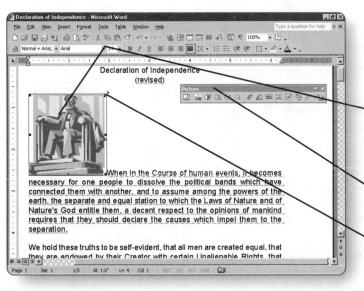

The image may not fit on the page exactly as you had envisioned it. You can easily make the image smaller or larger.

1. Click on the **art** image. The image will be selected and eight small handles will appear.

A special toolbar will appear with tools to modify the clip art.

2. Position the **mouse pointer** over one of the handles. The mouse pointer will turn into a double-headed arrow.

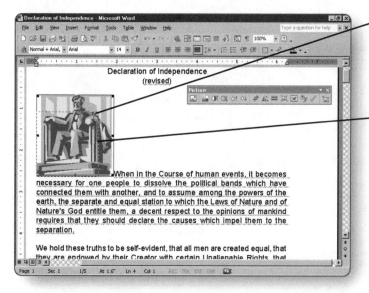

3. **Press** and **hold** your **mouse button** down on one of the selection handles. The pointer will turn into a plus sign.

4. **Drag** the **selection handle** out to make the picture larger, or inward to make it smaller. A dotted box will indicate the new size.

NOTE

Dragging on any corner handle will resize the height and width of the object at the same time; dragging on any side handle will resize the art in a single direction.

Moving Art

The picture you choose may need to be moved. As the art is inserted into the document, surrounding text adjusts to make room for it.

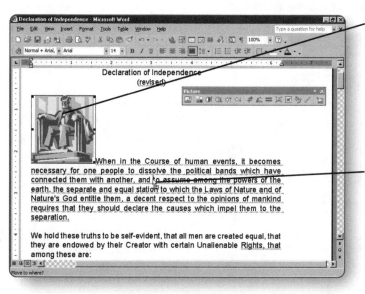

1. **Click** on the **art** image. The image will be selected.

2. **Position** the **mouse pointer** anywhere inside the frame of the graphic. Do not position it over one of the selection handles.

3. **Press and hold** the **mouse button** and **drag** the insertion point (in the form of a gray dotted line) to the new location. The mouse pointer will have a small box at the end of it.

4. Release the **mouse button**. The graphic will be in the new location. Notice that the text will move to make room for the picture.

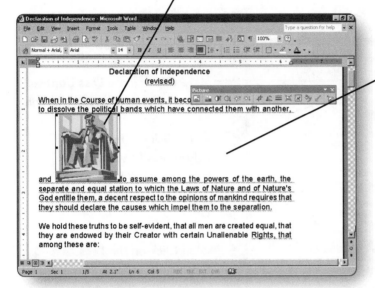

TIP

Click anywhere outside of the art image to deselect it. The Picture toolbar will also close.

Adjusting the Brightness or Contrast

Controls on the Picture toolbar work in the same way as the controls on your TV that adjust the brightness and contrast of the picture. With a picture in a Word document, adjusting this brightness affects the image on the screen and the printout of the picture by adjusting shades of gray.

1. **Click** on the **art** image. The image will be selected.

2a. **Click** on the **More Contrast button**. The contrast will brighten.

OR

2b. **Click** on the **Less Contrast button**. The contrast will lighten.

3a. **Click** on the **More Brightness button**. The brightness will increase.

OR

3b. **Click** on the **Less Brightness button**. The brightness will decrease.

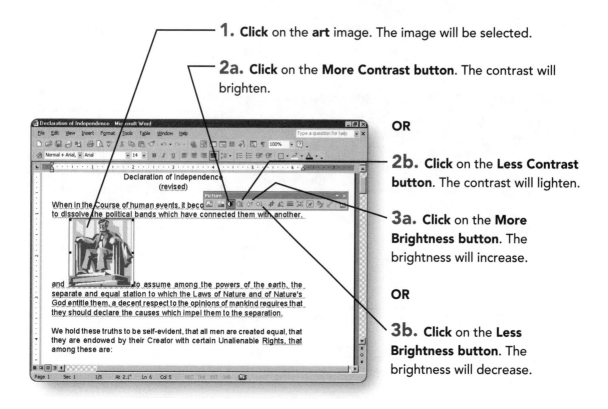

TIP

If the Picture toolbar does not appear when you click on the picture object, click on View, and then click on Toolbars. Click on Picture to display the Picture toolbar.

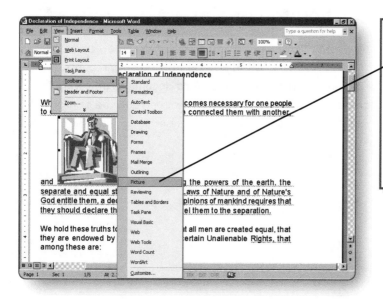

Cropping the Picture

You may want to use just a portion of the entire picture you've selected. You can easily modify the picture by using the Cropping tool.

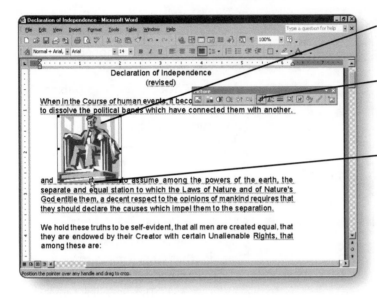

1. **Click** on the **art**. The image will be selected.

2. **Click** on the **Crop button**. The pointer will change to the Cropping tool.

3. **Position** the **mouse pointer** over one of the selection handles. The cropping tool will display over the handle.

4. **Press** and **hold** the **mouse button** and **drag toward** the center of the graphic. The pointer will change to a plus sign, and a dashed line will form a box. The edges of this box form the new edges of the picture, with only the portion inside the box remaining uncropped.

5. **Release** the **mouse** button. The art will be cropped.

6. **Click** on the **Crop button** again. The Cropping tool will be turned off.

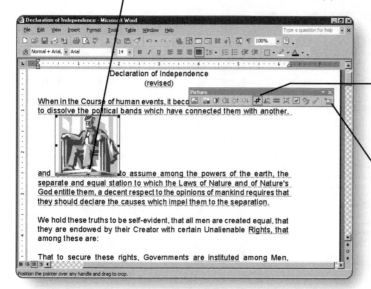

TIP

Click on the Reset Picture button on the Picture toolbar if you don't like any of the adjustments that you've made to your art and would like to start again. The art will return to the way it was originally inserted.

Wrapping Text Around Art

When you insert art into a document, lines of text move up or down to accommodate the art. Depending on the size of the art and the length of the lines of text, this effect may not be quite what you want. You might prefer to have the art sit within the lines of text, with the text stopping before the picture and starting again on the other side. This is called *text wrapping*.

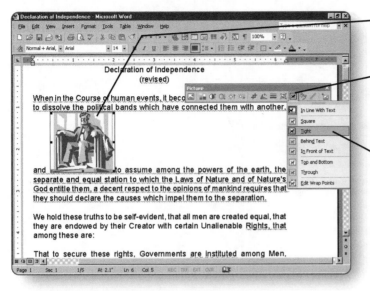

1. Click on the **art**. The image will be selected.

2. Click on the **Text Wrapping button**. A list of text wrapping selections will appear.

3. Click on **one** of the following **options**:

- **Square**. Wraps the text around all four sides of the picture boundaries.

- **Tight**. Wraps the text as tightly as possible to the shape of the image.

- **Behind Text**. Places the graphic image under the text so the text will appear on top of the image.

- **In Front of Text**. Places the graphic image on top of the text so the text will appear under the image.

- **Top and Bottom**. Places the text above and below the graphic object but not on either side.

- **Through**. Places text around the perimeter of the graphic object and through any open areas of the object.

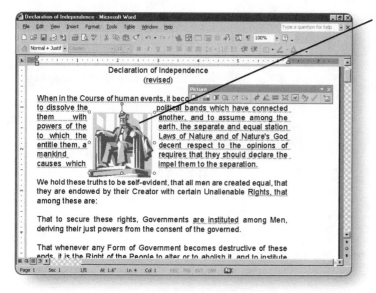

The image here has the text wrapped "tight" around the graphic.

Deleting Art

It's easy to delete any unwanted art from your document.

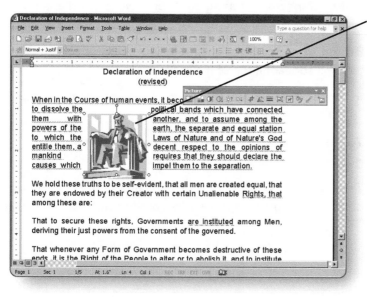

1. Click on the **art**. The image will be selected.

2. Press the **Delete key**. The image will be deleted.

12

Creating WordArt

Adding clip art to a document is one way to add visual excitement, but if you're the creative type, you might want to draw your own pictures using Word's drawing tools. If you want your text to have more impact, WordArt may be your solution. With WordArt, you can take headings or key words and add wonderful color schemes, shapes, and special effects. In this chapter, you'll learn how to:

- Create a WordArt object
- Change the object's size and shape
- Rotate and change the direction of a WordArt object

Adding WordArt

Adding WordArt to your document is simply a matter of selecting a predefined style and typing your text.

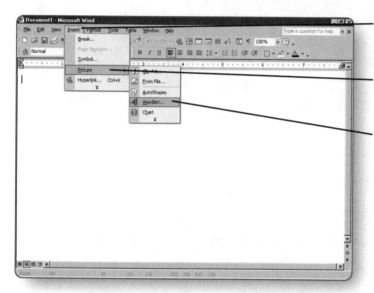

1. **Click** on **Insert**. The Insert menu will appear.

2. **Click** on **Picture**. The Picture submenu will appear.

3. **Click** on **WordArt**. The WordArt Gallery dialog box will open, containing predefined styles in which formats such as shape, color, or shadows are used to enhance text.

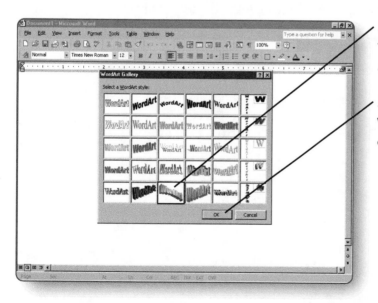

4. **Click** on a WordArt **style**. The selection will have a box around it.

5. **Click** on **OK**. The Edit WordArt Text dialog box will open.

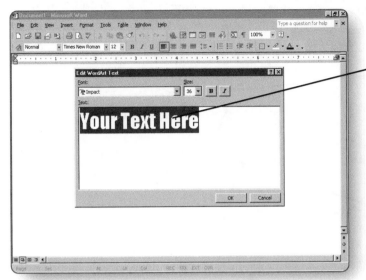

A placeholder in the Text box will say, "Your Text Here."

6. **Type** the **text** that you want to appear as WordArt. Your text will replace the highlighted text.

NOTE

Limiting WordArt to a single line of text is a good idea; the elaborate formatting can make lengthier text difficult to read.

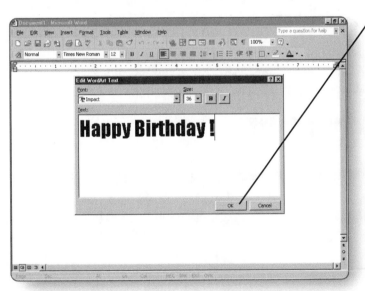

7. **Click** on **OK**. The text that you typed with the WordArt style you selected will be inserted in the document.

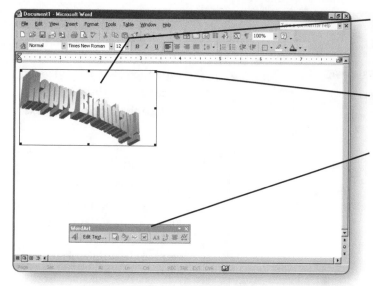

8. Click anywhere on the WordArt **text**. The object will be selected.

The WordArt object will have selection handles around it.

The WordArt toolbar will appear.

Making Adjustments to the WordArt

Even though it looks as though you've made a very specific design selection in the WordArt dialog box, you can actually make lots of adjustments to your selection.

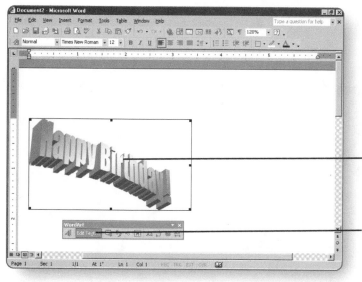

Editing WordArt

If you made a typing error or you want to adjust the size or font of the text, you can easily open the WordArt feature again.

1. Click on the WordArt **object**. The object will be highlighted with selection handles.

2. Click on the **Edit Text button**. The Edit WordArt Text dialog box will open.

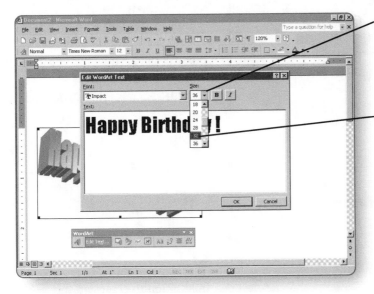

3. Click on the **down arrow** to the right of the Size drop-down box. A list of font sizes will appear.

4. Click on a **font size**. The font size will change.

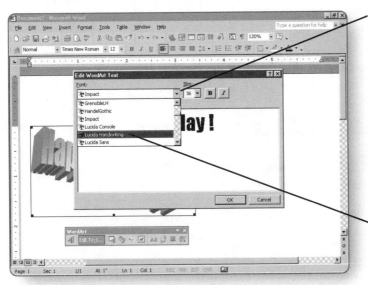

5. Click on the **down arrow** to the right of the Font drop-down box. A list of fonts will appear.

NOTE

Your selection of fonts may vary from the ones shown.

6. Click on a **font**. The font will change.

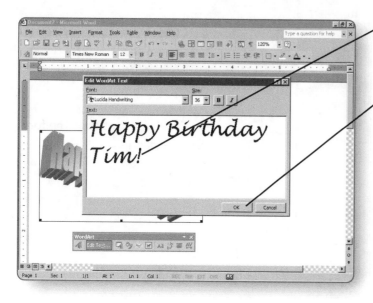

7. **Make** any **changes to** your **text** in the Text box. The text box will reflect the changes.

8. **Click** on **OK**. The object will be modified.

Reshaping an Object

In addition to changing the size of the WordArt text, you can also change the shape of the WordArt object. Modifying the proportions of the object and changing its overall height or width can give you some different effects.

1. **Click** on the **WordArt object**. The object will be highlighted with selection handles.

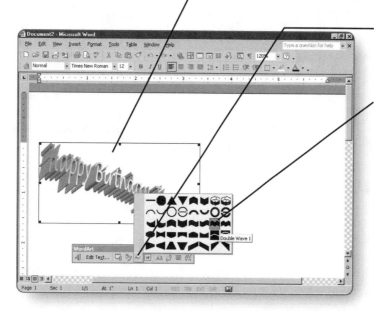

2. **Click** on the **WordArt Shape button** on the WordArt toolbar. A palette of shapes will appear.

3. **Click** on a **shape**. Your WordArt will change to the shape you selected.

NOTE

Some shapes will make your text hard to read, whereas others will add an exciting or fun tone to your words.

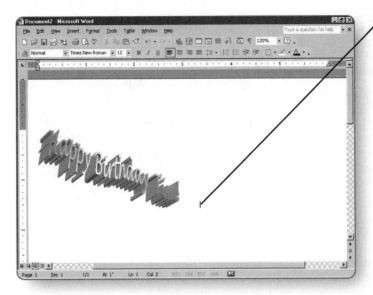

4. Click anywhere **on the document** outside of the WordArt object. The object will be deselected.

Moving Objects on a Page

You can easily move any object, including a WordArt object, around your document. If there is other text in your document, you can move a WordArt object as you learned in Chapter 11, "Communicating Ideas with Art." If, however, no other text exists on the page, you'll need to change the default "in line with text" wrap setting to move or rotate a TextArt object.

1. Click on the WordArt **object**. The object will be highlighted with selection handles.

2. Click on the **Text Wrapping button**. A list of text wrapping selections will appear.

3. Click on **Tight**. The selected object will appear with a green rotation handle.

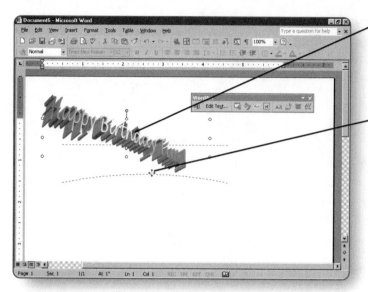

4. **Position** the **mouse pointer** over the middle of the WordArt object. The mouse pointer will turn into a four-headed arrow.

5. **Press** and **hold** the **mouse button** and **drag** the object to another position. The new position will be indicated on the screen.

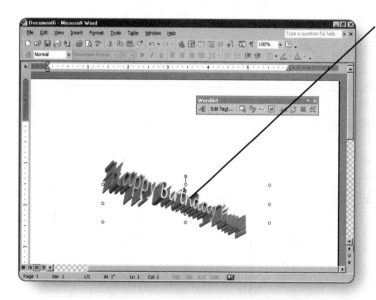

6. **Release** the **mouse button**. The WordArt object will be in its new position.

Rotating WordArt

Because WordArt is an object, it can be rotated to give you greater flexibility in designing the layout of your document page.

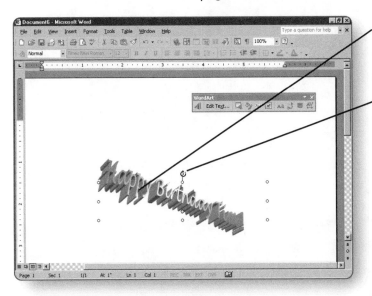

1. Click on the **WordArt object**. The object will be selected.

2. Click on the green **Rotate handle**. The mouse pointer will turn to an arrow with a circle around it.

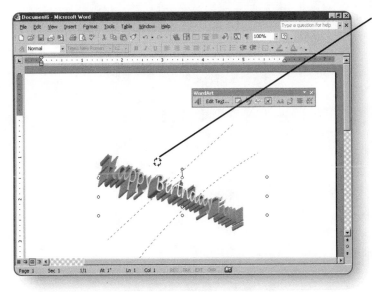

3. Press and **hold** the **mouse button** and **drag** the object. A dotted-line outline of the object in its new position will appear.

4. Release the **mouse button**. The object will display in its new position.

13

Using the Drawing Toolbar

WordArt is a nice shortcut to applying sets of predefined text effects. Many of those same effects, such as shadows, can be added to objects that you create in your Word document using the Drawing toolbar. This toolbar offers predefined drawing shapes, called *AutoShapes*, as well as tools to draw and format lines, boxes, circles, and more. In this chapter, you'll learn how to:

- Display the drawing toolbar
- Draw Autoshapes
- Add text to a drawing
- Give shapes a shadow effect
- Make a shape 3-dimensional

Displaying the Drawing Toolbar

The easiest way to work with drawn objects is to use the Drawing toolbar.

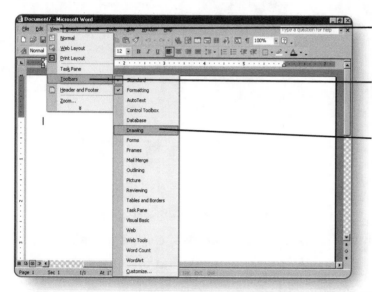

1. Click on **View**. The View menu will appear.

2. Click on **Toolbars**. A list of available toolbars will display.

3. Click on **Drawing**. The Drawing toolbar will display at the bottom of your screen.

Working with AutoShapes

Word has built-in sets of drawing shapes that make it easy to click and drag to draw anything on your document page—from a fancy banner to a pyramid.

Drawing AutoShapes

AutoShapes can help you create flow charts or text callout buttons.

1. Click on **AutoShapes**. A list of AutoShapes categories will appear.

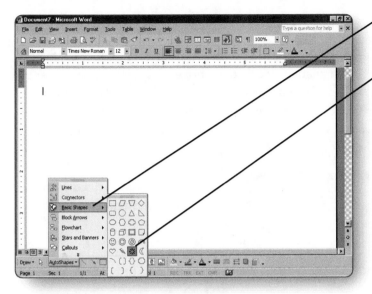

2. Click on a **category**. A selection of shapes will appear.

3. Click on a **shape**. The palette will close, and the pointer will change to a large crosshair.

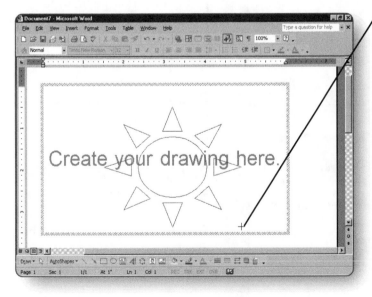

4. Click and **drag** the **mouse**. A shaped object will appear.

5. Release the **mouse button**. The new drawing shape will display with selection handles surrounding it.

Adding Text to Objects

In addition to drawing shapes, the Drawing toolbar contains a tool that enables you to draw boxes in which you can enter text. Because these text boxes are objects and not regular text, you can use drawing features such as rotating and layering with them to create interesting effects. You can even add text inside an AutoShape.

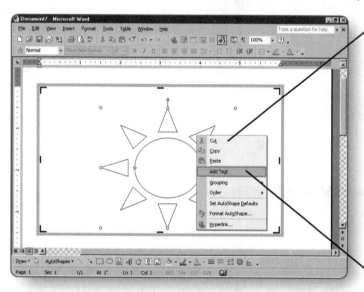

1. Right-click on the **drawn shape**. A shortcut menu will appear.

NOTE

If you selected a shape from the callout category, the shape will be ready for text to be entered. You can skip Steps 1 and 2.

2. Click on **Add Text**. The blinking insertion point will appear.

3. Type some **text**. The text will appear in the AutoShape object.

4. Click outside the **shape**. The blinking insertion point will disappear.

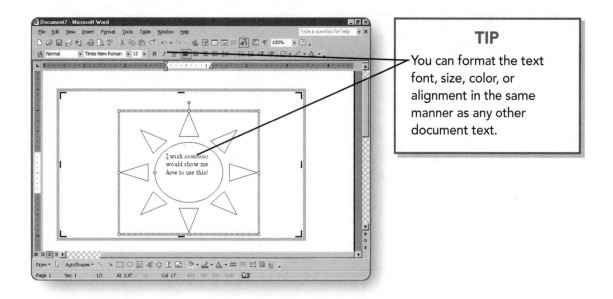

TIP

You can format the text font, size, color, or alignment in the same manner as any other document text.

Creating Shadows

Shadows can add depth and visual interest to objects.

1. Click on the shape **object**. The object will be selected.

2. Click on the **Shadow button**. A palette with selections of shadows will appear.

3. Click on a shadow **option**. The shadow palette will close.

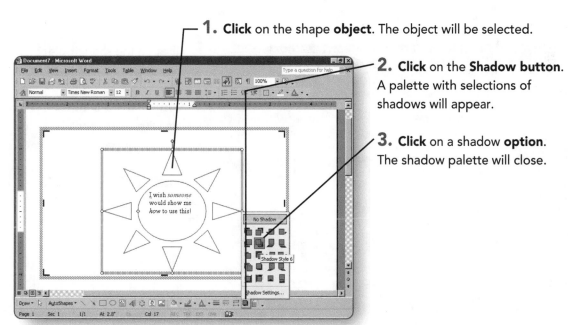

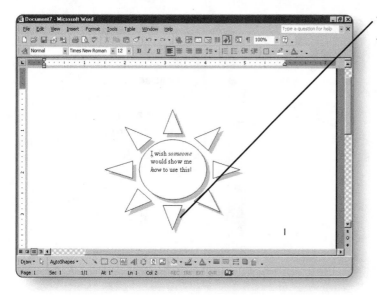

The Shadow will appear around the shape.

Making Shapes 3-Dimensional

Make objects come alive by adding 3-dimensional effects! Some objects won't work with 3-dimensional shapes, so the feature will not be available.

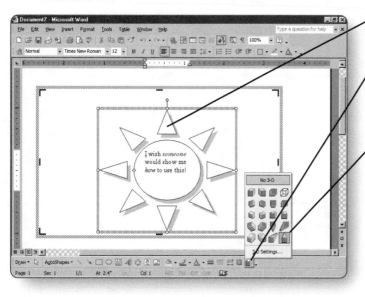

1. Click on the shape **object**. The object will be selected.

2. Click on the **3-D button**. A palette with selections of 3-D settings will appear.

3. Click on a 3-D **option**. The object will take on the added dimension.

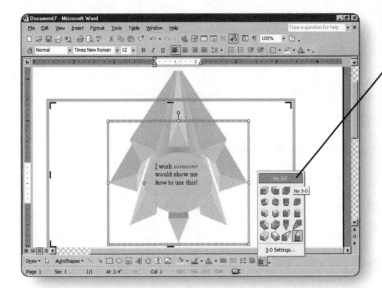

TIP

Remove 3-D settings by choosing No 3-D from the 3-D pallet.

Part III—Adding Visual Interest (11–13)

1. Where do you place your mouse pointer when you want to resize clip art? *See "Resizing Art" in Chapter 11*

2. What happens to surrounding text when you move a clip art object? *See "Moving Art" in Chapter 11*

3. What does "cropping" a picture do? *See "Cropping the Picture" in Chapter 11*

4. Where does text appear when you elect to wrap text tight around a picture? *See "Wrapping Text Around Art" in Chapter 11*

5. Why should text be kept short in a WordArt object? *See "Adding WordArt" in Chapter 12*

6. How do you deselect a WordArt object? *See "Reshaping an Object" in Chapter 12*

7. What do you click on to rotate a WordArt object? *See "Rotating WordArt" in Chapter 12*

8. How can you display the Drawing toolbar? *See "Displaying the Drawing Toolbar" in Chapter 13*

9. What are AutoShapes? *See "Working with AutoShapes" in Chapter 13*

10. Can any shape object work in 3-D? *See "Making Shapes 3-Dimensional" in Chapter 13*

PART IV

Using Tables, Charts, and Columns

Chapter 14
    Working with Tables **169**

Chapter 15
    Creating Charts **195**

Chapter 16
    Using Newspaper Columns **215**

14

Working with Tables

Tables are great for organizing information. When you need to compare data or follow information across several columns, it's easier if the information is displayed in a table. Tables can be used to place information side-by-side in a document, for example, in creating the various sections of an invoice or address list. In this chapter, you'll learn how to:

- Create a simple table
- Use the AutoSum feature
- Format a table
- Add and delete rows and columns
- Add borders around cells

Creating a Simple Table

You can insert a table in any of three different ways. You can insert it from a menu selection, create it from the toolbar, or draw it manually.

Inserting a Table Using the Menu

To create a simple table, all you need to do is estimate the number of rows and columns that you want to start working with, and you're ready to go. You don't even need to be accurate; you can add or delete columns and rows as you work.

1. Click on **Table**. The Table menu will appear.

2. Click on **Insert**. The Insert submenu will appear.

3. Click on **Table**. The Insert Table dialog box will open.

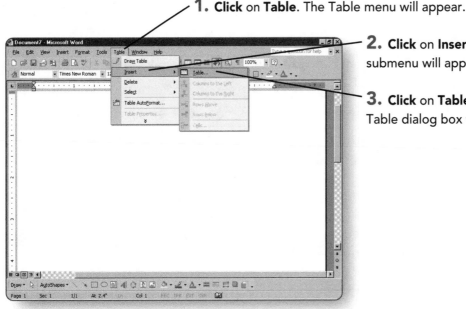

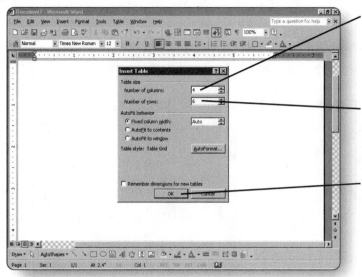

4. Enter the **number of columns** in the Number of columns text box. The number will be displayed.

5. Enter the **number of rows** in the Number of rows text box. The number will be displayed.

6. Click on **OK**. The table will be created.

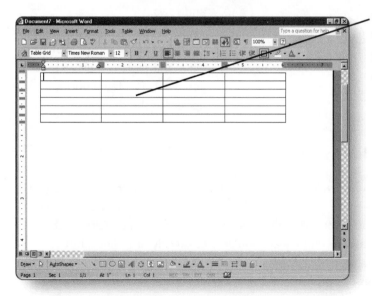

The table will appear in the Word document with the blinking insertion point ready to enter table information.

Creating a Table Using the Toolbar

A button is located on the Word standard toolbar to help you quickly create a table.

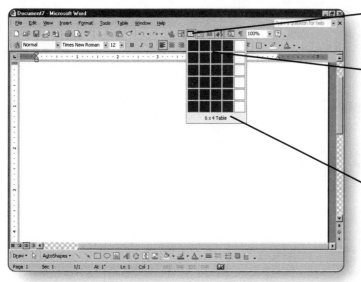

1. Click on the **Insert Table button**. A small grid will appear.

2. Press and **hold** the mouse button and **move** your **mouse pointer** down and across this grid. The selected squares of the grid will turn black.

Numbers at the bottom of the palette will appear, showing you the size of the table in columns and rows.

3. Release the **mouse button** when the table is the size that you want. The table grid will appear in the document.

Using the Draw Table Feature

The Draw Table feature enables you to just draw the grid you need on the screen by hand. This is particularly useful if you don't want all the lines inside the grid. With the Draw Table feature, not only are you able to quickly draw lines, but you also can quickly erase any parts of those lines that you don't need.

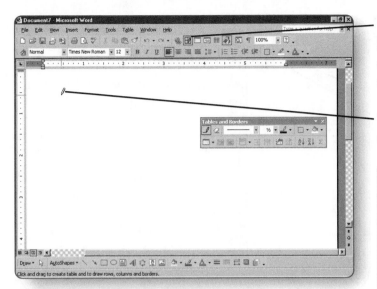

1. **Click** on the **Tables and Borders button**. The Tables and Borders toolbar will be displayed.

The pointer will immediately change to a pen.

NOTE

If you're not already in it, the view will automatically change to Print Layout view. Views were discussed in Chapter 6, "Working with Pages."

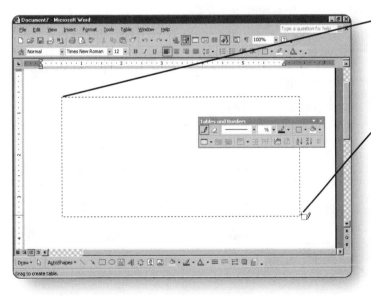

2. **Press** and **hold** the **mouse button** to anchor the upper-left corner of the table. The mouse pointer will turn into an arrow with a small box at the tip of it.

3. **Press** the **mouse button** and **drag** to draw a box that is the approximate size you need for your table. A dotted box will represent the table size.

4. **Release** the **mouse button**. The table border will appear.

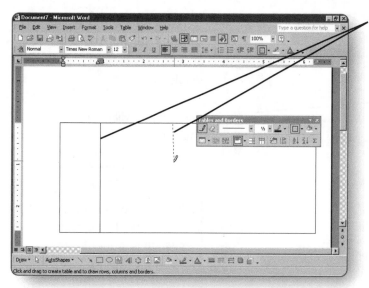

5. Press and **hold** the mouse button and **drag** to draw as many vertical lines as you need to create columns. The lines will appear as you draw them.

NOTE

Don't be concerned over exact placement and spacing of drawn lines. You'll learn how to space or move them later in this chapter.

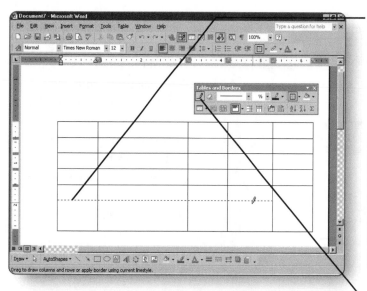

6. Press and **hold** the mouse button and **drag** to draw as many horizontal lines as you need to create rows. The lines will appear as you draw them.

NOTE

You'll notice as you draw these lines that they complete themselves when you reach a particular point.

7. Click on the **Draw Table button**. The feature will be deactivated.

Optionally, you can tell Word to make the rows and columns an equal size.

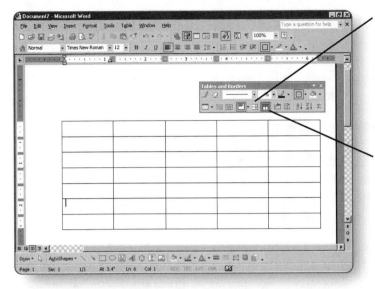

8a. **Click** on the **Distribute Rows Evenly button**. All of the rows you've created will be of equal size.

AND/OR

8b. **Click** on the **Distribute Columns Evenly button**. The table columns will be of equal size.

Entering Text

Each intersection of a column and row is called a cell. Text is typed into the individual cells. As you enter text in the cells, if you have more characters than will fit horizontally, the text automatically wraps to the next line, and the cell and the row it lies in expand vertically to hold the text.

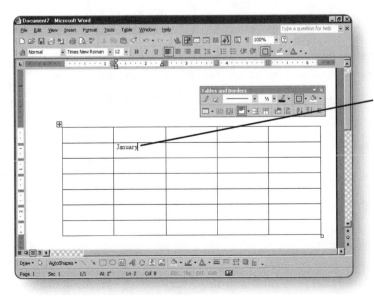

1. **Click** the **mouse pointer** in a cell. The blinking insertion point will appear.

2. **Type** some **text**. The text will display in a single cell.

NOTE

Edit text in cells in the same manner that you edit text in a regular document.

Moving Around in a Table

You can use your keyboard or mouse to move around in a table. To use the mouse, simply click in the cell you want to work with.

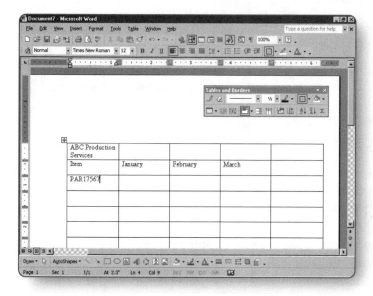

1. **Press** the **Tab key**. The insertion point will move to the cell to the right.

2. **Press** the **Down Arrow key**. The insertion point will move down to the next row.

3. **Press** the **Shift+Tab key**. The insertion point will move to the cell to the left.

4. **Press** the **Up Arrow key**. The insertion point will move up a row.

Adjusting Column Width

The text wrapping feature sometimes causes words to break oddly in the middle. When the text does not break in the position you expect, you may need to widen the column.

Changing Column Width Using the Mouse

You can easily modify any column width by clicking and dragging the mouse.

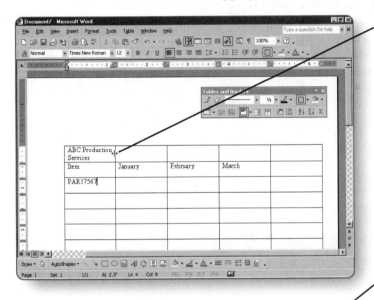

1. Place the **mouse pointer** over the border line of the column. The mouse pointer will change to a double-headed arrow.

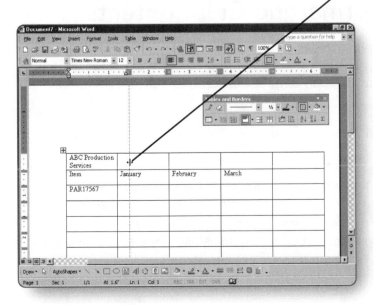

2. Press and hold the **mouse button** and **drag** to the right to increase the column width or to the left to decrease the column width. A dotted line will indicate the new position.

3. Release the **mouse button** when the column is at the width you want. The column width will change.

NOTE

Widening one column may make an adjacent column shrink so the table fits the document width.

Using AutoFit

The *Table AutoFit* feature will automatically adjust all columns to fit your text or the width of the document.

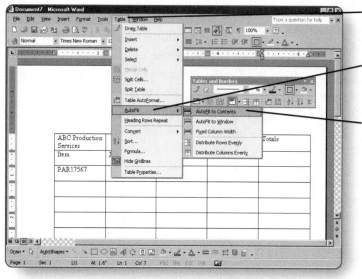

1. Click on **Table**. The Table menu will appear.

2. Click on **AutoFit**. The AutoFit submenu will appear.

3. Click on **AutoFit to Contents**. The columns will widen or shrink according to the cell contents.

Formatting Cell Contents

You can perform a variety of formatting effects on the contents of a cell, just as you do with any text in Word. However, you also can apply some unique formatting to cells themselves.

Aligning Cell Contents

As you make entries in the cells, by default they are all aligned at the top of the cell, along the left side. If you're using numbers in your table, you may want to make them right-align or maybe you would like to center column headings. You'll align your text both horizontally and vertically in each cell. You can align the contents of each cell separately.

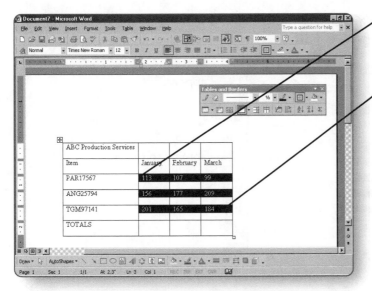

1. **Click** in the **first cell** you want to format. The blinking insertion point will appear.

2. **Press and hold** your **mouse button** and **drag** across any other cells that you want to format. The selected cells will be highlighted.

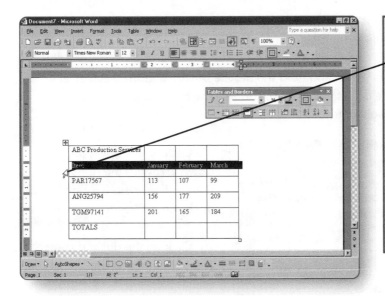

TIP

You also can select a whole row at a time by moving your insertion point to the left of the row until it becomes a white arrow, and then clicking. This works the same for selecting a column—move the insertion point to the top of the column until you see the same arrow.

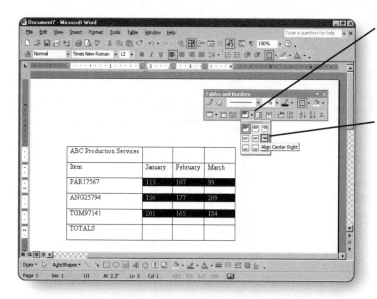

3. **Click** on the arrow to the right of the **Align Top Left button**. A grid of choices will appear.

4. **Click** on an alignment **option**. The option will be applied to the selected cells.

Formatting Text in Cells

Text inside tables is formatted exactly the same way any other text in the document is formatted.

1. **Press** and **hold** the **mouse button** and **drag** across any cells that you want to format. The selected cells will be highlighted.

2. **Click** on the appropriate **down arrow** to the right of the Font or Font size text box. A list of choices will appear.

3. **Click** on the desired **choice**. The option will be applied to the selected cells.

Using AutoFormat

You can add formatting to the lines that divide your rows and columns, and even add color or patterns to the interior of the cells. Of course, you don't want to spend hours trying different line sizes, colors, and patterns. Instead, you can use AutoFormat.

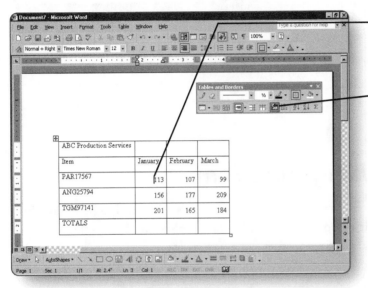

1. Click in any table **cell**. The blinking insertion point will appear.

2. Click on the **Table AutoFormat button**. The Table AutoFormat dialog box will open.

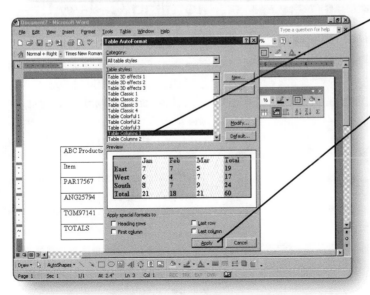

3. Click on a **format** in the Table styles: scroll box. A sample of the format will appear in the Preview window.

4. Click on **Apply**. The selected format is applied to your data.

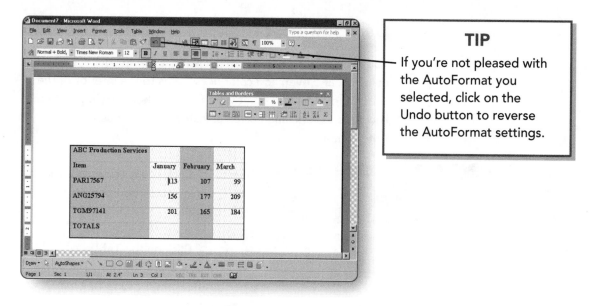

TIP

If you're not pleased with the AutoFormat you selected, click on the Undo button to reverse the AutoFormat settings.

Using AutoSum

Frequently, tables contain numbers that need to be added. For this reason, Word includes an AutoSum button on the Tables and Borders toolbar.

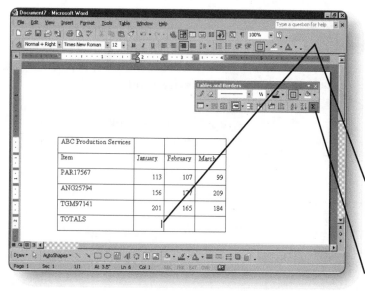

Totaling Cells with AutoSum

The AutoSum feature will first add the cells directly above it. If no values are available above it, the AutoSum feature will add the cells directly to the right of it.

1. Click in the **cell** where you want the total to appear. The blinking insertion point will appear.

2. Click on **AutoSum**. The total will be calculated.

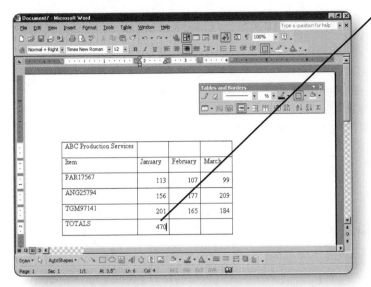

The answer will be displayed in the selected cell.

Updating AutoSum Totals

If you change any of the values in the cells that are totaled, the cell that has the total does not automatically update. You must update it manually.

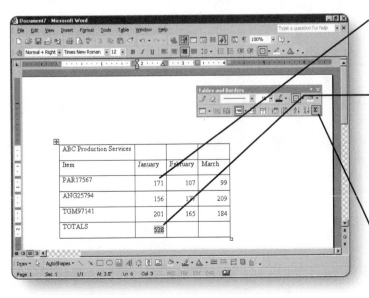

1. Make a **change** to a cell value. The cell will reflect the new number.

2. Click in the **cell** with the current total. Depending on exactly where you click in the cell, either a blinking insertion point will appear or a gray highlight will surround the total.

3. Click on **AutoSum**. The new total will be displayed.

Adding and Deleting Rows and Columns

When you're designing a table, it's easy to forget an essential row or column. However, Word makes it easy to add new rows and columns or delete ones you don't need.

Adding a Row to the End of a Table

You can easily add a row to the bottom of the table you originally created.

1. Click in the **last cell** of the last row. The blinking insertion point will appear.

2. Press the **Tab key**. A new row will automatically appear.

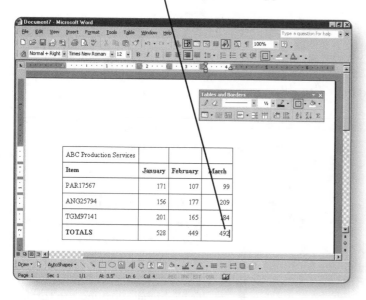

Inserting a Row Between Existing Rows

You may want to add a row at the beginning or in the middle of a table.

1. **Click** in the **row** where you want the new row. The blinking insertion point will appear.

2. **Click** on **Table**. The Table menu will appear.

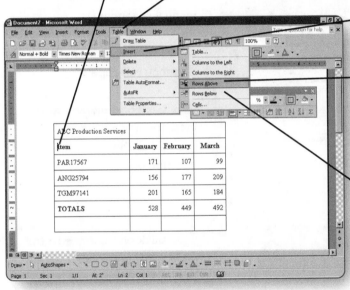

3. **Click** on **Insert**. The Insert submenu will appear.

4a. **Click** on **Rows Above**. The new row will be inserted above the insertion point row.

OR

4b. **Click** on **Rows Below**. The new row will be inserted below the insertion point row.

Inserting a Column

What if you decide you need another category of information in your table? That calls for a new column. Again, you can easily add a column between two existing columns or add one to the end of a set of existing columns.

1. **Click** in the **cell** where you want the new column. The blinking insertion point will appear.

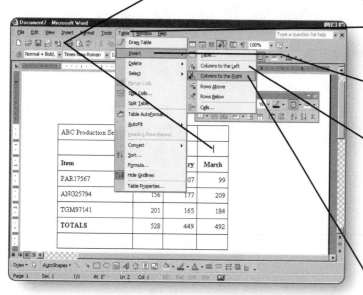

2. **Click** on **Table**. The Table menu will appear.

3. **Click** on **Insert**. The Insert submenu will appear.

4a. **Click** on **Columns to the Left**. The new column will be inserted to the left of the insertion point row.

OR

4b. **Click** on **Columns to the Right**. The new column will be inserted to the right of the insertion point row.

Deleting Rows or Columns

Deleting a row will delete an entire row across a table while deleting a column will delete an entire column.

1. Click the **mouse pointer** in the row that you want to delete. The blinking insertion point will appear.

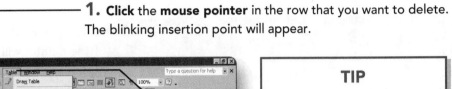

TIP

Optionally, select multiple rows or columns to delete them at the same time.

2. Click on **Table**. The Table menu will appear.

3. Click on **Delete**. The Delete submenu will appear.

4a. Click on **Columns**. The current column will be deleted.

OR

4b. Click on **Rows**. The current row will be deleted.

Erasing Cell Partitions

When you work with tables, you often find that you don't want all of the lines that divide cells. Erasing lines will combine connecting cells.

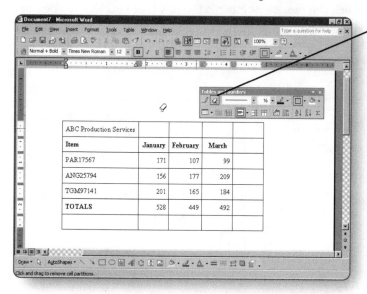

1. **Click** on the **Eraser button**. The pointer will change shape to look like an eraser.

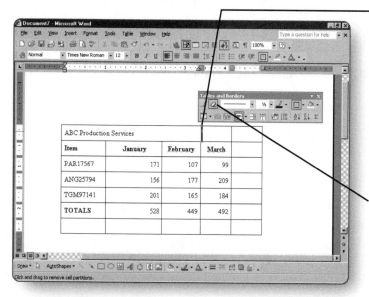

2. **Press** and **hold** the **mouse button** and **drag** the **eraser** over the lines you don't need.

3. **Release** the **mouse button**. The lines will change color and then disappear. The cells on each side of the erased line will be joined.

4. **Click** the **Erase button**. The erase feature will be deactivated.

Changing the Direction of Your Text

It may be more effective to have the text in some cells run vertically rather than horizontally.

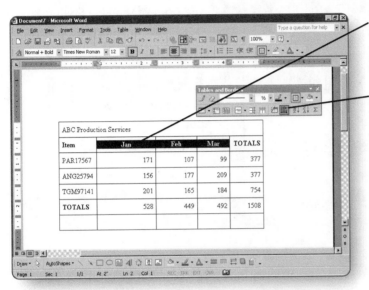

1. **Select** the **text** to be modified. The text will be highlighted.

2. **Click** on the **Change Text Direction button**. The text will display vertically.

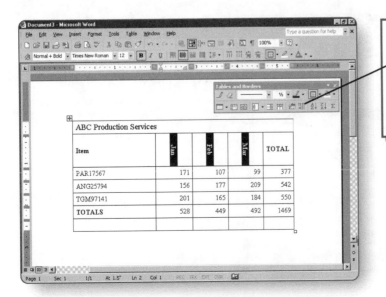

TIP

Each click of the Change Text Direction button modifies the text direction.

Modifying Table Cell Borders

You can modify the styles of the lines that surround your table cells.

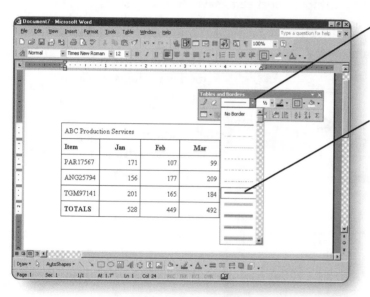

1. Click on the **down arrow** to the right of the Line Style text box. A list of line styles will appear.

2. Click on a **line style**. The mouse pointer will turn into a pencil.

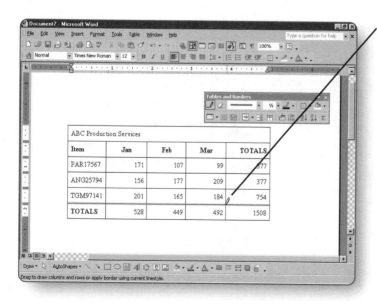

3. Press and **drag** the **mouse** across the lines that you want to have the new border line style. A gray line will appear.

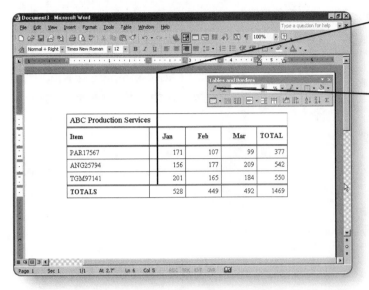

4. Release the **mouse button**. The style will be applied to the selected cells.

5. Click on the **Draw button**. The feature will be deactivated.

Adding a Table Heading Row

If a table extends to more than one page, you may want some of the top rows to repeat on each page.

1. Highlight the **rows** to be repeated. The rows will be highlighted.

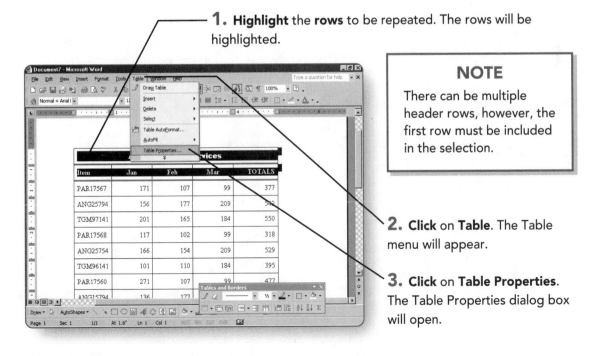

NOTE

There can be multiple header rows, however, the first row must be included in the selection.

2. Click on **Table**. The Table menu will appear.

3. Click on **Table Properties**. The Table Properties dialog box will open.

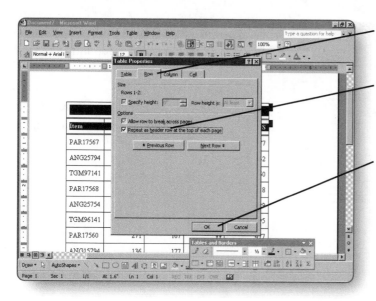

4. Click on **Row**. The Row tab will come to the front.

5. Click on **Repeat as header row at the top of each page**. The option will be selected.

6. Click on **OK**. The Table Properties dialog box will close.

Moving a Table

If you created the table in the wrong position in the document, you can easily move it to a new location.

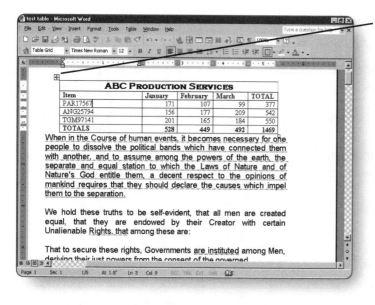

1. Position the **mouse** over the small black cross in the upper-left corner of the table. The mouse pointer will turn into a small black cross.

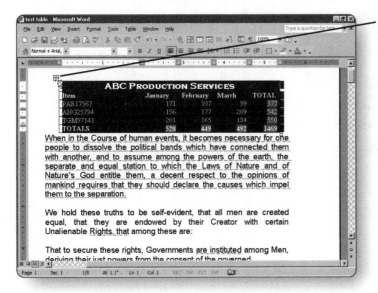

2. Click the **mouse** on the black cross. The entire table will become highlighted.

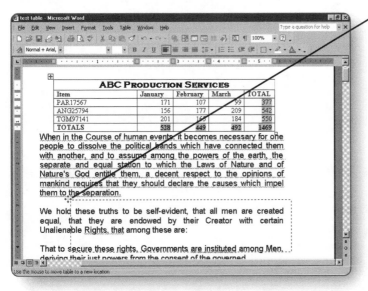

3. Press and **drag** the mouse pointer to a new location in the document. A dotted box indicating the boundaries of the table will appear with the mouse pointer.

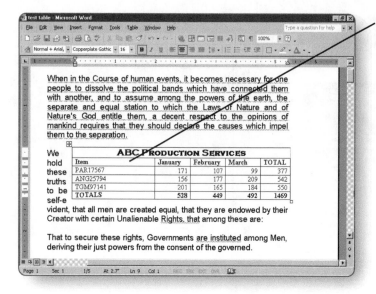

4. **Release** the **mouse button**. The table will move to the new location.

15

Creating Charts

Charts summarize data and make it easy for the reader to compare results. They also add color and interest to what otherwise may be a dull document. This chapter illustrates how to do the following:

- Create a column chart from the data in a table
- Add a chart title
- Adjust the size of your chart and format elements
- Create a chart without creating a table first

Creating a Chart from a Table

You can make a column chart from a table you've already created. Column charts are easy for readers to understand and are often used for comparing data from one year to another, one quarter to another, or estimated budget data against actual data.

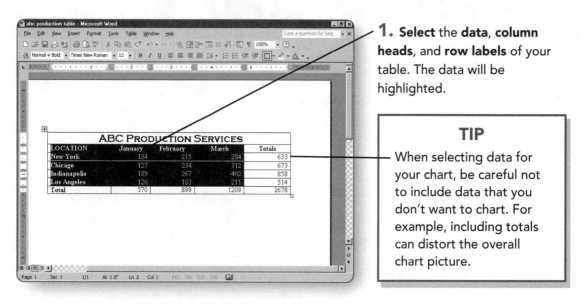

1. Select the **data, column heads,** and **row labels** of your table. The data will be highlighted.

TIP

When selecting data for your chart, be careful not to include data that you don't want to chart. For example, including totals can distort the overall chart picture.

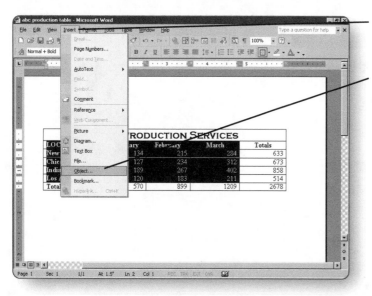

2. Click on **Insert.** The Insert menu will appear.

3. Click on **Object.** The Object dialog box will open.

4. If necessary, **click** on the **Create New tab**. The Create New tab will come to the front.

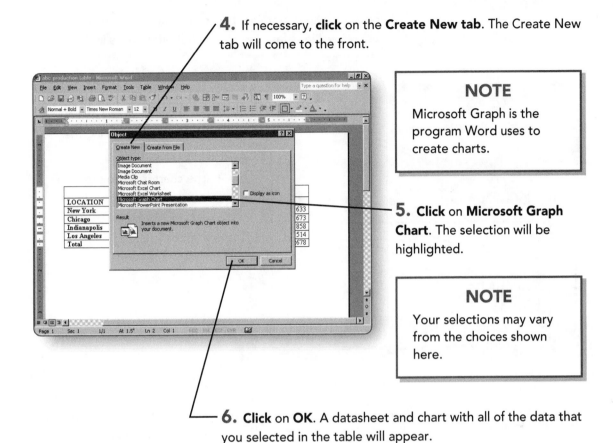

NOTE

Microsoft Graph is the program Word uses to create charts.

5. Click on **Microsoft Graph Chart**. The selection will be highlighted.

NOTE

Your selections may vary from the choices shown here.

6. Click on **OK**. A datasheet and chart with all of the data that you selected in the table will appear.

If you work with spreadsheet software such as Excel, the datasheet will look familiar. Notice the differences in the window now:

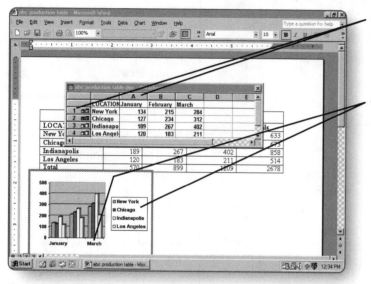

● The datasheet is set up with letters labeling the columns and numbers labeling the rows.

● The chart is complete with legend and category labels.

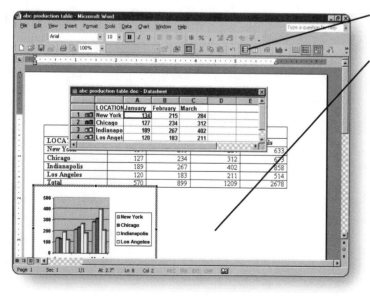

● The Standard toolbar changes to the Chart toolbar.

7. Click anywhere in the **document body**. The datasheet will close and your Word document will return with a chart inserted.

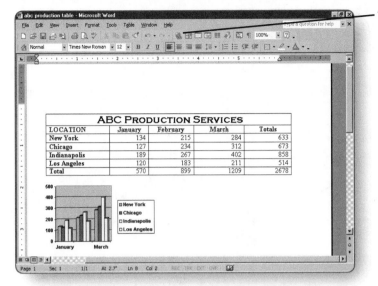

The standard toolbar will return.

Resizing a Chart

The chart is created automatically and won't always be the exact size you need in your document. Not only is it sometimes the wrong size, but you may need to adjust the width so that all the category labels are visible. In the example shown here, the word "February" is not displayed due to size constraints.

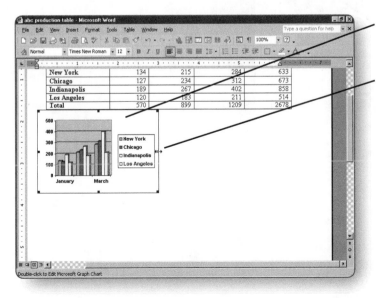

1. **Click** on the **chart**. Eight small handles will appear.

2. **Position** the **mouse pointer** over any of the handles. The mouse pointer will turn into a black double-headed arrow.

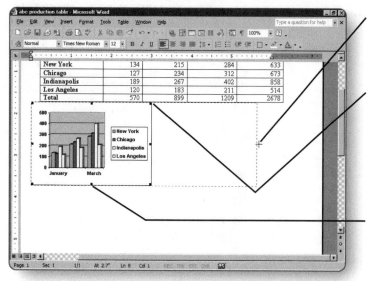

3. Press and drag the **handle**. A dotted line will indicate the chart's new size.

- Dragging corner handles will enlarge or shrink the window in both height and width in proportion to its original size.

- Dragging a side handle will modify the width only.

- Dragging a top or bottom handle will modify the height only.

4. Release the **mouse button**. The chart will be resized.

The category label "February" is now displayed.

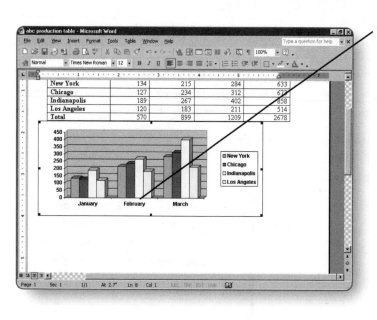

Editing a Chart

There are many options you can modify on a chart, ranging from adding a title or modifying font and color selections to changing the type of chart.

Hiding the Datasheet

Frequently the datasheet is lying on top of the chart, making it difficult to work with the elements of the chart. You can hide it and then redisplay it if necessary.

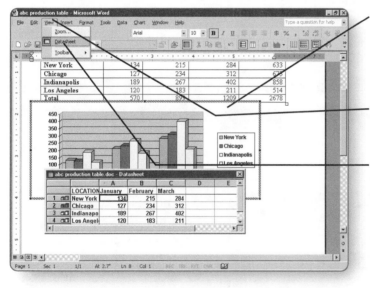

1. Double-click on the **chart**. The datasheet will reappear and the chart menu will be reactivated.

2. Click on **View**. The View menu will appear.

3. Click on **Datasheet**. The Datasheet will close.

Repeat the previous steps to redisplay the Datasheet.

Adding a Chart Title

A chart title helps your reader quickly interpret the information displayed in the chart.

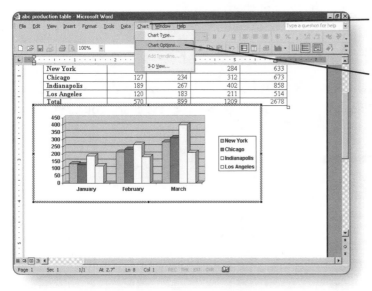

1. Click on **Chart**. The Chart menu will appear.

2. Click on **Chart Options**. The Chart Options dialog box will open.

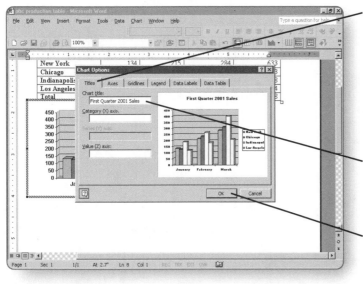

3. If necessary **click** on the **Titles tab**. The Titles tab will come to the front.

4. Click in the **Chart title: text box**. A blinking insertion point will appear.

5. Type a **title** for your chart. The title will display in the chart preview box.

6. Click on **OK**. The new title will be added to your chart.

Formatting Chart Text

Similar to standard Word documents, you can change the font, size, style, color, and other attributes for text on a chart. You can change the formatting of the Title, Legends, Category Axis, or Value Axis.

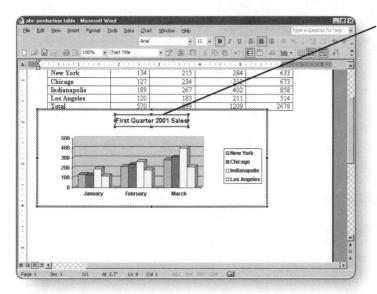

1. **Double-click** on the **text element** of the chart that you want to format. The Format dialog box will open.

NOTE

The dialog box name and the options displayed will vary with the chart element you selected.

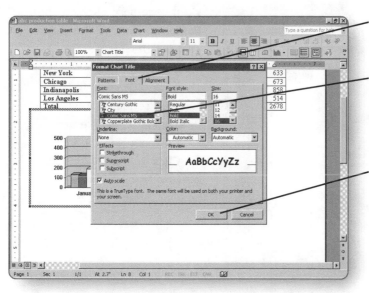

2. **Click** on **Font**. The Font tab will come to the front.

3. **Click** on the **Font**, **Font Style**, or **Font Size** you want for the selected object. The choices will be highlighted.

4. **Click** on **OK**. The Format dialog box will close.

Modifying Chart Colors and Patterns

Each series in the chart can be of any color or fill pattern you specify.

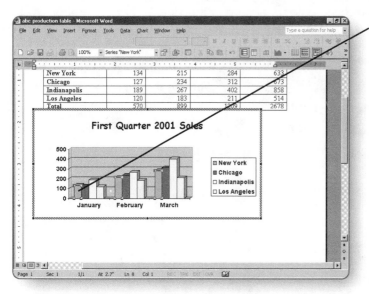

1. Double-click on the **first bar** of any series in the chart. The Format Data Series dialog box will open.

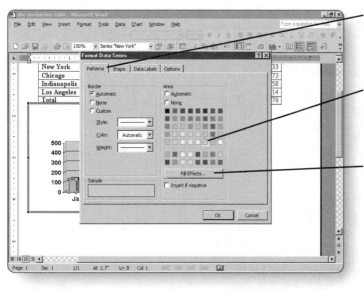

2. If necessary, **click** on **Patterns**. The Patterns tab will come to the front.

3. Click on a **color** for the selected series. A preview will display in the Sample box.

4. Click on the **Fill Effects button**. The Fill Effects dialog box will open.

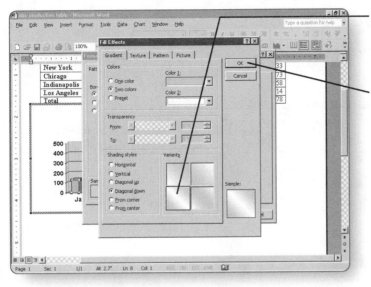

5. Click on a **fill choice** for the selected bar series. A sample will be displayed.

6. Click on **OK**. The Fill Effects dialog box will close.

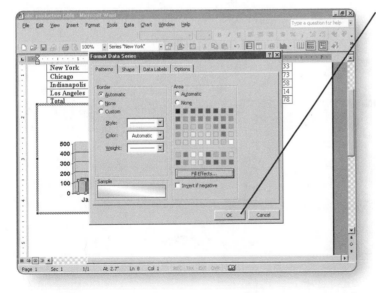

7. Click on **OK**. The Format dialog box will close and the series, including the legend, will change to the new color.

8. Repeat Steps 1-7 for each series to be modified.

Selecting Bar Shapes

Word includes several fun shapes you can use for column charts instead of the default rectangular bars.

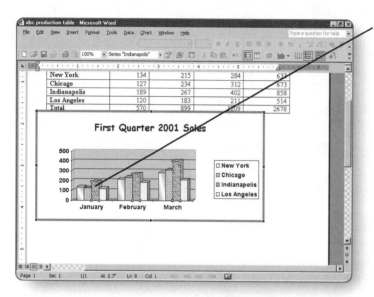

1. Double-click on the **first bar** of any series in the chart. The Format Data Series dialog box will open.

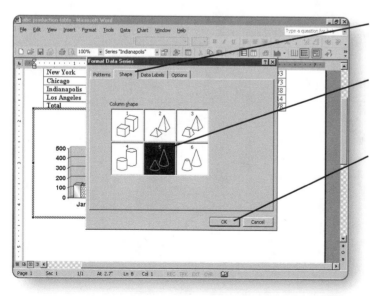

2. Click on the **Shape tab**. The Shape tab will come to the front.

3. Click on a **shape** for the selected series. The option will be selected.

4. Click on **OK**. The selected series on the chart will change to the new shape.

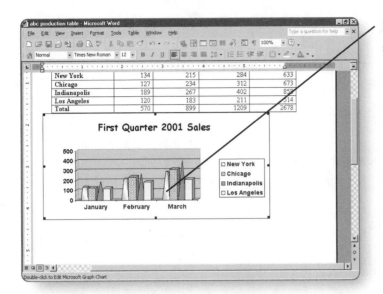

5. Repeat Steps 1-4 for each series to be modified.

Changing the Chart Type

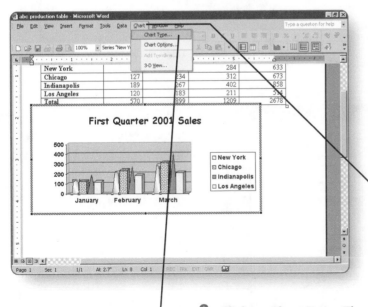

Several types of charts are available to you. Column charts are fine for comparing sets of data, and line charts are useful to show trends, such as population growth. Pie charts, on the other hand, show percentages that make up a whole.

1. Click on **Chart**. The Chart menu will appear.

2. Click on **Chart Type**. The Chart Type dialog box will open.

TIP

If the Chart menu is not displayed on the menu bar, double-click on the chart.

3. Click on a **Chart Type**. A selection of options will appear.

4. Click on a **chart sub-type** (style) for your chart. The option will be selected.

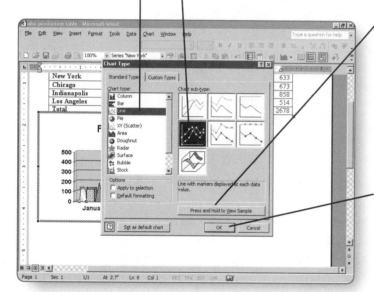

5. Press and hold the **mouse button** on **Press and Hold to View Sample**. A representative chart with your "live" data will display.

6. Release the **mouse button**. The options will reappear.

7. Click on **OK**. The chart type will change.

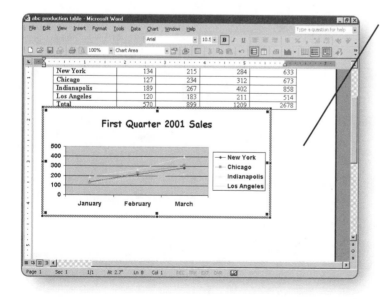

8. Click anywhere in the **document body**. The remainder of the Word document will return, ready for further editing.

Editing Chart Data

Changing the data in a table does not automatically reflect in a chart. If, after you've inserted the chart into your document, you need to make changes to the data, you can do so by modifying the datasheet.

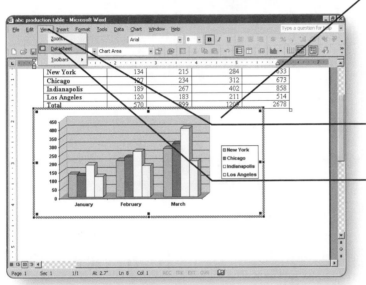

1. Double-click on the **chart**. The chart options will be reactivated.

If the datasheet is not displayed, you'll need to reveal it.

2. Click on **View**. The View menu will appear.

3. Click on **Datasheet**. The datasheet will redisplay.

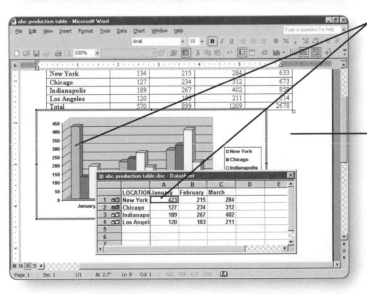

4. Click in any cell of the datasheet and **type** any desired **changes**. The chart will automatically update to reflect the changes.

5. Click anywhere in the **document body**. You will return to your Word document.

Deleting a Chart

If at any time a chart is no longer necessary, you can easily delete it.

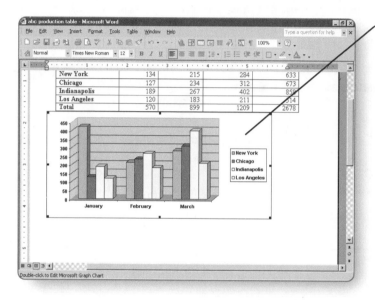

1. Click on the **chart**. The chart will be selected with eight black handles.

2. Press the **Delete key**. The chart will be deleted from the Word document.

Creating a Chart from Scratch

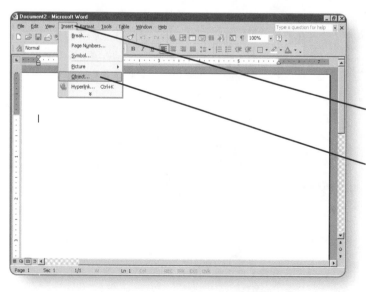

You don't need to create a table before you can create a chart. You can simply type your data directly into the datasheet.

1. Click on **Insert**. The Insert menu will appear.

2. Click on **Object**. The Object dialog box will open.

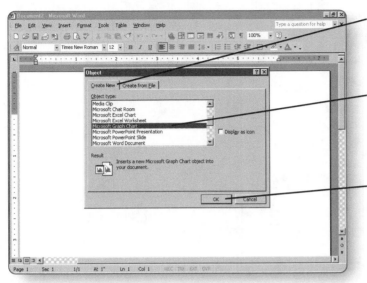

3. If necessary, **click** on the **Create New tab**. The Create New tab will come to the front.

4. **Click** on **Microsoft Graph Chart** in the Object type: text box. The selection will be highlighted.

5. **Click** on **OK**. A datasheet and chart will appear.

The datasheet will contain data, but not your data. This is sample data to help you figure out where to enter your data to create the chart. Notice the following:

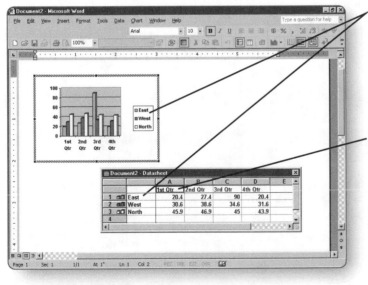

- The East, West, and North row labels appear as the legend.

- The column labels appear as category labels at the bottom of the chart.

6. **Click** in a **cell** in the datasheet. A black border will appear around the selected cell.

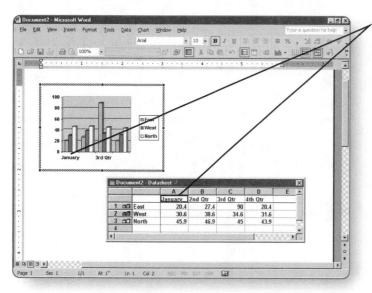

7. **Replace** the sample **data** with your data. You will immediately see the changes applied in the chart.

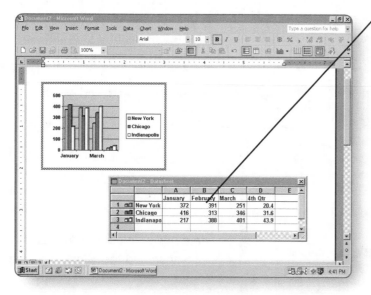

8. **Continue clicking** in cells and replacing sample data with your data. The chart will be updated.

If you find you have additional sample data, you'll need to delete it.

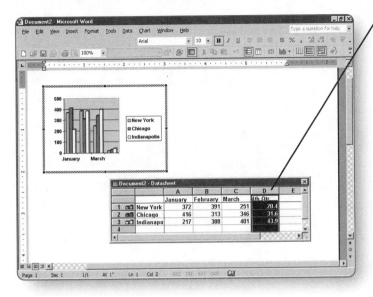

9. Click the **mouse** on the column letter or row number of the unwanted data. The cells will be highlighted.

TIP

Make sure you highlight the entire row or column. The next step won't work correctly if you just drag across unwanted cells.

10. Press the **Delete key**. The highlighted cells will be cleared and the data will be removed from the chart.

You can now edit the chart size, data, or formatting as you learned earlier in this chapter.

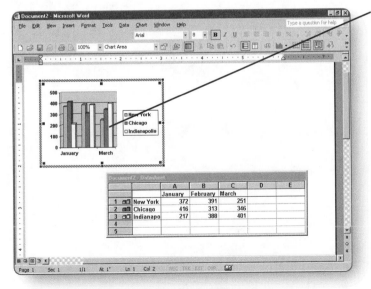

16

Using Newspaper Columns

When you think of columns you probably think of newspapers or newsletters, the kind that arrive through the mail from hospitals, schools, insurance companies, and other local businesses. These documents use columns to break up stories, with the text flowing from the bottom of one column to the top of the next. Of course, columns can be used for many other things, such as creating attractive forms or marketing materials. In this chapter, you'll learn how to:

- Create newspaper columns
- Change the number and width of columns
- Add vertical lines between columns
- Remove newspaper columns

Creating Newspaper Columns

Newspaper columns will apply to the entire document unless you select a portion before creating the columns.

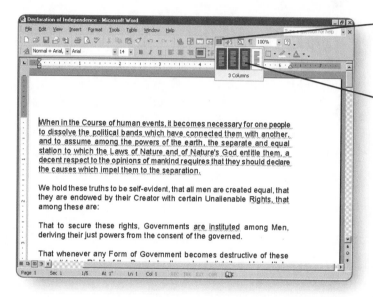

1. Click on the **Columns button**. A palette of column choices will appear.

2. Press and **hold** the **mouse button** and **drag across the palette** to select the number of columns. The number at the bottom of the palette will change as you drag over the selections.

3. Release the **mouse button** on the number of columns that you want to use. The columns button will close.

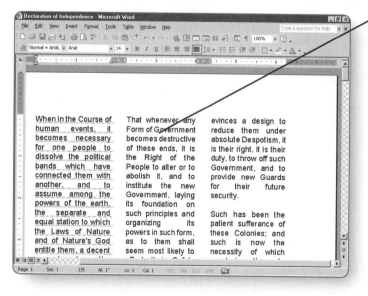

The selected text will flow into the number of columns that you chose, from the top to the bottom of the left-most column, and then up to the top of the column to its right, and so on.

Changing the Number of Columns

Perhaps you decide after formatting text in columns that you want one more column or one less column. Word enables you to change the number of columns easily.

Again, if you want to make this change to only a portion of the document, you must select that portion before continuing with these steps.

1. Click on the **Columns button**. The palette of column choices will appear.

2. Press and **hold** the **mouse button** and **drag across the palette** to make your new selection. The number at the bottom of the palette will change as you drag over the selections.

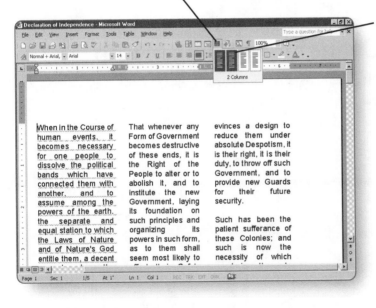

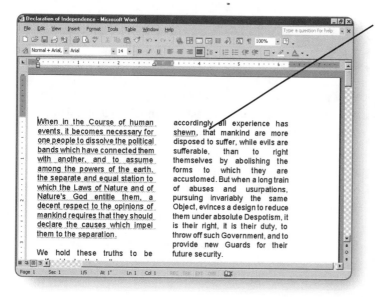

3. Release the **mouse button** on your new column choice. The selected text will flow into the new number of columns that you chose.

Changing Column Width

When you select the number of columns to be created, Word divides the text into columns of equal width. However, you can modify column width, and you can adjust the space between columns, called the *gutter*.

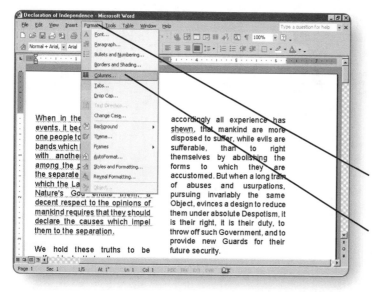

Changing the Width of Columns

If you don't want your columns to be of equal width, Word enables you to set the width of each column individually.

1. Click on **Format**. The Format menu will appear.

2. Click on **Columns**. The Columns dialog box will open.

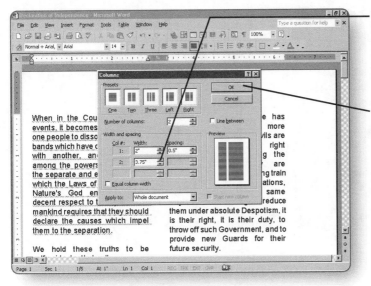

3. **Click** on the **up/down arrows** for each column you want to modify. The remaining columns will adjust accordingly.

4. **Click** on **OK**. The column widths will be modified.

Changing the Width of Space Between Columns

The space between each column is called the gutter. You can individually adjust the gutter between any two columns.

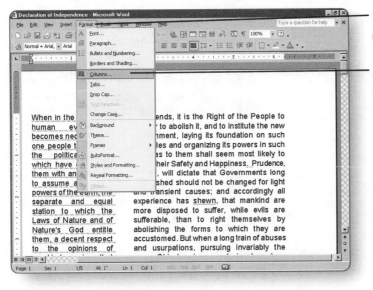

1. **Click** on **Format**. The Format menu will appear.

2. **Click** on **Columns**. The Columns dialog box will open.

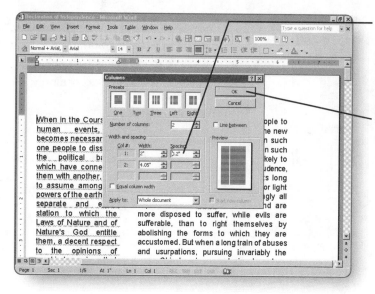

3. Click on the **up/down arrows** for each gutter spacing you want to modify. The width of the gutter will be displayed.

4. Click on **OK**. The gutter widths will be modified.

Creating Vertical Lines Between Columns

Newspapers and magazines often add vertical lines between columns to make it easier to read the text.

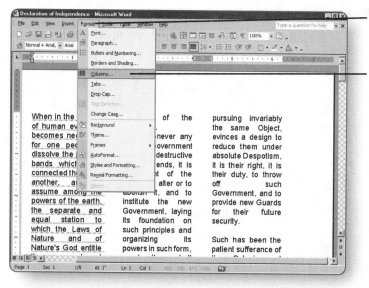

1. Click on **Format**. The Format menu will appear.

2. Click on **Columns**. The Columns dialog box will open.

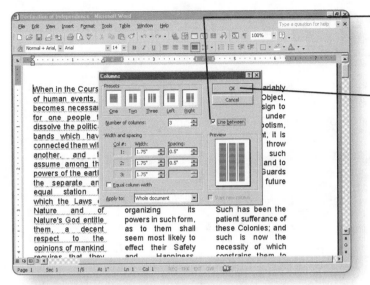

3. Click in the **Line between check box**. The option will be selected.

4. Click on **OK**. A vertical line will be inserted between columns on pages where there is more than one column.

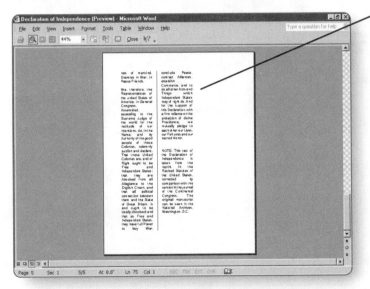

On the final page, if all columns are not used, the vertical line will not appear behind the last column.

Removing Newspaper Columns

If you prefer your text without multiple columns, the columns and vertical lines can be easily removed. This is really just a matter of returning the text to a one-column format.

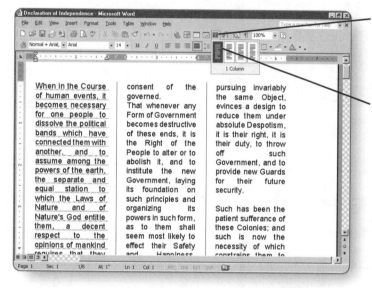

1. **Click** on the **Columns button**. The Columns palette will appear.

2. **Click** on **1 Column**. The vertical line(s) will disappear and the text will expand across the entire page.

Part IV—Using Tables, Charts, and Columns (14–16)

1. How many methods does Word provide to create a table? *See "Creating a Simple Table" in Chapter 14*

2. If you type more text than will fit in a cell, what happens to the text? *See "Entering Text" in Chapter 14*

3. What does AutoFit do? *See "Using AutoFit" in Chapter 14*

4. What button can you click to automatically add table cell values? *See "Totaling Cells with AutoSum" in Chapter 14*

5. When might you use a table heading row? *See "Adding a Table Heading Row" in Chapter 14*

6. What program does Word use to create charts? *See "Creating a Chart from a Table" in Chapter 15*

7. What happens to the standard toolbar when you create a chart? *See "Creating a Chart from a Table" in Chapter 15*

8. What type of data is traditionally represented in a pie chart? *See "Changing the Chart Type" in Chapter 15*

9. How does text flow when using multiple newspaper columns? *See "Using Newspaper Columns" in Chapter 16*

10. What is the blank space between columns called? *See "Changing Column Width" in Chapter 16*

PART V

Using the Word Tools

Chapter 17
Discovering Tools for Speed **227**

Chapter 18
Discovering Tools for Quality **243**

Chapter 19
**Using Mail Merge to Create
Form Letters** **253**

Chapter 20
Creating Envelopes and Labels **267**

17

Discovering Tools for Speed

Word includes tools that help speed up the process of creating and editing documents. In this chapter, you'll learn how to:

- Work with AutoCorrect
- Use AutoText
- Make corrections quickly with Find and Replace
- View document statistics

Working with AutoCorrect

AutoCorrect is a great feature. You type something wrong, and Word automatically corrects it. Or, you type something like (c), and Word understands that what you really want is a symbol for copyright, and it inserts ©.

Turning AutoCorrect Features On and Off

To take full advantage of this wonderful automatic correction feature, you have to understand how it works and how to customize it.

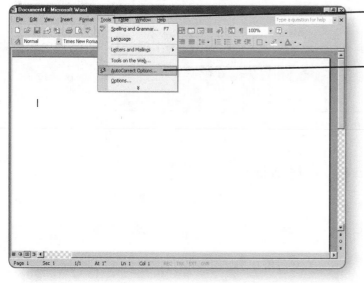

1. **Click** on **Tools**. The Tools menu will appear.

2. **Click** on **AutoCorrect Options**. The AutoCorrect dialog box will open with the AutoCorrect tab in front.

A check mark will appear next to the features that are activated.

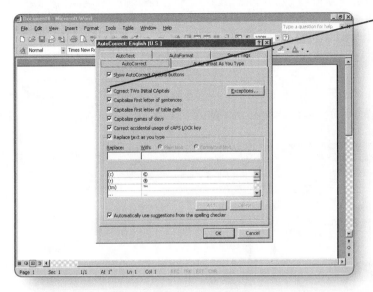

3. **Click** on an **option** to remove the check mark. The option will be turned off. If an option doesn't have a check mark next to it, **click** on the **option** to add a check mark. The option will be turned on.

Adding AutoCorrect Entries

If you know that you commonly make the same typing mistake, such as "clcik" when it should be "click," you can tell Word to fix it for you.

1. **Type** your **common mistake** in the Replace: text box. The text will display.

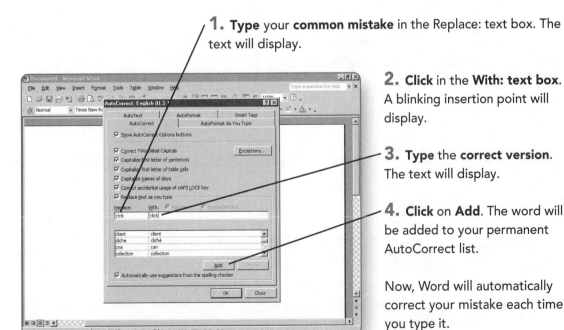

2. **Click** in the **With: text box**. A blinking insertion point will display.

3. **Type** the **correct version**. The text will display.

4. **Click** on **Add**. The word will be added to your permanent AutoCorrect list.

Now, Word will automatically correct your mistake each time you type it.

Deleting AutoCorrect Entries

What if you're typing an article on common misspellings and you *want* to type the word "the" spelled "teh?" Or, you use "(c)" to indicate headings in a report, and Word keeps changing this to the copyright symbol?

1. **Click** on an **entry** from the AutoCorrect list. The entry will appear in the Replace: and With: text boxes.

2. **Click** on **Delete**. The entry will be deleted.

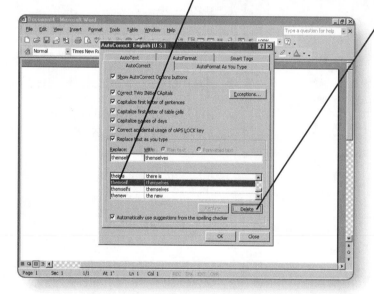

Exploring AutoFormat as You Type

Word can also format text as you are typing it. This can include automatically creating bulleted and numbered lists or replacing fractions with fraction characters.

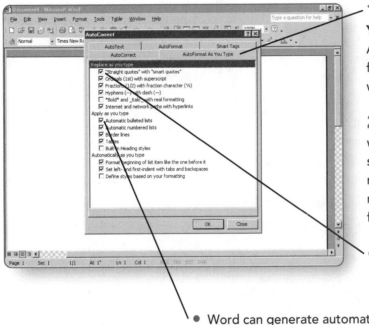

1. **Click** on the **AutoFormat As You Type tab**. The AutoFormat As You Type tab will come to the front. More automatic features will be available from this tab.

2. **Click** on any **option** to select what you want to apply. A selected option will have a check mark in the box next to it. You'll notice options such as the following:

- Word can apply "curly quotes," change 1st to 1st, make 1/2 into $^1/_2$, and more!

- Word can generate automatic bulleted or numbered lists (refer to Chapter 10, "Working with Lists," for more information on this feature).

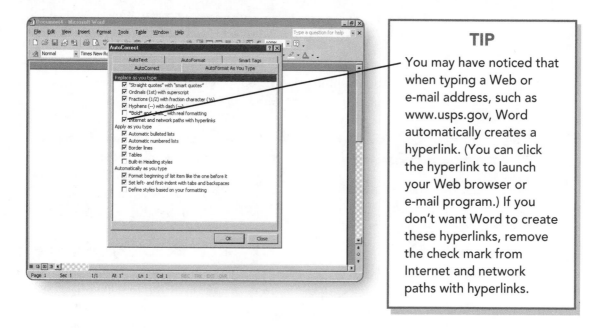

TIP

You may have noticed that when typing a Web or e-mail address, such as www.usps.gov, Word automatically creates a hyperlink. (You can click the hyperlink to launch your Web browser or e-mail program.) If you don't want Word to create these hyperlinks, remove the check mark from Internet and network paths with hyperlinks.

3. Click on **OK**. The AutoCorrect dialog box will close.

Using AutoText

Word is not only able to fix mistakes, it also can type commonly used text for you. Word calls this function AutoText.

Working with AutoComplete

AutoText includes the AutoComplete feature, with which Word attempts to anticipate what you are typing and offers to finish typing it for you. When typing text such as the names of Months or Days or even some commonly used phrases (such as "Best wishes") you only need to type a few characters before Word attempts to finish the typing for you.

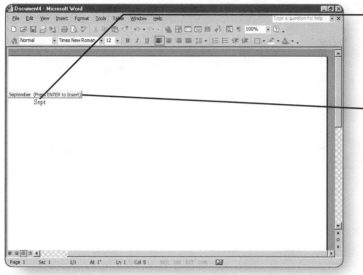

1. **Type** the **first few characters** of a month or a day. In this example, the letters Sept have been typed.

A yellow tip box pops up, offering the suggestion of September.

2. **Press** the **Enter** key. Word will complete the typing.

Creating Your Own AutoText Entry

You also can add your own AutoText entries, for example, the address of a business you write to often or a paragraph you use every week in your weekly report. A standard letter closing is also a perfect entry for AutoText.

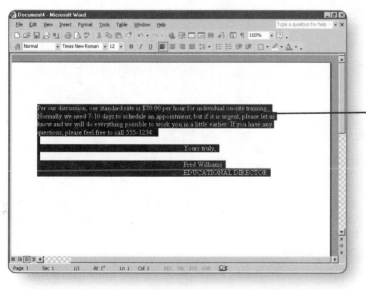

1. **Type** the **text** you want to include as an AutoText entry. The text will appear in the current document.

2. **Select** the **text** to be included as an AutoText entry. The text will be highlighted.

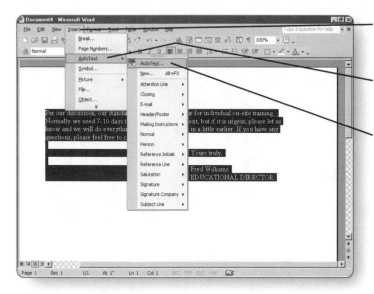

3. Click on **Insert**. The Insert menu will appear.

4. Click on **AutoText**. A submenu will appear.

5. Click on **AutoText**. The AutoCorrect dialog box will open with the AutoText tab in front.

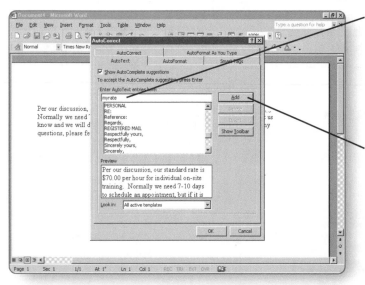

6. Type an **abbreviation** you would like to use that represents the highlighted text. The abbreviation will appear in the Enter AutoText entries here: text box.

7. Click on **Add**. The AutoText entry will be added to the list and the dialog box will close.

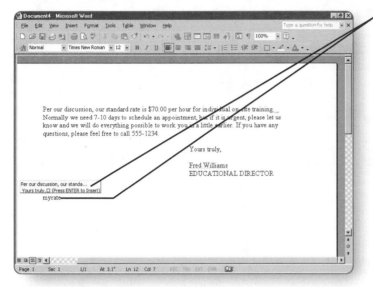

Now when you type the abbreviation you suggested, Word offers to type the balance of the text.

Inserting AutoText Using the Menu

Save typing time by using your AutoText entries, as well as many predefined AutoText entries, to complete your typing for you.

1. **Click** the **mouse pointer** in the document where the text is to appear. A blinking insertion point will appear.

2. **Click** on **Insert**. The Insert menu will appear.

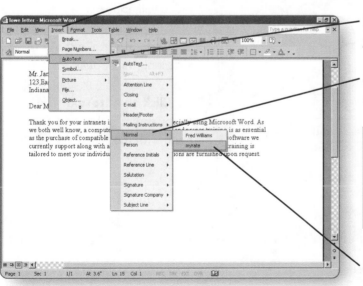

3. **Click** on **AutoText**. The AutoText submenu will appear.

4. **Click** on a **Category**. Another submenu will appear.

> ### TIP
> All entries you create will be stored in the Normal category.

5. **Click** on the **AutoText** shortcut entry.

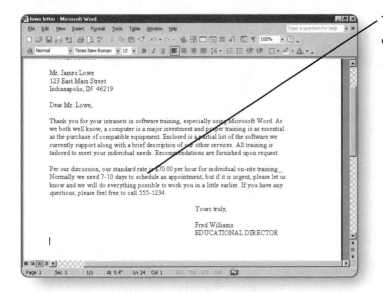

The AutoText entry text will be entered into your document.

Deleting AutoText Entries

If you no longer want a particular AutoText entry, you can easily delete it from the list.

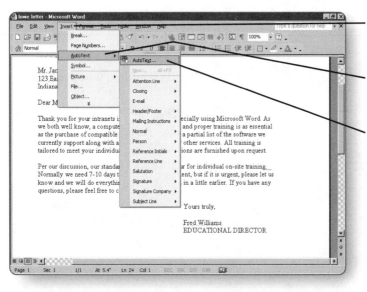

1. Click on **Insert**. The Insert menu will appear.

2. Click on **AutoText**. A submenu will appear.

3. Click on **AutoText**. The AutoCorrect dialog box will open with the AutoText tab in front.

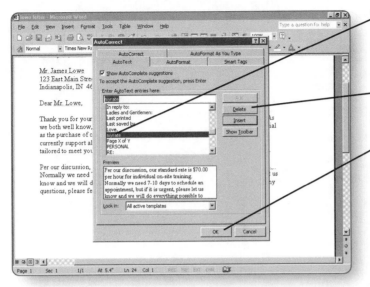

4. **Click** on the **entry** you would like to delete. The entry will be highlighted.

5. **Click** on **Delete**. The entry will be deleted.

6. **Click** on **OK**. The dialog box will close.

Using Find and Replace

Find and Replace is a real time-saver. You can quickly find out if you covered a topic in a lengthy report, or you can change names, dates, and prices throughout documents with just a few keystrokes.

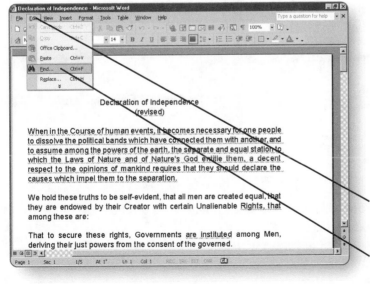

Using Find

The Word Find command is useful to seek out text in a document you may have trouble visually locating. The Find command does not change any text; it simply locates and highlights it for you.

1. **Click** on **Edit**. The Edit menu will appear.

2. **Click** on **Find**. The Find and Replace dialog box will open.

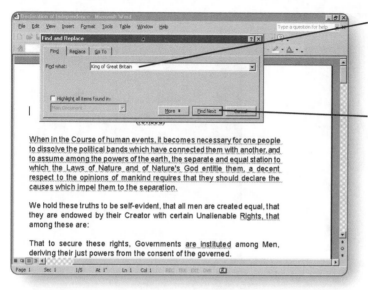

3. Type the **word** or **phrase** that you want to search for. The typed text will appear in the Find what: text box.

4. Click on **Find Next**. Word will take you to the first occurrence of the word or phrase that you're looking for.

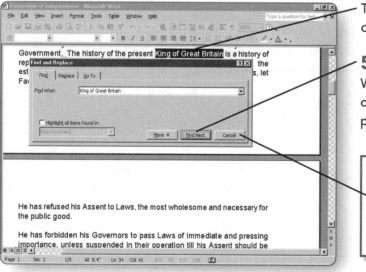

The first occurrence of the word or phrase is highlighted.

5. Click on **Find Next** again. Word will take you to the next occurrence of the word or phrase that you're looking for.

TIP

Click on Cancel if you want to discontinue the search.

Word will notify you when no more occurrences of the search text occur.

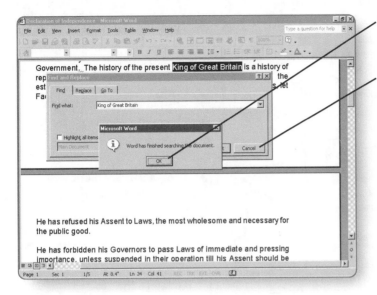

6. Click on **OK**. The message box will close.

7. Click on **Cancel**. The Find and Replace dialog box will close.

Using Replace

If you want to locate text and change it to something else, let Word do it for you with the Replace feature.

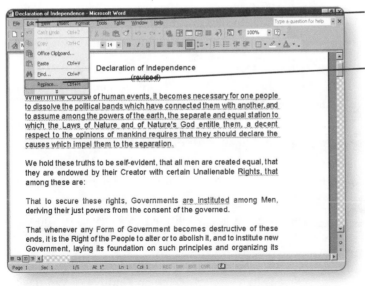

1. Click on **Edit**. The Edit menu will appear.

2. Click on **Replace**. The Find and Replace dialog box will open.

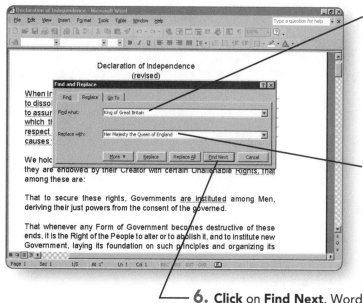

3. Type the **text** you want to search for. The text will appear in the Find what: text box.

4. Click in the **Replace with: text box**. The blinking insertion point will appear.

5. Type a **replacement word** or phrase. The text will appear in the Replace with: text box.

6. Click on **Find Next**. Word will highlight the first match.

7. Choose one of the following:

TIP

To delete the "found" text, leave the Replace with: text box empty. You'll be replacing the found text with nothing.

- **Click** on **Replace** if this is text you want to change. The text will be replaced and Word will highlight the next text match.

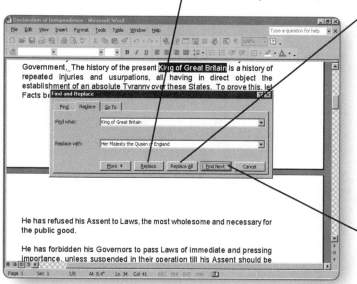

- **Click** on **Replace All**. Word will replace all occurrences of the found text with the "replace text" and notify you of the total number of replacements. Use this feature cautiously. Remember that Word will take you very literally. Make sure the find and replace options are exactly as you want them.

- **Click** on **Find Next**. Word will not make any changes and will locate the next occurrence of the text.

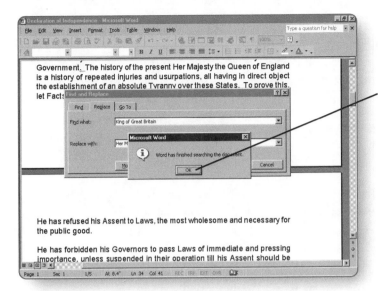

Word will notify you when no more occurrences of the search text occur.

8. Click on **OK**. The message box will close.

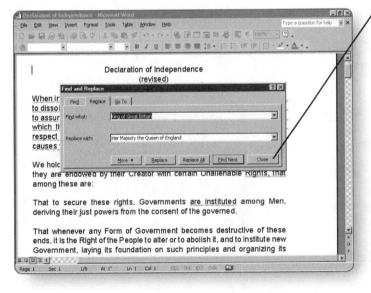

9. Click on **Close**. The Find and Replace dialog box will close.

Finding Document Statistics

There may be occasions when you need to know how many words you've typed. Possibly, you're finishing a term paper that needs to be at least 1,000 words, or perhaps you're transcribing medical documents for which you'll be paid by the word.

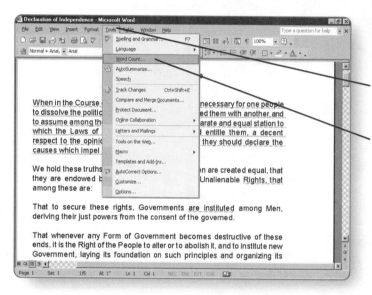

1. Click on **Tools**. The Tools menu will appear.

2. Click on **Word Count**. The Word Count dialog box will open.

The dialog box will tell you exactly how many pages, words, paragraphs, lines, and even characters you have in your document.

3. Click on **Close**. The dialog box will close.

18

Discovering Tools for Quality

Whether you're writing the great American novel, a standard business letter, or a resume, spelling or grammatical errors can ruin the impression that you're trying to create. Not only does Word have spelling and grammar checkers to correct these errors, but it also has an online Thesaurus so that you can find just the right word to convey your ideas. In this chapter, you'll learn how to:

- Find and correct spelling mistakes
- Identify and correct grammatical errors
- Use the Thesaurus

Correcting Spelling and Grammatical Errors

Word has built-in dictionaries and grammatical-rule sets that it uses to check your document. Word can identify possible problems as you type, and it also can run a special spelling and grammar check, which provides you with more information about the problems and tools for fixing them. These features aren't infallible; if you type air instead of err, Word probably won't be able to tell you that you're wrong. However, combined with a good proofreading, these tools can be very helpful.

Checking Spelling as You Go

By default, Word identifies problems right in your document as you type. Potential spelling errors have a red wavy line underneath them.

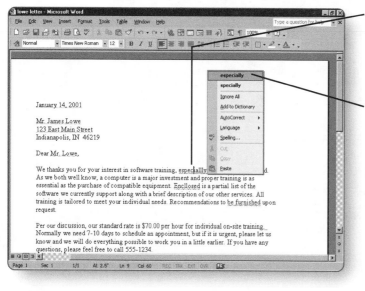

1. **Right-click** on an unrecognized **word**. The shortcut menu will appear with suggested corrections.

2. **Click** on the **correct spelling**. The erroneous word will be replaced with your selection.

Checking Grammar as You Go

Similar to spelling errors, Word identifies some potential grammatical errors with green wavy lines underneath them.

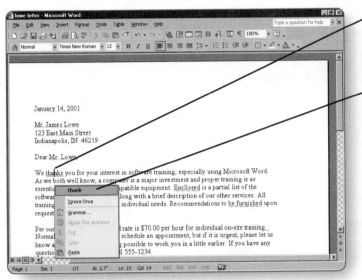

1. Right-click on the **word or phrase**. The shortcut menu will appear.

2. Click on the correct **grammatical suggestion**. The incorrect word or phrase will be replaced with your selection.

Sometimes, Word cannot give a grammatical suggestion. In those cases, you'll need to correct the error yourself.

TIP

Do *not*, repeat do *NOT*, rely on the Spell Check and grammar features to catch all your errors. They are far from perfect and can miss many items. They also can flag errors when your text is really OK and can suggest wrong things to do to fix both real problems and false error reports. You alone know what you want your document to say. Proofread it yourself!

Running a Spelling and Grammar Check

Word is set up to run both a spelling and grammar check at the same time.

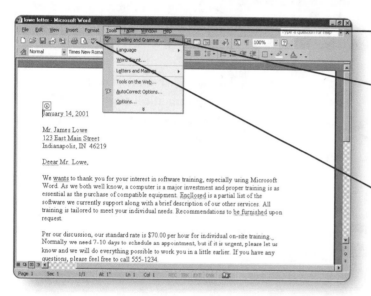

1. **Click** on **Tools**. The Tools menu will appear.

2. **Click** on **Spelling and Grammar**. The Spelling and Grammar dialog box will open.

TIP

Optionally, click on the Spelling and Grammar button.

The first error encountered, whether spelling or grammar, will be displayed. If the error is in spelling, it is identified in the Not in Dictionary: text box. In the Suggestions: text box, there are possible correct spellings for the word. In this example, the correct spelling is already highlighted.

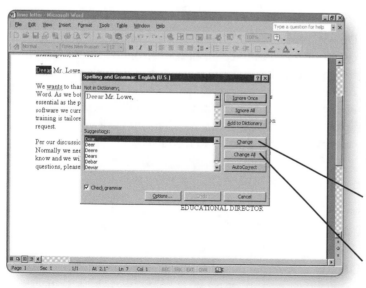

3. **Click** on **one** of the following:

- **Click** on **Change** to change just this incident of the spelling mistake.

- **Click** on **Change All** if you think you could have made the mistake more than once.

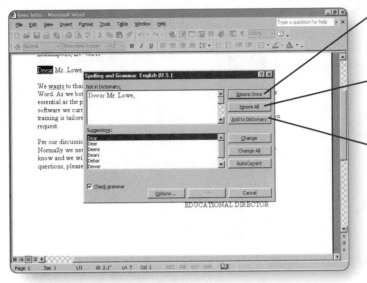

- **Click** on **Ignore Once** if you don't want to correct this instance of the spelling.

- **Click** on **Ignore All** if you don't want to correct any instances of the spelling.

- **Click** on **Add to Dictionary** to add a word, such as a proper name or legal term, to Word's built-in dictionary so that it won't be flagged as an error in the future.

After you choose one of these actions, the check will proceed to the next possible error.

If Word finds a grammatical error, it will display it in the top text box, with a suggested revision or explanation of the error in the Suggestions: text box.

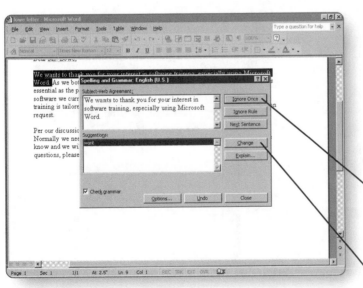

4. Click on **one** of the following:

- **Click** on **Ignore Once** if you don't want to change this instance of the grammatical problem.

- **Click** on **Change** to make the suggested change.

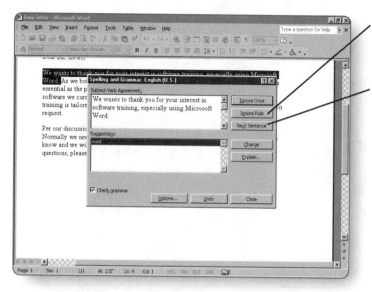

- **Click** on **Ignore Rule** to ignore all instances of the type of grammatical problem.

- **Click** on **Next Sentence** to continue the check. All instances of the same word or phrase will be ignored.

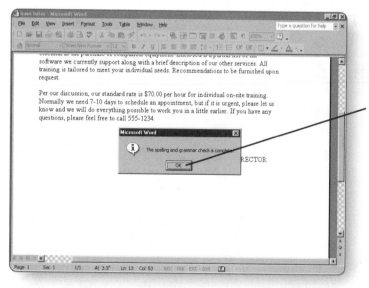

When all potential mistakes have been identified, Word will notify you that the spelling and grammar check is complete.

5. **Click** on **OK**. The message box will close.

Disabling Grammar Check

If you want to have a spelling check but not a grammar check, you can disable it.

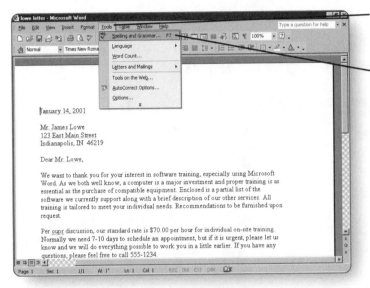

1. Click on **Tools**. The Tools menu will appear.

2. Click on **Spelling and Grammar**. The Spelling and Grammar dialog box will open.

3. Click in the check box next to **Check grammar**. The check mark will be removed and the spell check will begin.

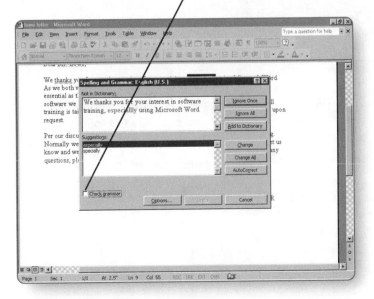

NOTE

In some instances, a message box may appear. Click on Yes. The grammar check will be disabled, and Word will look only for misspelled words.

4. Continue with the **spell check** as you learned in the previous section.

Finding That Elusive Word with the Thesaurus

When you just can't remember the word you need, the Thesaurus is invaluable.

1. **Select** the **word** that you want to replace with a better word. The word will be highlighted.

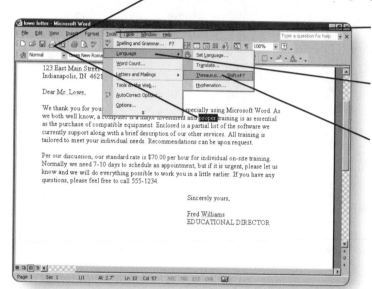

2. **Click** on **Tools**. The Tools menu will appear.

3. **Click** on **Language**. A submenu will appear.

4. **Click** on **Thesaurus**. The Thesaurus dialog box will open.

TIP

If the Thesaurus is not installed, you'll be prompted to install it. You'll need your Word or Office CD to install the feature.

Many words have multiple meanings. Word frequently lists many of the possible meanings of your word.

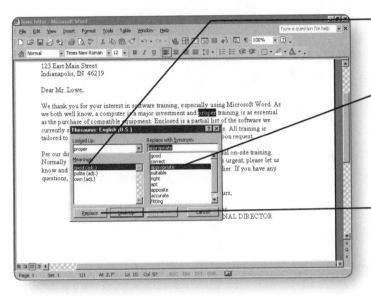

5. Click on a **meaning**. A selection of synonyms will appear on the right.

6. Click on a **word** in the Replace with Synonym: text box that fits your document better than the original. The word will be highlighted.

7. Click on **Replace**. The word will be replaced with the suggestion.

19

Using Mail Merge to Create Form Letters

You know the letter you get from the famous celebrity telling you that you have won TEN MILLION DOLLARS? (OK, in teeny tiny print it says you "may" have won ten million dollars.) It has your name printed in big letters right there on the certificate!

You need two things to create a personalized mailing with a mail merge: a letter, which is called the *main document* and contains the information that doesn't change, and codes, called *merge fields*, that act as placeholders for the variable information. This variable information is usually a list of names and addresses, called the *data source*, and contains the information that does change for each letter. When you merge the two, the result is an individualized form letter, called the *merge document*. In this chapter, you'll learn how to:

- Create a main document
- Create a data source
- Insert merge fields
- Merge the data with the document to create a form letter

Creating the Main Document

You can use a letter that you've previously created as the main document, or you can create a letter from scratch. Type your letter without filling in any return address or name in the salutation. If you want to add variables in the body of the letter, such as the addressee's first name, you can do this too. You just need to remember to leave a space for a field.

1. Type or open the **letter** to be used as the main document. The document will appear on the screen.

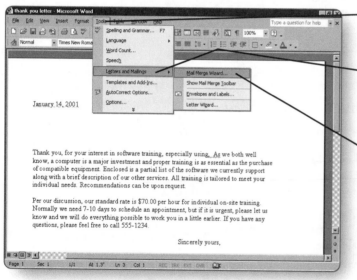

2. Click on **Tools**. The Tools menu will appear.

3. Click on **Letters and Mailings**. The Letters and Mailings submenu will appear.

4. Click on **Mail Merge Wizard**. The Mail Merge Task Pane will open.

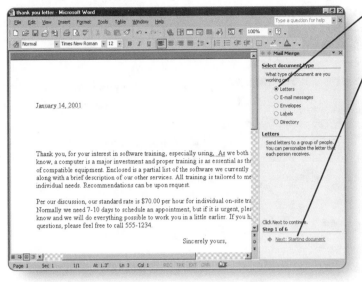

5. Click on **Letters**. The option will be selected.

6. Click on **Next: Starting Document**. The select recipients screen will appear.

Specifying Data for Your Mail Merge

The next stage of the mail-merge process is to designate or create the data source and then enter the names, addresses, and other information that will be merged into your letter.

You can select recipients from Outlook, from an existing data list created in Word, Excel, or Access, or create the customer list as you go.

Creating the Data Source

Fields and records are two of the common terms used with merge data files. A *field* is an individual piece of information about someone or something, such as a zip code or first name. A *record* is the complete picture of information about someone with all the fields put together.

For this example, we'll create a mailing list, but you'll learn in Chapter 20, "Creating Envelopes and Labels," how to select an existing data file.

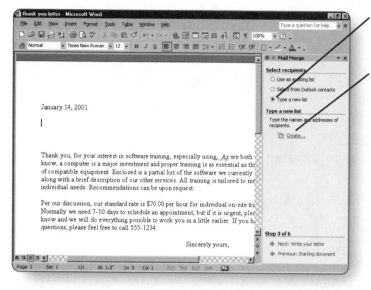

1. **Click** on **Type a new list**. The option will be selected.

2. **Click** on **Create**. The New Address List dialog box will open.

Word has tried to anticipate your needs by providing the most commonly used fields.

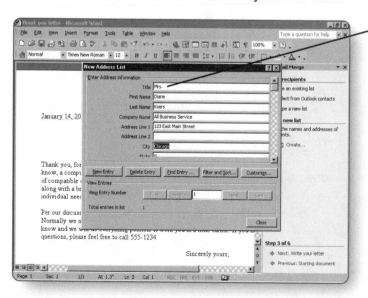

3. **Enter** the **data** for the first recipient. Press Tab to move from one field to the next. Data does not need to be entered in every field.

TIP

Press Shift+Tab to return to a previous field.

Adding Additional Data Fields

Although Word includes the commonly used fields, you may need to add your own. You can customize the data file.

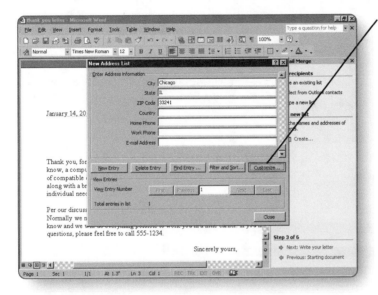

1. Click on **Customize**. The Customize Address List dialog box will open.

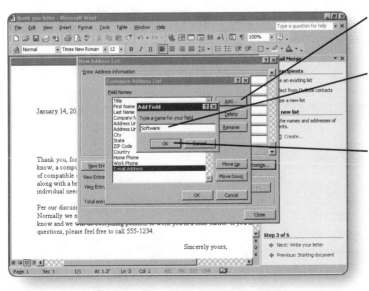

2. Click on **Add**. The Add Field dialog box will open.

3. Type a **field name** to be added. The text will appear in the text box.

4. Click on **OK**. The field will be added to the list.

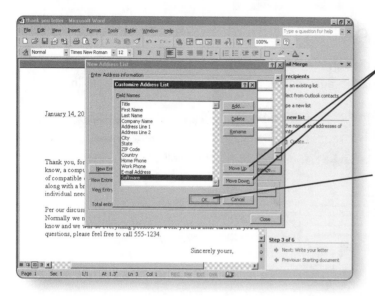

TIP

If a field is listed in an inappropriate order, click on the field name and click on the Move Up or Move Down button.

5. Click on **OK**. The Customize Address List dialog box will close.

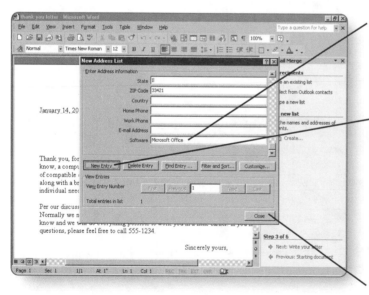

6. Enter the necessary **data** in the new field.

TIP

Click on New Entry to add additional records.

When you've completed entering your data records, close the New Address List dialog box.

7. Click on **Close**. The Save Address List dialog box will open.

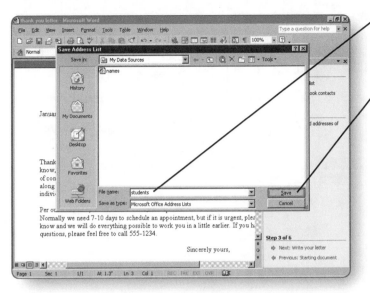

8. **Type** a **name** for the address list. The file name will appear in the File name text box.

9. **Click** on **Save**. The Mail Merge Recipients dialog box will open.

Selecting Recipients

You may have a number of names in your data file, but perhaps you don't want to send the merged letter to everyone. Word now allows you to pick and choose which recipients you want to receive a letter.

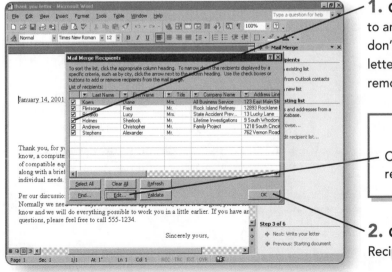

1. **Click** on the **check box** next to any recipient to whom you don't want to send the form letter. The check mark will be removed.

TIP

Click on Edit to edit any record data.

2. **Click** on **OK**. The Mail Merge Recipients dialog box will close.

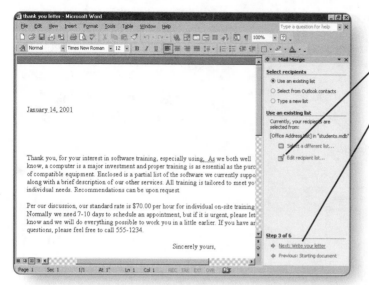

TIP

Click on Edit recipient list to reselect recipients.

3. Click on **Next: Write your letter**. The Write your letter screen will appear.

Inserting Merge Fields

You've now created a main document (a letter) and a data source. The next step is to enter the codes (merge fields) into your form letter for the data source fields telling Word exactly where you want those data fields to be placed.

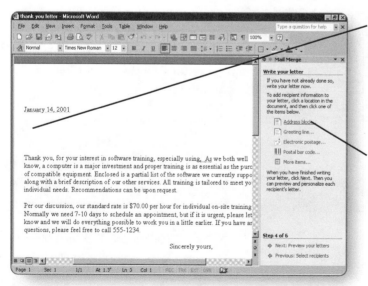

1. Click the **mouse** where you want the first piece of information (generally the recipient name and address). A blinking insertion point will appear.

2. Click on **Address Block**. The Insert Address Block dialog box will open.

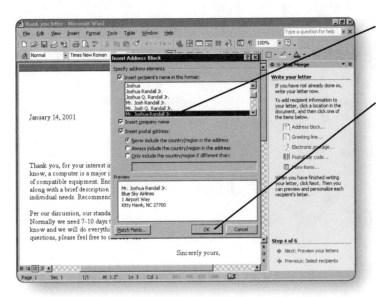

3. Click on an **address format**. A sample will preview in the Preview pane.

4. Click on **OK**. The Insert Address Block dialog box will close.

The field << <<AddressBlock>> >> will appear at the position of the insertion point. This is a hidden code to Microsoft Word. Don't try to just type << <<AddressBlock>> >>.

Most letters also include a personalized greeting. Word has a Greeting Line field available to assist you.

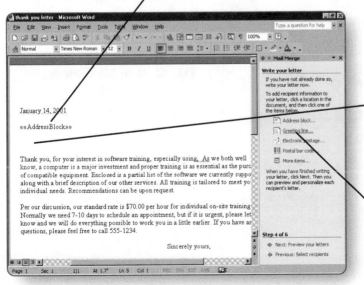

5. Click the **mouse** where you want the greeting line to be placed. A blinking insertion point will appear.

6. Click on **Greeting line**. The Greeting Line dialog box will open.

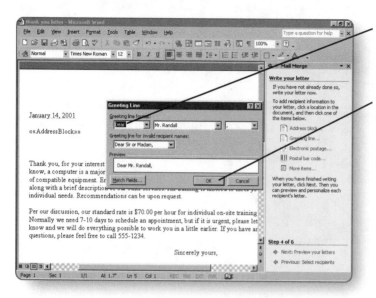

7. Choose from the various **styles of greeting**. A sample will appear in the preview pane.

8. Click on **OK**. Word will insert another code called << <<Greeting Line>> >> into your document.

If the field information you want to insert into your document doesn't fall into the designated categories of Address block, Greeting line, Electronic Postage, or Postal bar code, you can select it for yourself.

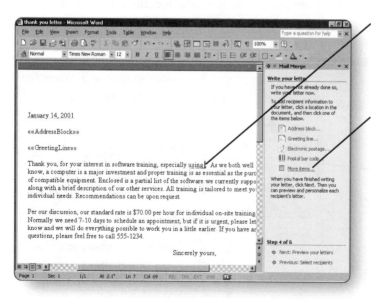

9. Click the **mouse** where you want the special field to appear. The blinking insertion point will appear.

10. Click on **More Items**. The Insert Merge field dialog box will open.

11. **Click** on the **field name** you want to insert. The field name will be highlighted.

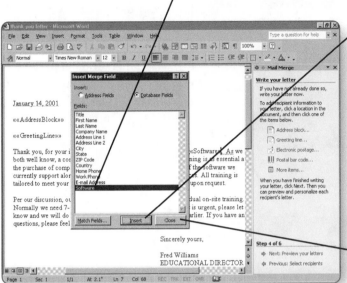

12. **Click** on **Insert**. The selected field name code will be inserted into your document.

NOTE

It is not necessary to use all fields in a form letter, and fields may be used multiple times in the same document.

---

13. **Click** on **Close**. The Insert Merge field dialog box will close.

Previewing the Mail Merge

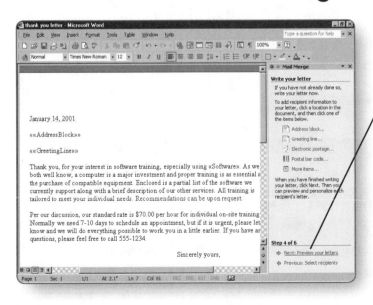

The next step is to preview the merged records and if necessary, edit and further personalize any recipient's letter.

1. **Click** on **Next: Preview your letters**. Your first record will be merged with the main document and appear on the screen.

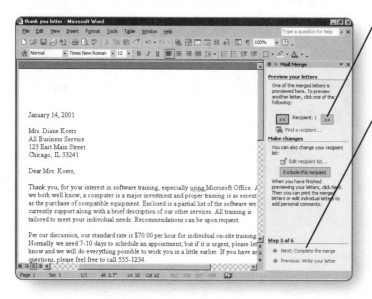

2. Click on the **Next Record button**. The next letter merged from your data source will appear.

3. Click on **Next: Complete the merge**. The Complete the merge screen will appear.

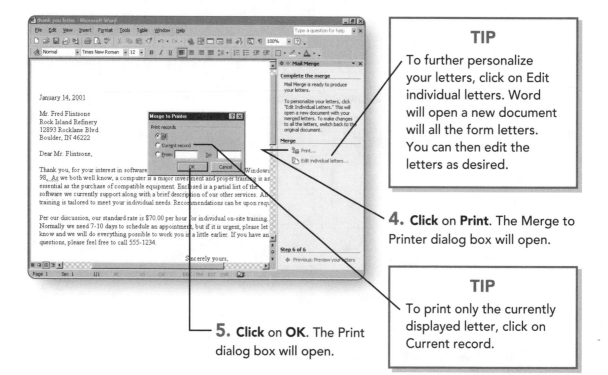

TIP

To further personalize your letters, click on Edit individual letters. Word will open a new document will all the form letters. You can then edit the letters as desired.

4. Click on **Print**. The Merge to Printer dialog box will open.

5. Click on **OK**. The Print dialog box will open.

TIP

To print only the currently displayed letter, click on Current record.

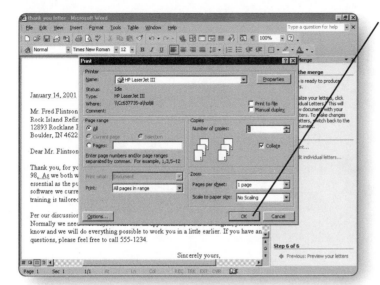

6. Click on **OK**. The merged letters will print.

20

Creating Envelopes and Labels

Now that you have created your letters or form letters, you'll need envelopes to mail them. Or . . . maybe you'd prefer to use mailing labels. Word makes it easy to create either one using the mail merge feature. In this chapter, you'll learn how to:

- Create a single envelope
- Open an existing data source file
- Create and print envelopes for your merged letters
- Merge labels from a data source file

Generating a Single Envelope

Need a single envelope? Generating envelopes in Word is a very easy process. Word can pick up the address from an open letter or you can type it in yourself.

1. Open a **document** (usually a letter) containing an address. The document will appear on your screen.

2. Click on **Tools**. The Tools menu will appear.

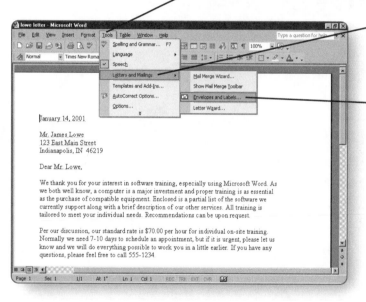

3. Click on **Letters and Mailings**. The Letters and Mailings submenu will appear.

4. Click on **Envelopes and Labels**. The Envelopes and Labels dialog box will open.

Word copied the address block from the body of the letter.

TIP

If your document was blank, or if you need to make any changes, click in the Delivery address box and type any corrections.

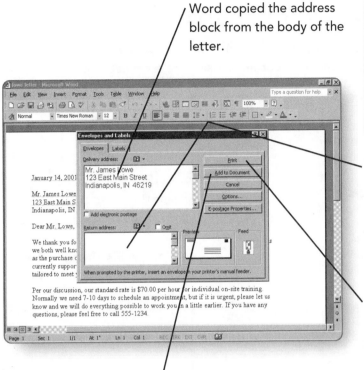

5. Optionally, **click** in the **Return address box and type** a return **address**.

You can print the envelope by itself or add it to the existing document.

6a. Click on **Print**. The envelope will automatically print.

OR

6b. Click on **Add to Document**. The envelope will be added to the existing document.

Envelopes are added at the top of the document.

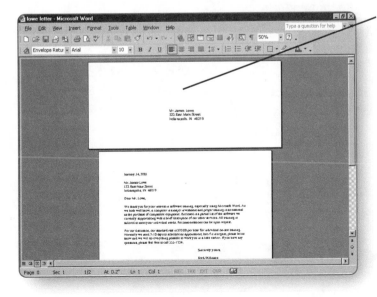

Creating Merged Envelopes

You can use the mail-merge process to go back and create an envelope main document using the same data source.

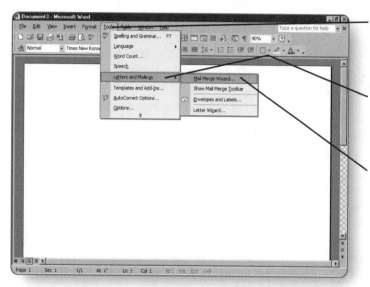

1. From a blank document, **click** on **Tools**. The Tools menu will appear.

2. **Click** on **Letters and Mailings**. The Letters and Mailings Submenu will appear.

3. **Click** on **Mail Merge Wizard**. The Mail Merge task pane will open.

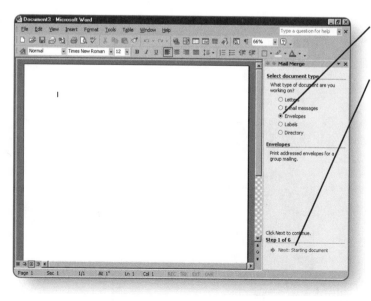

4. **Click** on **Envelopes**. The option will be selected.

5. **Click** on **Next: Starting document**. The Select starting document screen will appear.

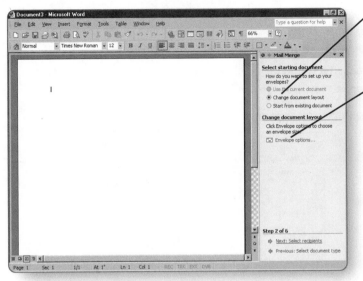

6. Click on **Change document layout**. The option will be selected.

7. Click on **Envelope options**. The Envelope options dialog box will open.

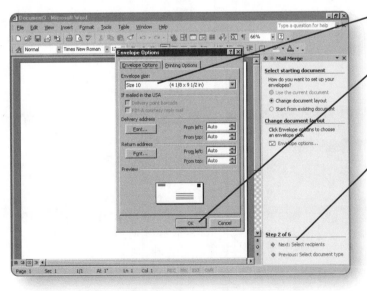

8. Change any desired **options**, including envelope size.

9. Click on **OK**. The Envelope Options dialog box will close and your document will resemble an envelope.

10. Click on **Next: Select Recipients**. The Select recipients screen will appear.

Opening a Data File

In Chapter 19 "Using Mail Merge to Create Form Letters," you created a data source file as you were working on the mail merge. You can use that same file again, or even open an Excel worksheet, Access database, or Outlook contact list to use as your data source.

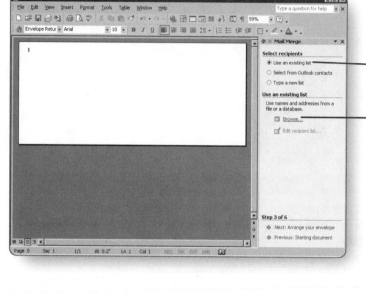

1. Click on **Use an existing list**. The option will be selected.

2. Click on **Browse**. The Select Data Source dialog box will open.

3. Locate and click on the **file name** to be used for your data source. The file name will be highlighted.

4. Click on **Open**. A Mail Merge Recipients window will appear.

You may have a number of names in your data file, but perhaps you don't want to send the merged letter to everyone.

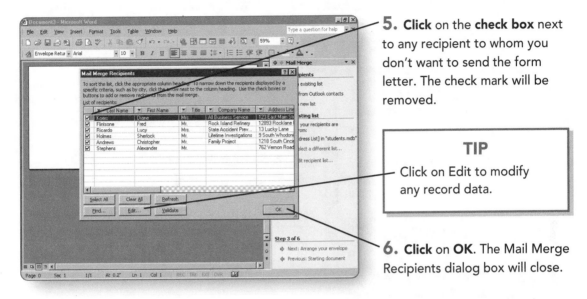

5. Click on the **check box** next to any recipient to whom you don't want to send the form letter. The check mark will be removed.

TIP

Click on Edit to modify any record data.

---

6. Click on **OK**. The Mail Merge Recipients dialog box will close.

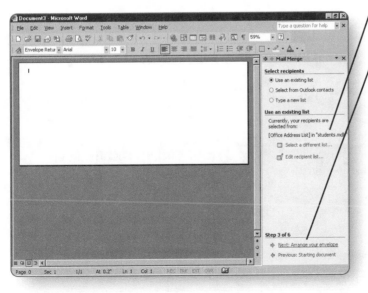

The currently selected data file appears in the task pane.

7. Click on **Next: Arrange your envelope**. The Arrange your envelope screen will appear.

Arranging Data on the Envelope

Next you'll need to tell Word how you want the envelope addressed. Adding an address block in an envelope is very similar to adding an address block in a form letter.

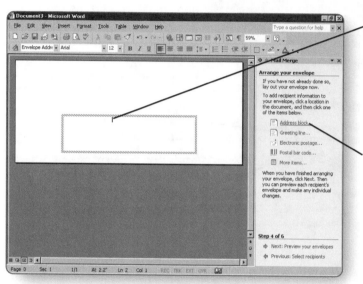

1. **Click** in the approximate **envelope address location**. A box will appear around the envelope address area and a blinking insertion point will appear.

2. **Click** on **Address block**. The Insert Address Block dialog box will open.

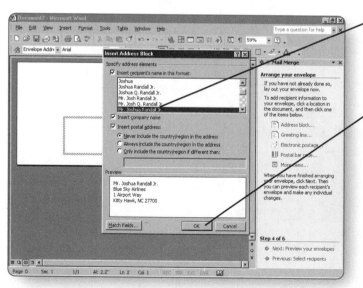

3. **Click** on an **address format**. The format option will be highlighted and a sample will display in the preview pane.

4. **Click** on **OK**. The Insert Address Block dialog box will close.

Completing the Merge

Now that you've laid out the envelope, you can merge and print them.

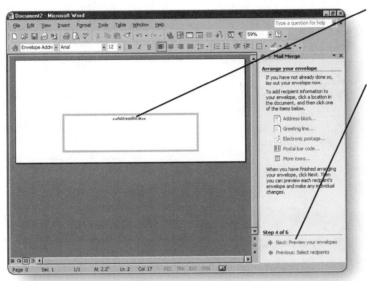

The Word field << <<Address Block>> >> appears in the body of the envelope.

1. Click on **Next: Preview your envelopes**. The first name from your data list will appear on an envelope.

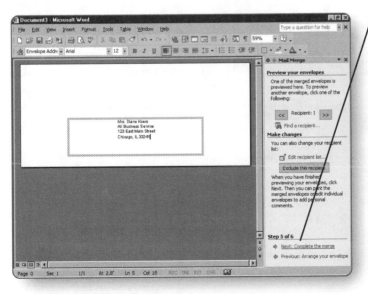

2. Click on **Next: Complete the merge**. The Complete the merge screen will appear.

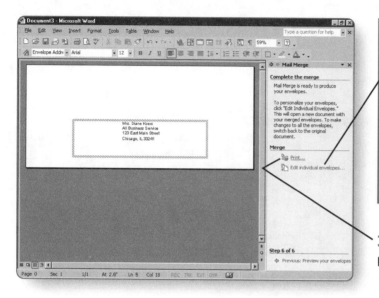

TIP

To further personalize your current merged envelopes, click on Edit individual envelopes. Word will open a new document with all the envelopes, which you can edit as desired.

3. **Click** on **Print**. The Merge to Printer dialog box will open.

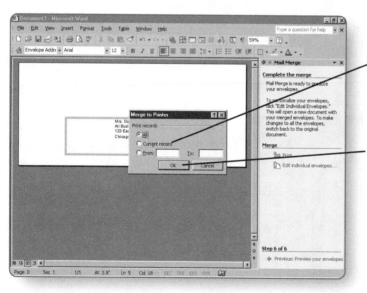

TIP

To print only the currently displayed envelope, click on Current record.

4. **Click** on **OK**. The Print dialog box will open.

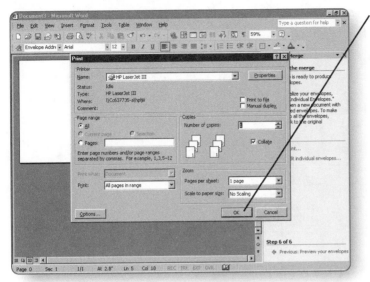

5. Click on **OK**. The merged letters will print.

Creating Merged Mailing Labels

Now that you can buy sheets of labels that feed easily into both inkjet and laser printers, mailing labels and envelopes are equally easy to produce using Word's Mail Merge feature. Labels can be especially useful if you have large quantities of letters to mail.

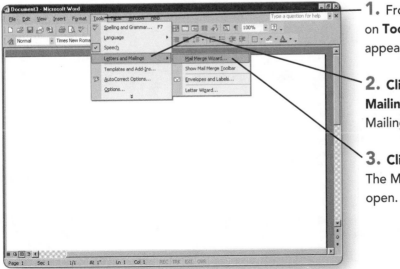

1. From a blank document, **click** on **Tools**. The Tools menu will appear.

2. Click on **Letters and Mailings**. The Letters and Mailings submenu will appear.

3. Click on **Mail Merge Wizard**. The Mail Merge task pane will open.

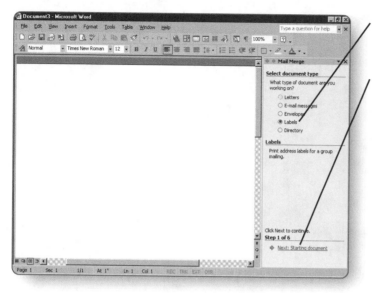

4. **Click** on **Labels**. The option will be selected.

5. **Click** on **Next: Starting document**. The Select starting document screen will appear.

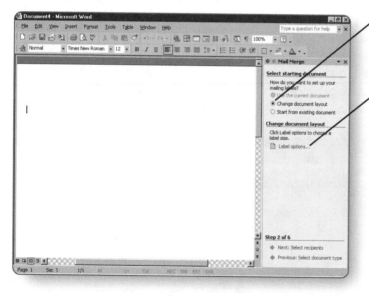

6. **Click** on **Change document layout**. The option will be selected.

7. **Click** on **Label options**. The Label options dialog box will open.

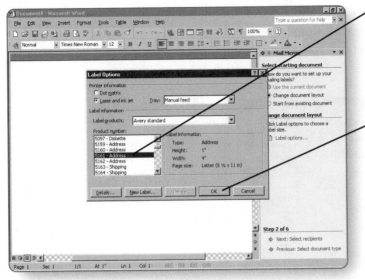

8. Click on the **label style** you intend to use. The label information will appear on the right side of the Label options dialog box.

9. Click on **OK**. The Label options dialog box will close.

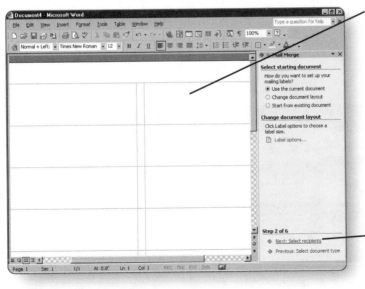

The document screen resembles a sheet of blank labels.

TIP

Word uses tables when creating labels. If you don't see the gridlines indicating labels, click on Table, Show Gridlines.

---

10. Click on **Next: Select Recipients**. The Select recipients screen will appear.

Similar to letters and envelopes, you can create a new data file, or select from an existing one, or even choose from your Outlook contact list. For this example, we'll use our Outlook contacts.

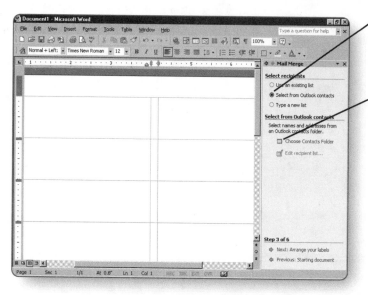

11. Click on **Select from Outlook contacts**. The option will be selected.

12. Click on **Choose Contacts folder**. The Choose Profile dialog box will open.

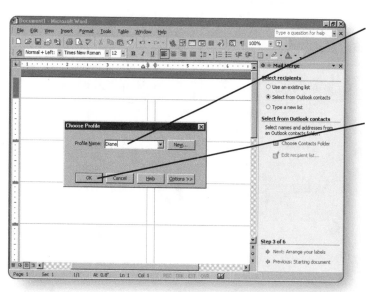

13. Click on the **profile name** to be used for your data source. The profile name will appear in the Profile name list box.

14. Click on **OK**. Select Contact List folder will open.

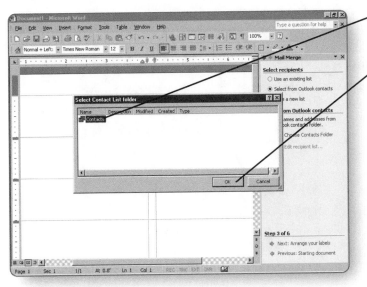

15. **Click** on **Contacts**. The selection will be highlighted.

16. **Click** on **OK**. A Mail Merge Recipients window will appear.

You may have a number of names in your data file, but perhaps you don't want to send the merged letter to everyone.

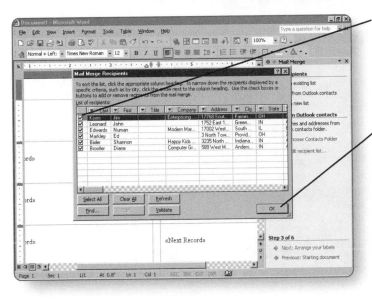

17. **Click** on the **check box** next to any recipient to whom you don't want to send the form letter. The check mark will be removed.

18. **Click** on **OK**. The Mail Merge Recipients dialog box will close.

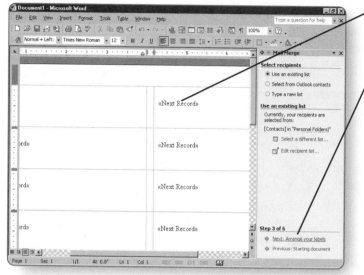

Word placed a <<Next Record>> command into the label document.

19. **Click** on **Next: Arrange your labels**. The Arrange your labels screen will appear.

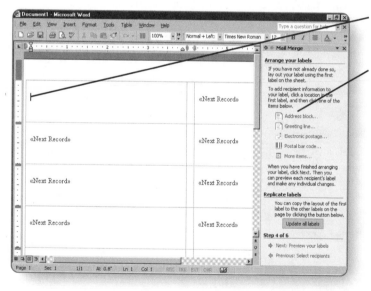

Make sure the blinking insertion point is still in the first label.

20. **Click** on **Address block**. The Insert Address Block dialog box will open.

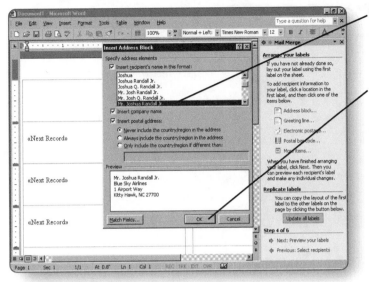

21. Choose an **address layout**. A sample will appear in the preview window.

22. Click on **OK**. The Insert Address Block dialog box will close.

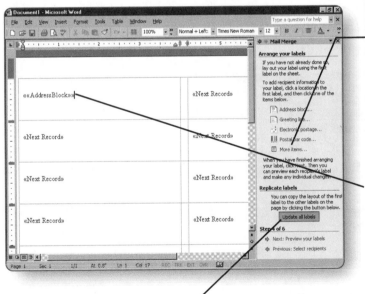

TIP

If you want the label to include additional or different fields than the address block, click on More items and choose from the available fields.

Word will insert a << <<Address Block>> >> code into the first label. You'll need a code like that in each label, but you don't have to repeat the steps for each label. Let Word do the work for you!

23. Click on **Update all labels**. The << <<AddressBlock>> >> code will be inserted on all labels.

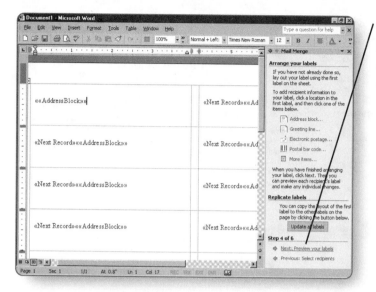

24. Click on **Preview your labels**. A sheet of labels displaying the names from your data file will appear.

You can now continue to edit or print your labels as you learned in the "Completing the Merge" section earlier in this chapter.

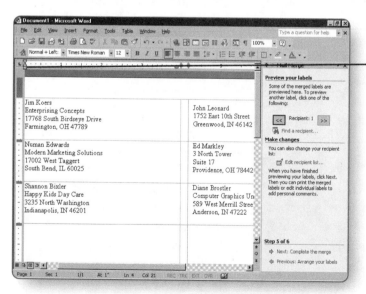

TIP

If you find that your labels are printing too close to the left edge of the label, press Ctrl+A (to select all the labels) and drag the left indent mark a little to the right.

Part V—Using the Word Tools (17–20)

1. What feature does Word include that will automatically fix common typing errors? *See "Working with AutoCorrect" in Chapter 17*

2. What is AutoText? *See "Using AutoText" in Chapter 17*

3. Does the Find command modify text in any way? *See "Using Find" in Chapter 17*

4. How can you quickly determine the total number of words in a document? *See "Finding Document Statistics" in Chapter 17*

5. How does Word indicate potential spelling errors? *See "Checking Spelling as You Go" in Chapter 18*

6. What Word feature can locate a synonym? *See "Finding That Elusive Word with the Thesaurus" in Chapter 18*

7. What are the two documents needed to create a mail merge? *See Chapter 19 "Using Mail Merge to Create Form Letters"*

8. In a mail merge, what is the difference between a field and a record? *See "Creating the Data Source" in Chapter 19*

9. Besides a Word document, what other types of data source documents can Word use in a Mail Merge? *See "Opening a Data File" in Chapter 20*

10. Why might you want to indent mailing labels to the right? *See "Creating Merged Mailing Labels" in Chapter 20*

PART VI

Working with Long Documents

Chapter 21
Working with Paragraph Styles. 289

Chapter 22
Discovering Templates 301

Chapter 23
Adding Headers and Footers 313

Chapter 24
Working with Footnotes or Endnotes. . . 319

21

Working with Paragraph Styles

Whether you're creating a letter or a memo, a report or an invitation, each paragraph within that document has a *paragraph style*: a style can include its font, font size, any special effects, alignment, and spacing—any characteristics in the Font or Paragraph dialog box accessed through the Format menu. When you work with short documents, you probably need only one paragraph style. However, when you use Word to tackle longer documents, such as reports, you will find that paragraph styles can make formatting your document a breeze. In this chapter, you'll learn how to:

- Display the style area
- Apply a Word style
- Modify a style
- Use an example to create a new style
- Use the New Style dialog box to create a new style

Displaying the Style Area

The first text box on the Formatting toolbar shows only the style of the paragraph where the insertion point is. To see all the styles used in your document, you need to display the style area.

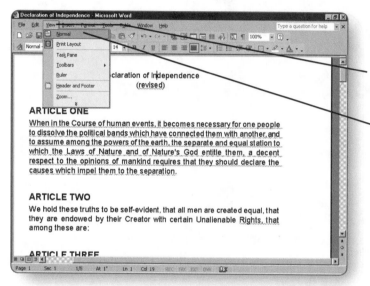

To view the style area, you'll need to be in Normal view.

1. **Click** on **View**. The View menu will appear.

2. **Click** on **Normal**. The on-screen document will be displayed in Normal view.

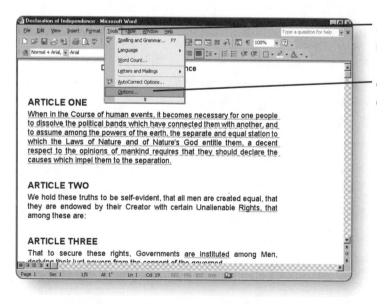

3. **Click** on **Tools**. The Tools menu will appear.

4. **Click** on **Options**. The Options dialog box will open.

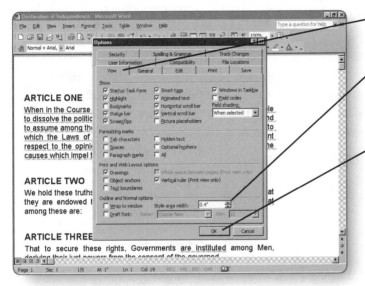

5. **Click** on the **View tab**. The View tab will come to the front.

6. **Click** on the **up arrow** in the Style Area width text box until .6" appears in the text box.

7. **Click** on **OK**. The Options dialog box will close.

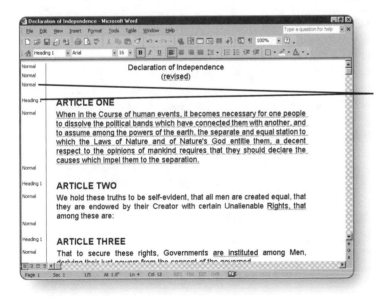

The style area will appear in every document until you change the Style Area width.

In this example you can see some of the text is set in the style called "Normal" while "Heading 1" is set for other text.

Working with Word Styles

Word comes with a wide selection of styles for formatting titles, section heads, and so on. Remember that Word's definition of a paragraph isn't the one taught in grammar classes, where two or more sentences are set apart. To Word, a paragraph is any body of text ended by a pressing of the Enter key. Even one word can be a paragraph to Word.

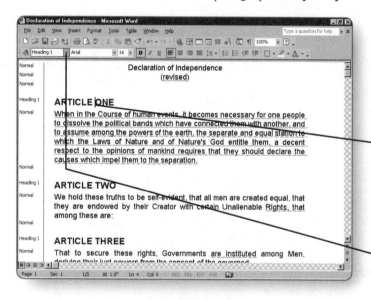

The default style applied to all newly typed text is called "Normal."

1. Click the **mouse pointer** in the paragraph that you want to format with one of the Word styles. The blinking insertion point will appear.

2. Click on the **drop-down list arrow** to the right of the Style text box. A list of styles will appear.

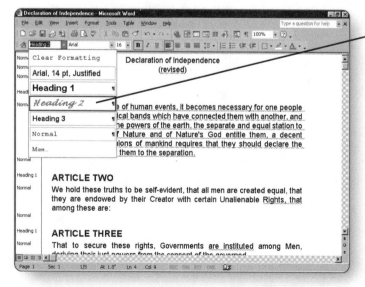

3. Click on the **style** you want. Word will apply the style to the paragraph.

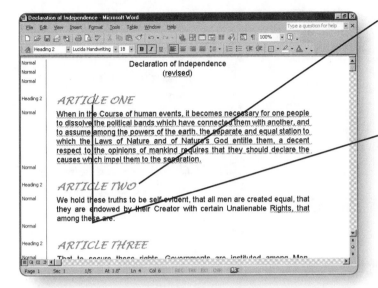

4. Repeat Steps 1 through 3 for any paragraphs you want new styles applied to. Those selections will have the new styles applied.

In this example, the Heading 2 style was applied, and the font name, size, and color attributes were changed.

Creating New Styles

Sometimes you may find that the style Word offers doesn't exactly meet your needs. Word can create a new style by using an example, or it can create a new style from scratch.

Using an Example to Create a New Style

There are several ways to create new styles. One way is to format a paragraph with the attributes you need, then tell Word to look at that paragraph and create a new style from it.

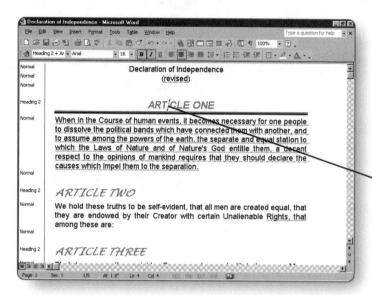

1. **Format** a **paragraph.** Formatting attributes will be applied to the text. In this example, the font is changed to 18 point Arial, a border is applied, and the paragraph spacing is centered.

2. **Click** the **mouse pointer** in the formatted paragraph. The blinking insertion point will appear.

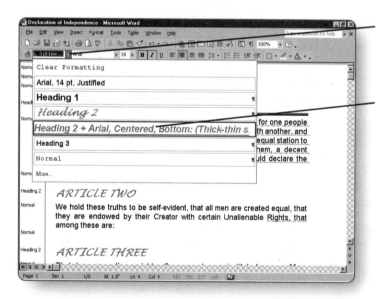

3. **Click** on the **Style down arrow.** A list of styles will appear.

The new style will appear in the Style drop-down list in the Formatting toolbar. You can now apply this style to any other paragraphs using the techniques you learned in the previous section.

Creating a New Style from Scratch

Another way to create a style is to simply create a style name and tell Word exactly what formatting you want applied. When creating styles you'll use the Styles and Formatting task pane, which you discovered in Chapter 8, "Using Fonts Effectively."

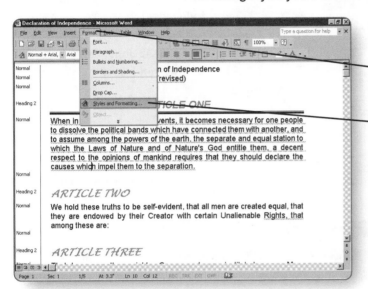

1. Click on **Format**. The Format menu will appear.

2. Click on **Styles and Formatting**. The Styles and Formatting task pane will open.

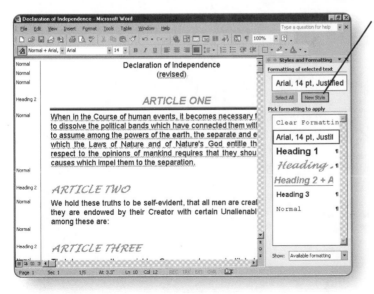

3. Click on **New Style**. The New Style dialog box will open.

4. **Type** a **name** for the new style in the Name text box. The name will appear in the Name: text box.

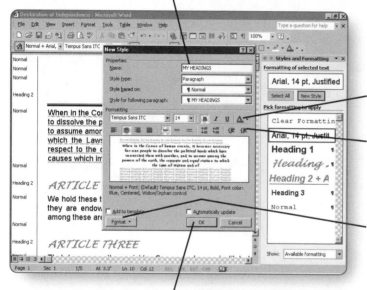

5. **Select** the desired **formatting**. Choose from the following:

- **Font Options:** Font, Size, Style, and Color

- **Paragraph Options:** Alignment, Line Spacing, Paragraph Spacing, and Indentation

Additional formatting options are available from the Format button.

6. **Click** on **OK**. The Styles and Formatting task pane will display the new style.

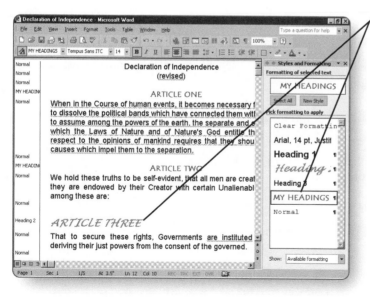

You can now apply the new style to any text in the document.

Deleting a Style

If you've created a style you no longer are using, you can easily delete it.

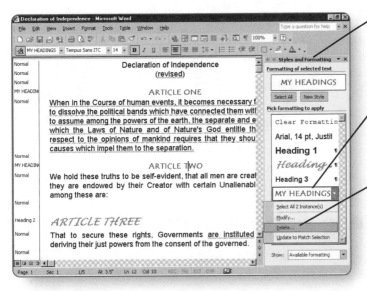

1. **Display** the **Styles and Formatting task pane.** (Hint: click on Format, Styles and Formatting.)

2. **Right-click** on the **style name** to be deleted. A shortcut menu will appear.

3. **Click** on **Delete**. A confirmation box will appear.

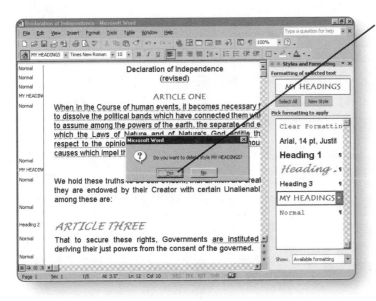

4. **Click** on **Yes**. The style will be deleted.

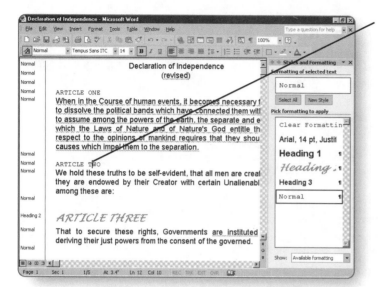

Any paragraphs that had the deleted style will return to the Normal style.

Revealing Formatting

New to this version of Microsoft Word is the Reveal Formatting feature, which is similar in nature to the WordPerfect Reveal Codes function. The Reveal Formatting feature is displayed in a task pane window.

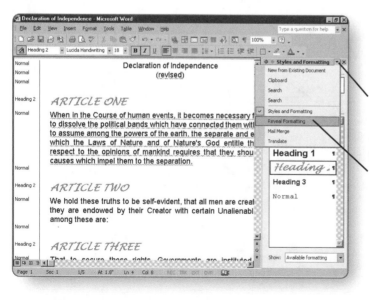

1. Display any **task pane window**. Click on View, Task Pane.

2. Click on the **task pane drop-down arrow**. A list of other task panes will appear.

3. Click on **Reveal Formatting**. The Reveal Formatting task pane will appear.

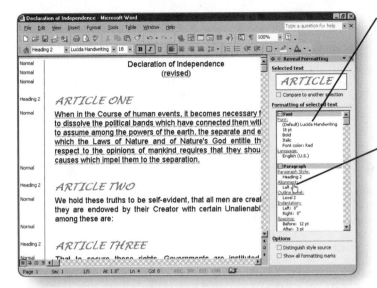

Word displays the font and paragraph information at the current insertion point location.

TIP

Click on any attribute category to display a dialog box allowing you to change the characteristics of the current text.

22

Discovering Templates

Every Microsoft Word document is based on a template. A *template* determines the basic structure for a document and contains settings such as styles, AutoText, fonts, macros, menus, page layout, and special formatting. Word provides a variety of document templates, and you can create your own document templates.

- Use a template
- Save a file as a template
- Use and apply a template
- Edit a template

Using a Word Template

Using templates, you can automatically create memos, faxes, or other documents with the formatting already applied.

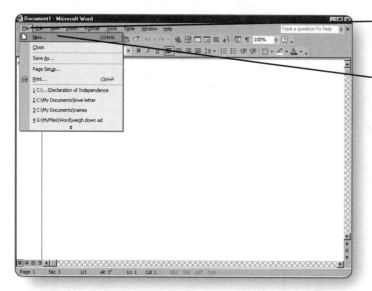

1. Click on **File**. The File menu will appear.

2. Click on **New**. The New Document task pane window will open.

NOTE

You cannot access the Word templates by clicking on the New button. The New button only creates a new document based on the "Normal" template.

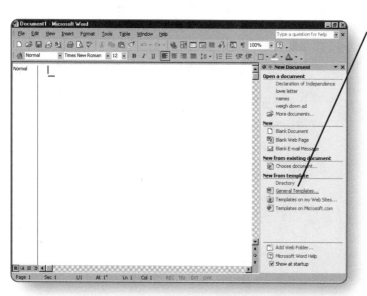

3. Click on **General Templates**. The Templates dialog box will open.

NOTE

You may be prompted to insert the Microsoft Office CD.

There are several categories of predefined templates available for your use. Some templates are marked Wizards. You'll learn how to use a wizard in Chapter 25, "Using Word to Create Web Pages."

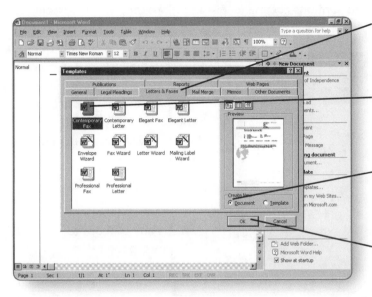

4. **Click** on a **category**. A selection of templates will appear.

5. **Click** on the **template name** you want to use. The template name will be highlighted.

6. If necessary, **click** on **Document**. The option will be selected.

7. **Click** on **OK**. An untitled document will appear with the text, graphics, formatting, and other attributes applicable to that template.

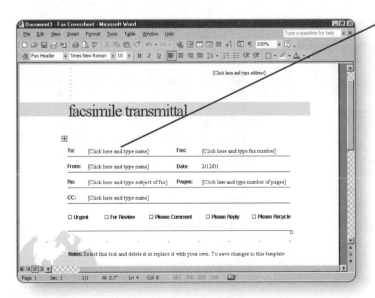

8. **Add** additional **text or** otherwise **edit** the **document** using methods you've already learned and following any on-screen instructions. The document will be modified.

Saving a File as a Template

When you save a template, Word will switch to the User templates location as specified in the Options menu (Tools menu, Options command, File Locations tab), which by default is the Templates folder. If you save a template in a different location, the template will not appear in the New dialog box.

1. Create or open a **document** to be saved as a template. The document will appear on the screen.

TIP

Make any changes to the text, page setup, formatting, or styles you want to be applicable to all new documents of this type. The new settings will be available in the current document.

2. Click on **File**. The File menu will appear.

3. Click on **Save As**. The Save As dialog box will open.

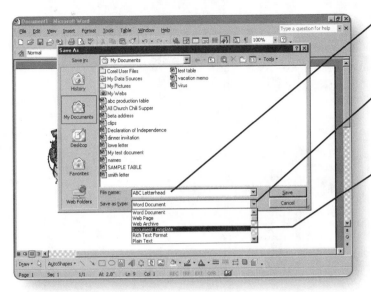

4. **Type** a **name** for the new template. The name will appear in the File name: text box.

5. **Click** on the **Save as Type: arrow**. A list of choices will display.

6. **Click** on **Document Template**. The option will appear in the Save as Type: list box.

Word will automatically switch to the templates folder.

7. **Click** on **Save**. The document will be saved as a template.

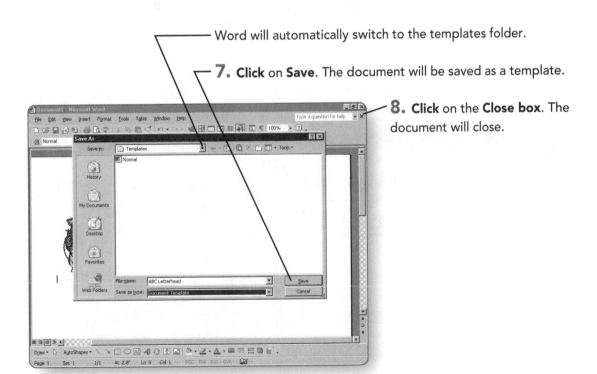

8. **Click** on the **Close box**. The document will close.

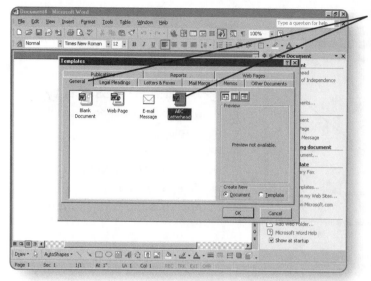

The custom template will appear in the General category of the Template dialog box.

Applying a Template

As you've seen, you can open a document based on a template. You also can attach a template to a file that is already open. When a template is attached to a file, only the styles are added to the current document. Text, graphics, and page settings are not included.

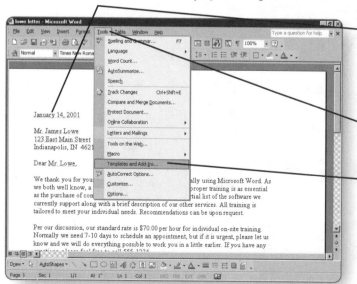

1. Create or open the **document** to which you plan to apply the new template. The document will display onscreen.

2. Click on **Tools**. The Tools menu will appear.

3. Click on **Templates and Add-ins**. The Templates and Add-ins dialog box will open.

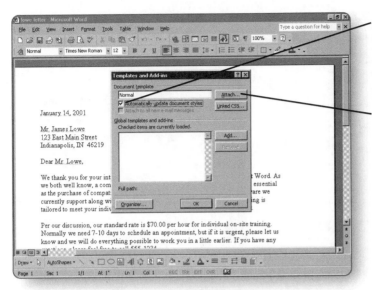

4. If not already checked, **click on Automatically update document styles**. The option will display a check mark.

5. Click on **Attach**. The Attach Template dialog box will open.

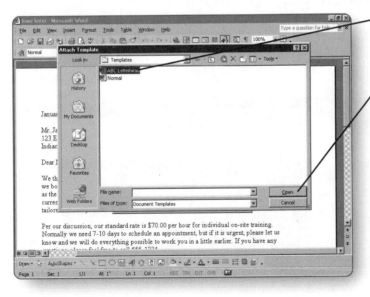

6. Click on the **template name** that you plan to attach to the document.

7. Click on **Open**. The selected template will appear in the Templates and Add-ins dialog box.

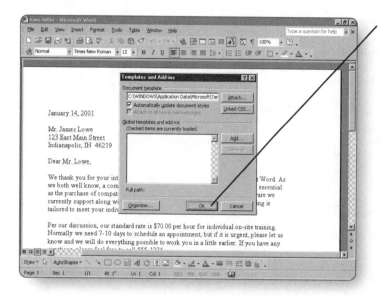

8. Click on **OK**. Word will attach the template to the open document.

Any styles from the attached template will now be available in the current document.

Editing a Template

If you need to make changes to a template, you'll need to create a new template, modify it, and save it with the old template name.

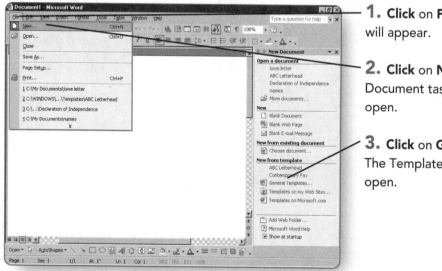

1. Click on **File**. The File menu will appear.

2. Click on **New**. The New Document task pane window will open.

3. Click on **General Templates**. The Templates dialog box will open.

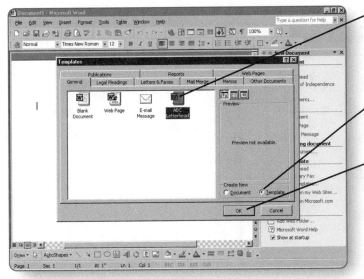

4. Click on the **template name** you want to modify. The template name will be highlighted.

5. Click on **Template**. The option will be selected.

6. Click on **OK**. An untitled template will appear with the text, graphics, formatting, and other attributes available in that template.

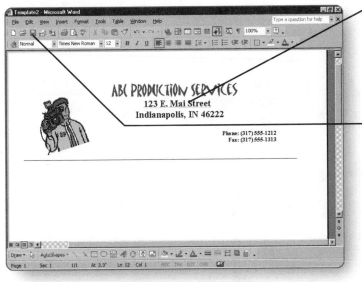

7. Add additional **text** or **edit** the document using methods you've already learned. The document will reflect the changes.

8. Click on the **Save button**. The Save As dialog box will open.

TIP

Optionally, click on File, Save As.

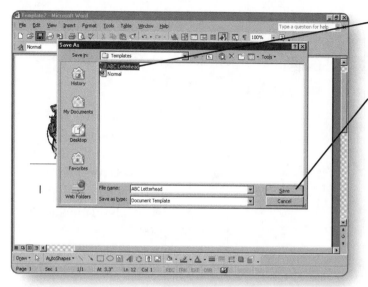

9. Click on the **name** of the original template. The template name will be highlighted.

10. Click on **Save**. A confirmation message box will appear.

11. Click on **OK**. The template will be saved and new documents based on the template will reflect any changes you made.

12. Click on the **Close box**. The open template will close.

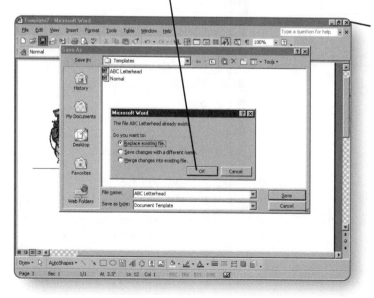

Deleting a Template

If you no longer need a customized template, you can easily delete it.

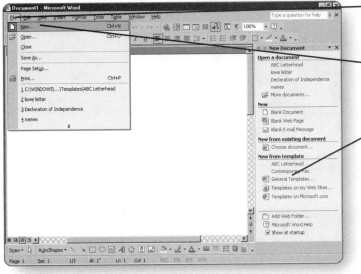

1. Click on **File**. The File menu will appear.

2. Click on **New**. The New Document task pane window will open.

3. Click on **General Templates**. The Templates dialog box will open.

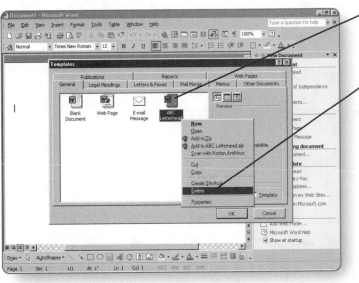

4. Right-click on the **template name** to be deleted. A shortcut menu will appear.

5. Click on **Delete**. A confirmation message will display.

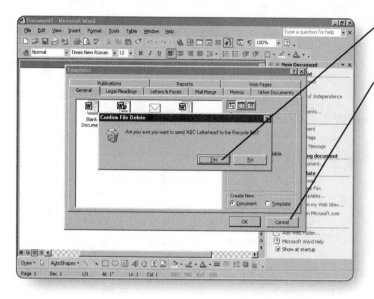

6. **Click** on **Yes**. The template will be deleted.

7. **Click** on **Cancel**. The New dialog box will close.

23

Adding Headers and Footers

Headers and footers are features used for placing information at the top or bottom of every page of a document. You can place any information in headers and footers: the author of the document, the date of last revision, or a company logo. When you start working with documents of more than one page, it's possible for the printed pages to get out of order or mixed up with another document. To easily identify which printouts belong to which document, it's a good idea to add headers and footers with dates and page numbers. In this chapter, you'll learn how to:

- Insert a header or footer
- Add page numbers and dates
- Align text in headers and footers
- Set up headers and footers to print differently on different pages

Inserting a Header or Footer

As you'd expect, a header prints at the top of every page, and a footer prints at the bottom.

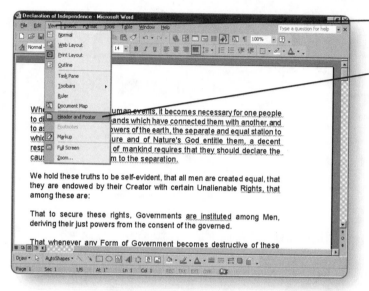

1. Click on **View**. The View menu will appear.

2. Click on **Header and Footer**. The screen will change to Print Layout view, and the Header box will appear along with the Header and Footer toolbar.

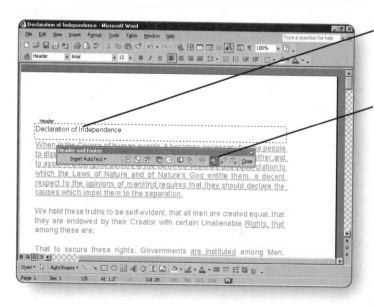

3. Type and format some **text**. Your text will appear in the Header box.

4. Click on the **Switch Between Header and Footer button**. The Footer box will appear.

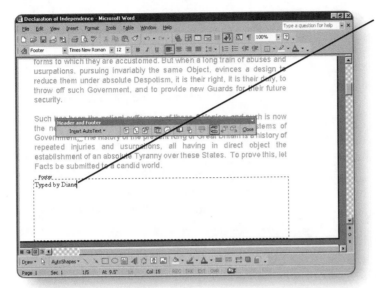

5. Type some **text**. The text will appear in the Footer box.

Adding Date, Time, or Page Number

When the Header or Footer box is open, you can add the date and/or time to either. This places a field for the current date or time; Word will insert the current date and time in that field based on the computer's clock and calendar settings when you print the document. The Insert Page Number feature places the correct page number on each page.

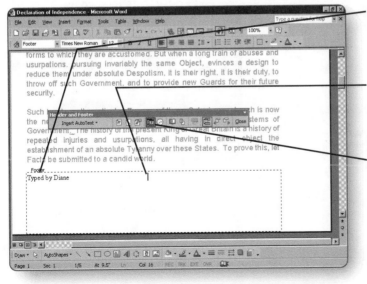

1. Type and format some **text**. The text will appear along the left margin.

2. Press the **Tab key**. The insertion point will jump to the center of the page.

3. Click on the **Insert Date button**. The current date will be inserted.

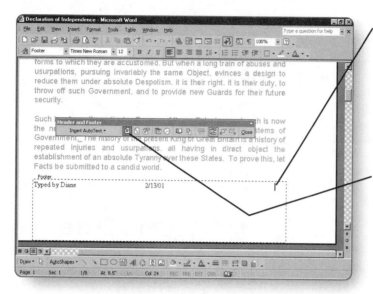

4. Press the **Tab key**. This will right align the next text you insert.

When adding page numbering, Word will use a code. Don't just type a number in.

5. Click on the **Insert Page Number button**. The page number will be inserted.

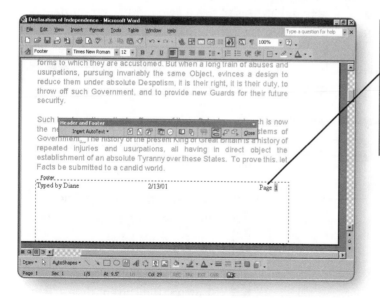

TIP

Optionally, precede the insertion of the page numbering with any desired text, such as "Page."

Arranging Headers and Footers on Different Pages

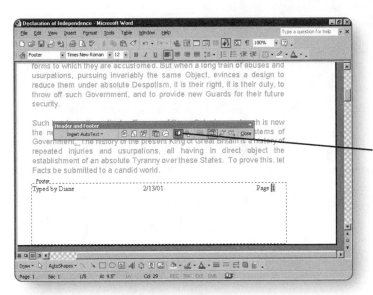

When the Header or Footer box is open, you can choose to have different headers and footers on odd or even pages, or a different header or footer on just the first page of the document.

1. Click on the **Page Setup button**. The Page Setup dialog box will open.

2. Click on the **Layout tab**. The layout tab will come to the front.

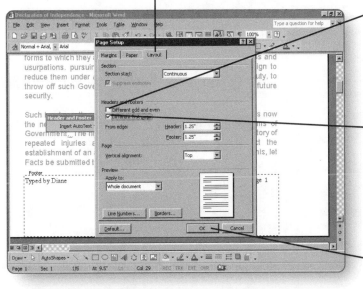

3. Optionally, **click** in the **Different odd and even check box** to have a different header or footer on odd and even pages. The option will be selected.

4. Click in the **Different first page check box** to allow the first page of the document to have a different or blank header or footer. The option will be selected.

5. Click on **OK**. The Page Setup dialog box will close.

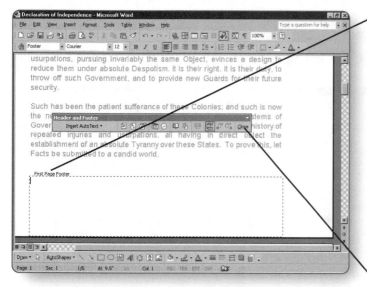

Notice that Word now refers to the footer as "First Page Footer."

TIP

Don't enter anything in the Header or Footer boxes for the first page if you don't want a header of footer on the first page of your document.

6. Click on **Close** on the Header and Footer toolbar. You will return to your document window.

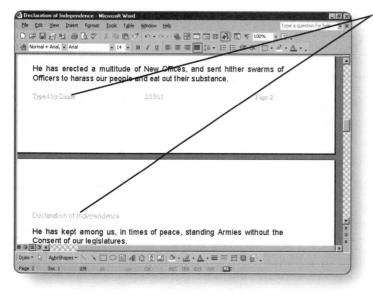

Headers and footers are visible only when you are using Print Layout view or Print Preview.

24

Working with Footnotes or Endnotes

Often reports present material that requires notes set off from the regular text, for example, when you credit material from another source. You can use the Word Footnote or Endnote feature to add these explanatory or source notes to your document. In this chapter, you'll learn how to:

- Create and copy footnotes and endnotes
- Move and delete footnotes and endnotes
- View and convert footnotes and endnotes

Creating a Footnote or Endnote

To give credit where credit is due, you can use the Word Footnote or Endnote feature. Word places footnotes on the page where the note reference mark appears and places endnotes at the end of the document.

When creating a footnote, Word will automatically add a number or character to mark the reference as well as add a separating line. If you have both footnotes and endnotes in a document, Word will number them independently.

Footnotes and endnotes are easiest to create if you are working in Normal view.

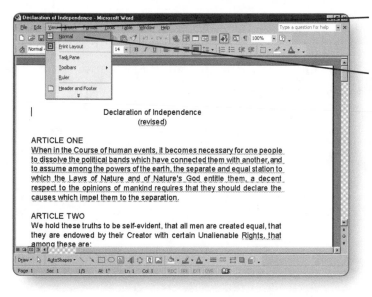

1. **Click** on **View**. The View menu will appear.

2. **Click** on **Normal**. The document will display in Normal view.

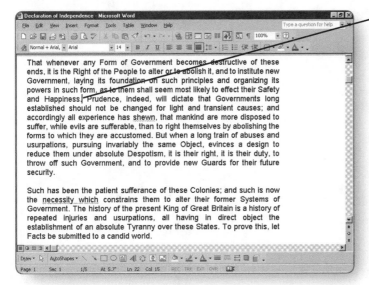

3. Click the **mouse pointer** where you want the note reference mark to appear. A blinking insertion point will appear.

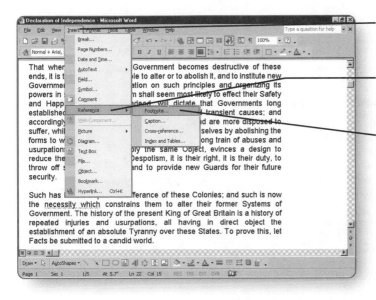

4. Click on **Insert**. The Insert menu will appear.

5. Click on **Reference**. The Reference submenu will appear.

6. Click on **Footnote**. The Footnote and Endnote dialog box will open.

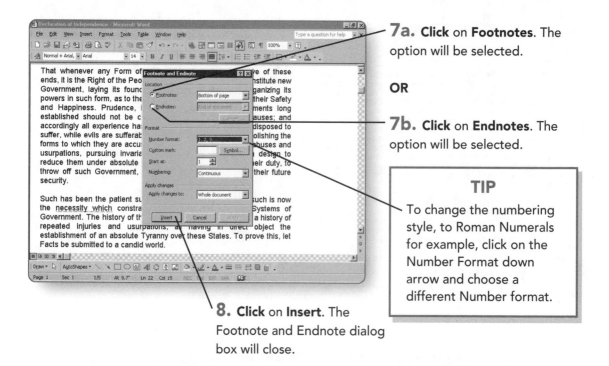

7a. Click on **Footnotes**. The option will be selected.

OR

7b. Click on **Endnotes**. The option will be selected.

TIP

To change the numbering style, to Roman Numerals for example, click on the Number Format down arrow and choose a different Number format.

8. Click on **Insert**. The Footnote and Endnote dialog box will close.

A note reference mark will appear in the document, and a note text area will appear at the bottom of the page.

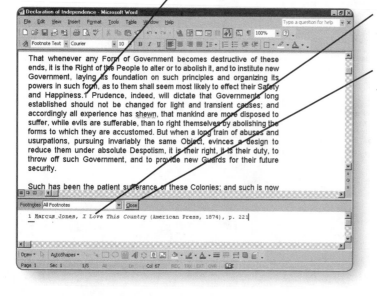

9. Type the **note text**. The text will appear in the note text area.

10. Click on **Close**. The note text area will close.

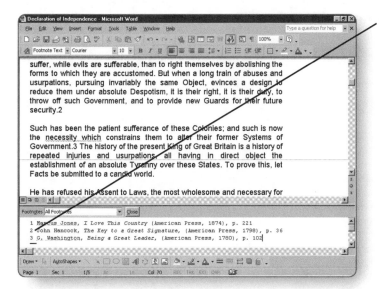

11. **Repeat Steps 3 through 10** to add additional notes. Word will automatically assign the next number to each additional note.

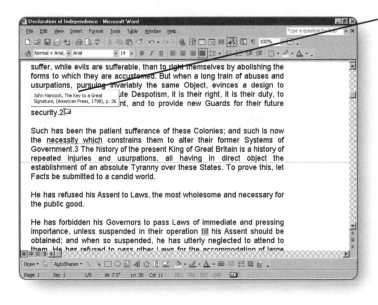

If you position the mouse pointer over the note reference mark in the body of the document, the note text will appear in a box similar to a Tool Tip.

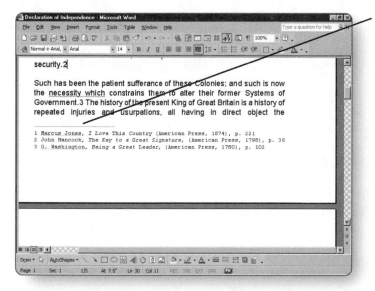

When looking at a footnote in Print Layout view you can see the separating line.

Copying Notes

Sometimes you will refer to a source more than once in a document. Fortunately, you don't have to retype the text for the footnote; you can copy and paste it into a new location. Word will renumber all the notes affected by the change.

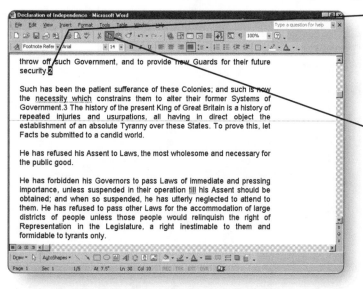

1. **Select** the **note reference mark** of the footnote or endnote that you plan to copy. The reference mark will be highlighted.

2. **Click** on the **Copy button**. The text will be copied to the Windows Clipboard.

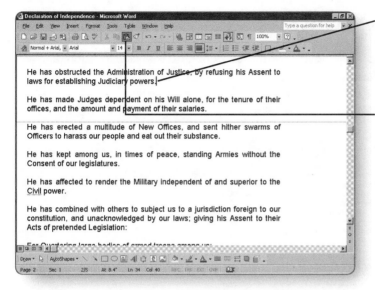

3. **Click** the **mouse pointer** at the location for the duplicated note. A blinking insertion point will appear.

4. **Click** on the **Paste button**. The duplicate note will be placed in the document.

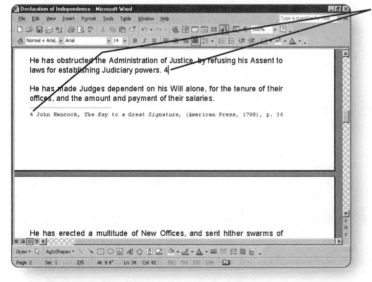

The note reference mark of the copied footnote or endnote will appear in the original and new locations, and the footnote or endnote will appear in the footnote or endnote text area with the correct numbering.

Moving Notes

You can move a footnote or endnote to a new location, and Word will renumber all of the notes affected by the move.

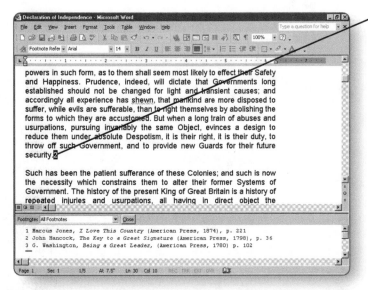

1. **Select** the **note reference mark** of the note that you plan to move. The reference mark will be highlighted.

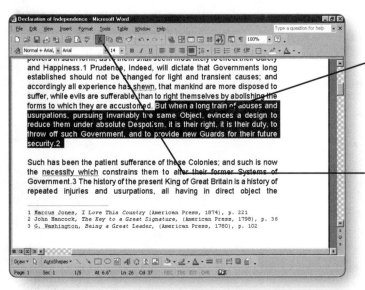

TIP

If you want to move any surrounding document text along with the reference number, highlight it as well.

---

2. **Click** on the **Cut button**. The text will be copied to the Windows Clipboard and removed from the document.

3. Click the **mouse pointer** at the new location for the note. A blinking insertion point will appear.

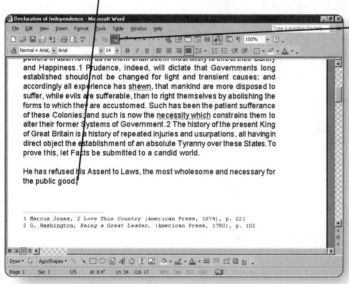

4. Click on the **Paste button**. The note will be placed in the new location in the document and renumbered if necessary.

Deleting a Footnote or Endnote

As you've already noticed, the role of the note reference mark in Word is important. You insert a footnote or endnote by indicating where to place the note reference mark, and then you type the footnote or endnote. You delete a footnote or endnote by deleting the note reference mark, not by deleting the footnote or endnote.

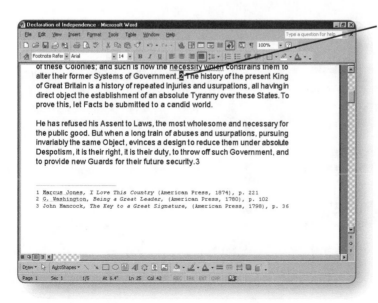

1. Select the **note reference mark** of the footnote or endnote that you plan to delete. The reference mark will be highlighted.

2. Press the **Delete key**. Word will delete the note reference mark and the footnote or endnote in the text area and then renumber all the notes affected by the deletion.

Converting a Footnote to an Endnote

What happens if you create footnotes throughout your report and then decide that you should have used endnotes? Word can convert footnotes to endnotes and endnotes to footnotes—saving you the headache of retyping each entry.

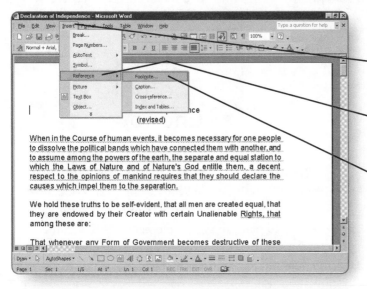

1. Click on **Insert**. The Insert menu will appear.

2. Click on **Reference**. The Reference submenu will appear.

3. Click on **Footnote**. The Footnote and Endnote dialog box will open.

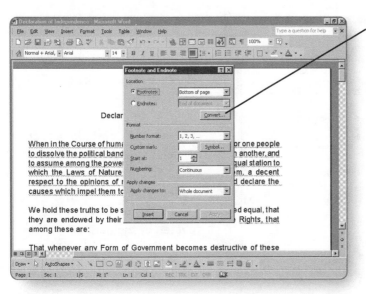

4. Click on **Convert**. The Convert Notes dialog box will open, with the option to convert the type of note you're using to the other type already selected.

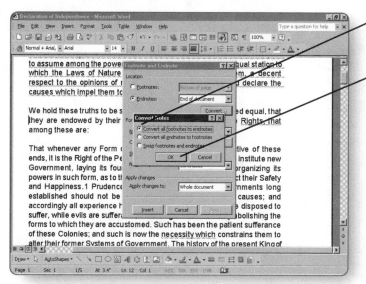

5. **Click** on an **option**. The option will be selected.

6. **Click** on **OK**. The Convert Notes dialog box will close.

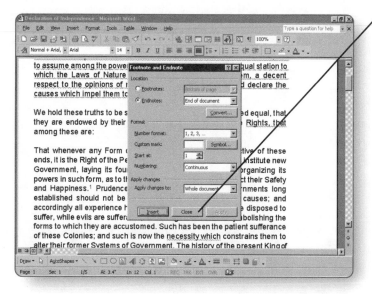

7. **Click** on **Close**. The Footnote and Endnote dialog box will close and the conversion will begin.

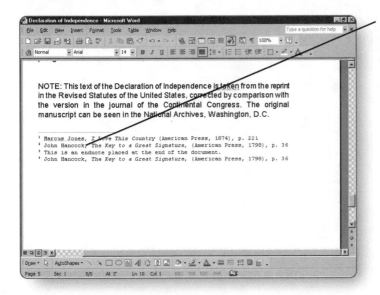

In this example, all footnotes have been converted to endnotes.

Part VI—Working with Long Documents (21–24)

1. What types of elements are included in a style? *See Chapter 21 "Working with Paragraph Styles"*

2. What is the name of Word's default style? *See "Working with Word Styles" in Chapter 21*

3. If you delete a style, what happens to text that had that style applied to it? *See "Deleting a Style" in Chapter 21*

4. What does a template determine about a Word document? *See Chapter 22 "Discovering Templates"*

5. When applying a template to an open document, what is added to the current document? *See "Applying a Template" in Chapter 22*

6. Where does a header print? *See "Inserting a Header or Footer" in Chapter 23*

7. Where do Word's date and time fields get their information? *See Chapter 23 "Adding Date, Time, or Page Numbers"*

8. What views can be used to see headers or footers? *See "Arranging Headers and Footers on Different Pages" in Chapter 23*

9. Where does Word place endnotes? *See "Creating a Footnote or Endnote" in Chapter 24*

10. What do you highlight to delete a footnote or endnote? *See "Deleting a Footnote or Endnote" in Chapter 24*

PART VII

Using Word Technology

Chapter 25
Using Word to Create Web Pages **335**

Chapter 26
Speaking with Word **357**

25

Using Word to Create Web Pages

Word makes creating a Web page almost as easy as creating a standard document. You can actually create Web pages in two different ways: you can use a wizard or template, or you can convert an existing Word document to Web page format—known as HTML (*Hypertext Markup Language*). Although the name sounds complicated, the process is very easy. In this chapter, you'll learn how to:

- Create a Web page from a Word document
- Use the Web Page Wizard to create a Web page
- Insert links and graphics
- View your Web page

Saving a Word Document as a Web Document

When a document is saved as a Web document, Word will insert the HTML tags for you—you won't even see them.

You don't need to create HTML documents from scratch if you want to use a document you've already created.

1. Open or create the Word **document** you want to save as a Web page. The document will display on the screen.

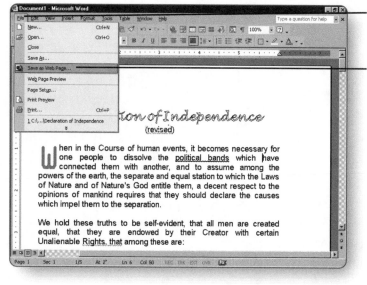

2. Click on **File**. The File menu will open.

3. Click on **Save As Web Page**. The Save As dialog box will open.

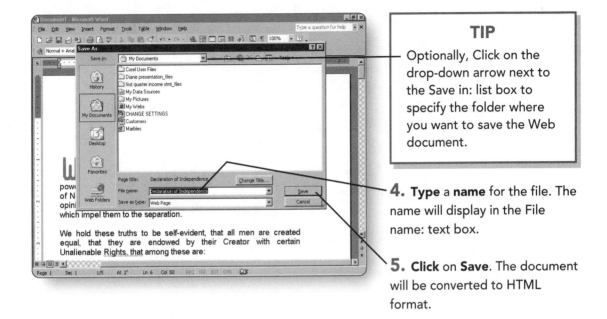

TIP

Optionally, Click on the drop-down arrow next to the Save in: list box to specify the folder where you want to save the Web document.

4. **Type** a **name** for the file. The name will display in the File name: text box.

5. **Click** on **Save**. The document will be converted to HTML format.

Most Word formatting choices are acceptable in a Web document; however, there are a few formats that most Web Browsers cannot support. The following table lists a few of the specialized character formats that do not convert properly when converting a Word document to HTML.

Format	*Reaction in a Web Browser*
Animated Text	No animation and will appear as italicized text
Emboss or Engrave	Will turn into a light-gray shaded text
Shadowed Text	Text will become bold
Character borders	No border around text
Special Underlining	Appears as a single underline
Color underline	Black underline
Small Caps	All Caps

If you have any of the non-supported formats in your Word document, a dialog box will advise you of what will happen to the non-supported formats.

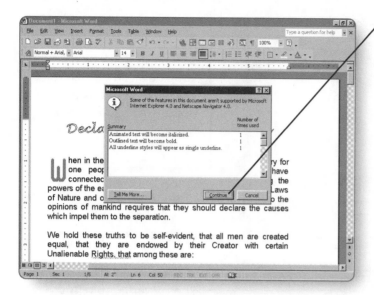

6. Click on **Continue**. The conversion will continue and the document will be displayed in Word's Web Layout view.

Creating a New Web Page

Studies have shown that Web surfers lose patience with Web pages that take longer than 20 seconds to load, therefore, try to design your Web pages to load quickly. Large graphic images often slow the loading of a Web page.

Using the Web Page Wizard

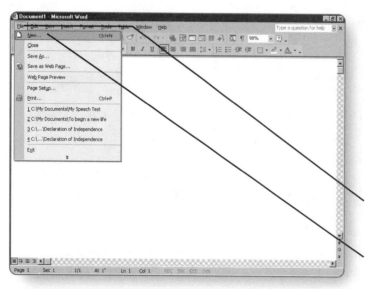

Some people think that only a wizard can understand all the ins and outs of the World Wide Web. By using the Web Page Wizard you have the capacity to become a master Web page builder. Using the Web Page Wizard is the easiest way to create a Web page.

1. Click on **File**. The File menu will appear.

2. Click on **New**. The New document task pane will open.

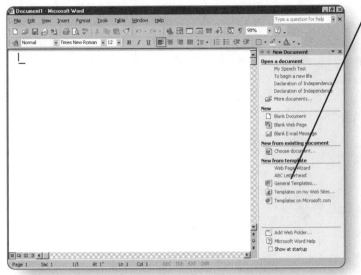

3. Click on **General Templates**. The Templates dialog box will open.

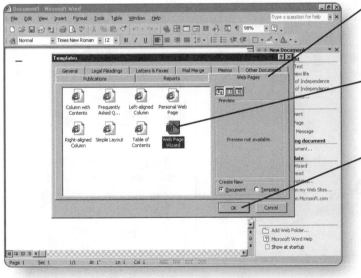

4. Click on the **Web Pages tab**. The Web Pages tab will come to the front.

5. Click on the **Web Page Wizard icon**. The icon will be highlighted.

6. Click on **OK**. The beginning screen of the Web Page Wizard will appear.

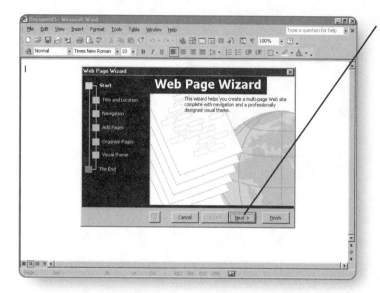

7. **Click** on **Next**. The next page of the wizard will display.

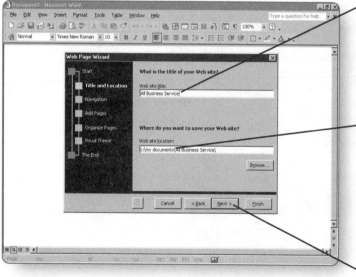

8. **Type** a **title** for the Web site. The text will appear in the Web site title: text box.

TIP

You can optionally specify a file location for your Web pages. Generally however, it's best just to leave them where Word is trying to place them.

9. **Click** on **Next**. The next page of the Web Page Wizard will appear.

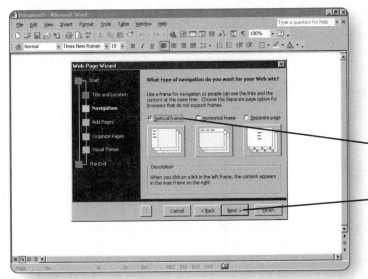

Next you need to specify a format of *frames*, which are independent boxes on a Web page. Frames help to organize links and other options on a page.

10. **Click** on a **frame style**. The option will be selected.

11. **Click** on **Next**. The Add Pages screen will display.

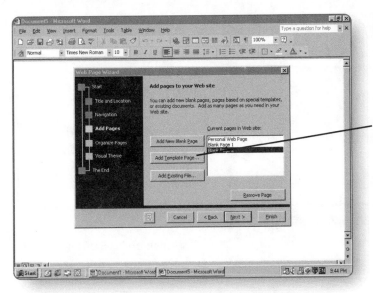

Now you need to decide what types of additional pages you want for your Web site. The easiest method is to use Word's predefined templates.

12. **Click** on **Add Template Page**. A dialog box displaying the different types of templates will open.

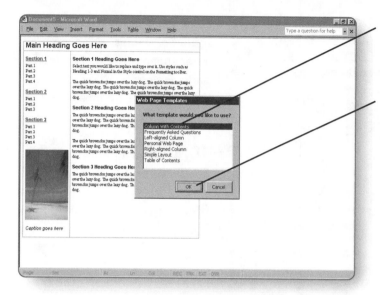

13. **Click** on an **option**. A sample of the selection will appear behind the dialog box.

14. **Click** on **OK**. The Web Page Wizard will reappear.

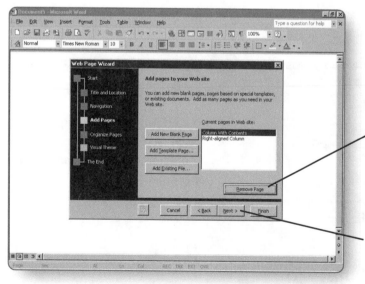

15. **Repeat Steps 10 through 12** for each additional page you want to include.

TIP

To remove unwanted pages, click on the page and click the Remove Page button.

16. **Click** on **Next**. The Organize Pages screen will display.

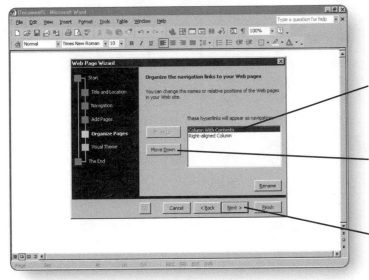

Here you can decide the order in which you want the various pages to appear.

17. **Click** on a page **description**. The description will be highlighted.

18. **Click** on **Move Up or Move Down**. The page order will be rearranged.

19. **Click** on **Next**. The Themes page will display.

Using Word Themes

Themes are a collection of background colors/patterns, bullet styles, line styles, heading styles, and font styles. When you select a theme, you make available, in your document, all the styles associated with the theme. Most people use themes when designing Web pages.

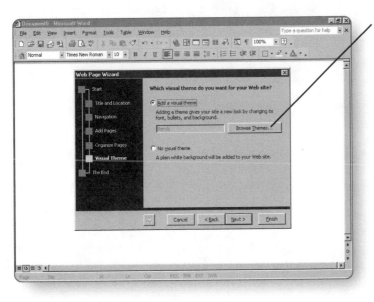

1. **Click** on **Browse Themes**. A list of available themes will display.

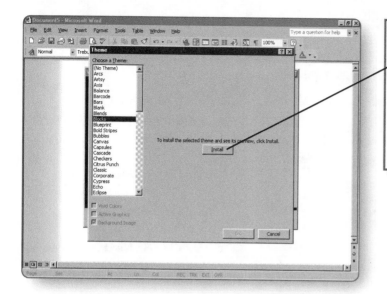

TIP

If, after clicking on a theme name, you don't see a preview, you'll need to click on Install and insert your Word CD to install Themes.

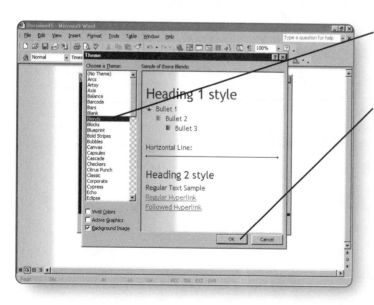

2. Click on a **Theme**. A sample of the theme will display in the preview box.

3. Click on **OK**. The Theme dialog box will close and the Web Page Wizard will redisplay.

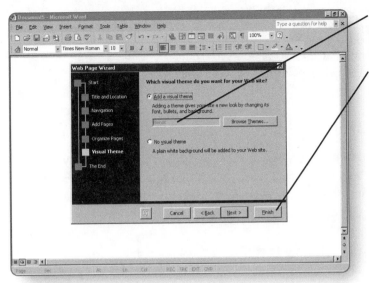

The name of the theme you selected will display.

4. Click on **Finish**. The Wizard will close.

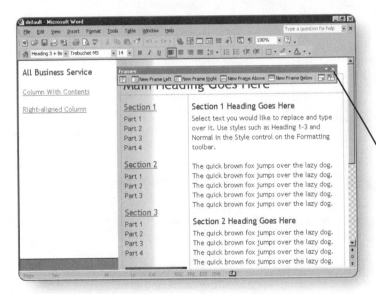

The individual pages will be saved and Word will display the opening (default) page as well as the Frames toolbar. You'll now be ready to edit the page with your information.

5. Click on the Frames toolbar **close box**. The Frames toolbar will close.

Editing a Web Page

Now that the Web Page Wizard has supplied a skeleton Web page, you'll want to make changes to it.

Typing Text

The Web Page Wizard supplies "dummy" text where you should supply real text. You change the text on a Web page document the same way that you change text in any Word document.

1. Select some **text**. The text will be highlighted.

2. Type the **replacement text**. The new text will replace the highlighted text.

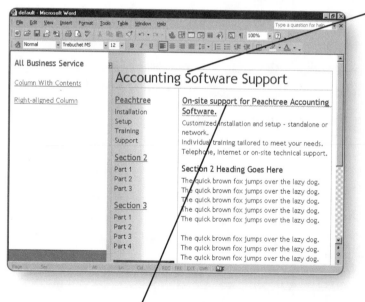

TIP

If you have text stored in a Word document that you want to use on the Web page, use the Windows Copy and Paste commands to transfer text from the standard document to the Web page document.

3. Repeat Steps 1 and 2 for each portion of text to be modified. The text will appear onscreen.

Adding Scrolling Text

Scrolling text on a Web page provides quite a dramatic effect. Unfortunately, not all Web browsers support scrolling text. Any surfer who happens to be using a browser that doesn't support scrolling text will see regular text.

To create scrolling text, you'll need to use the Web Tools toolbar.

1. Click on View. The View menu will appear.

2. Click on **Toolbars**. The Toolbars submenu will appear.

3. Click on **Web Tools**. The Web Tools toolbar will display.

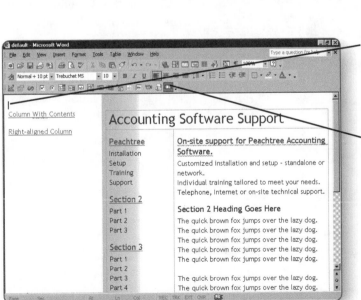

4. Click the **mouse pointer** at the location you want the scrolling text. The blinking insertion point will appear.

5. Click on the **Scrolling Text** tool from the Web Tools toolbar. The Scrolling Text dialog box will open.

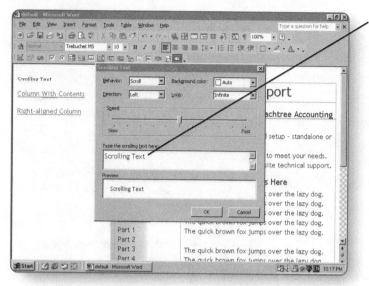

6. Select the words **Scrolling Text** in the Type the scrolling text here: text box. The text will be highlighted.

7. Type the **text** you want to appear. The new text will replace the original text.

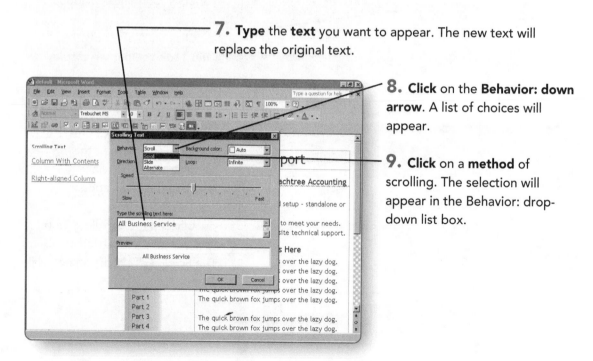

8. Click on the **Behavior: down arrow**. A list of choices will appear.

9. Click on a **method** of scrolling. The selection will appear in the Behavior: drop-down list box.

10. Click on **Direction: down arrow**. A list of choices will appear.

11. Click on a **direction** for the text to scroll. The selection will appear in the Direction: drop-down list box.

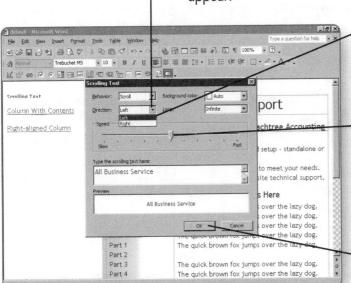

12. Drag the **speed knob** to the left or right. Dragging to the left will slow down the speed of the scrolling text, while dragging to the right will increase the speed.

13. Click on **OK**. The Scrolling Text dialog box will close and you will return to your Web page.

TIP

You can now further edit the scrolling text object. Click on the appropriate choices from the Standard toolbar to edit size, font, or color.

Including a Background Sound

You can have a background sound play when someone views your Web page; background sounds don't slow Web browsers because they load and begin to play while the Web page is loading.

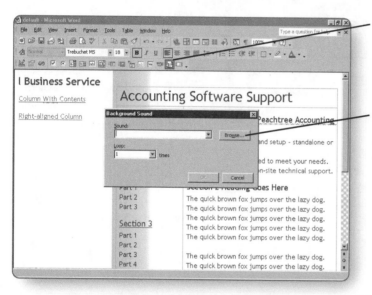

1. On the Web tools toolbar, **click** on the **Sound button**. The Background Sound dialog box will open.

2. Click on **Browse**. A list of sounds available on your hard drive will display.

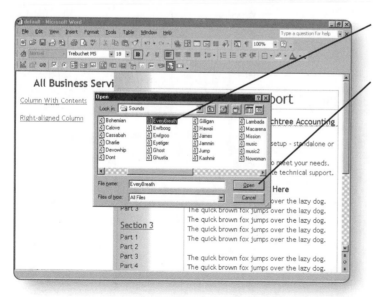

3. Click on a **sound**. The file name will be highlighted.

4. Click on **Open**. The Background Sound dialog box will reopen.

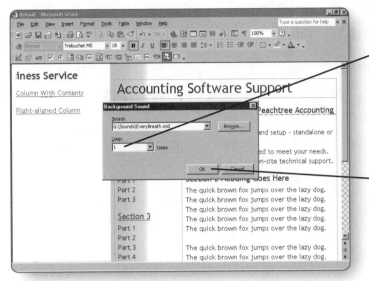

TIP

Changing the number in the Loop: drop-down list box determines the number of times the sound will play.

5. Click on **OK**. The Background Sound dialog box will close.

Inserting Links

A *hyperlink* is text that allows you to jump from one area to another. Links are frequently used in Web pages and in Word's help menus.

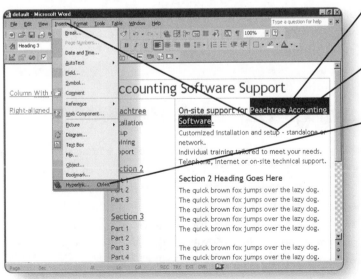

1. Select text to be a link. The text will be highlighted.

2. Click on **Insert**. The Insert menu will appear.

3. Click on **Hyperlink**. The Insert Hyperlink dialog box will open.

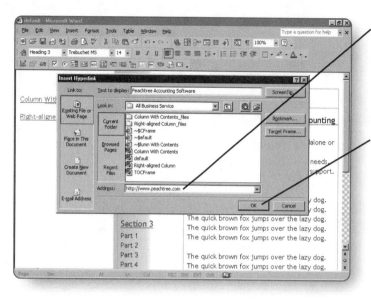

4. **Type** the **path** and **file name** of the Web page or document you want to link to your Web page. The name will display in the Address: text box.

5. **Click** on **OK**. Word will create a link to the document.

Inserting a Picture

Web pages usually include some graphics to create visual interest. You can insert and edit a drawing or picture into a Web page by following the directions in Chapter 11, "*Communicating Ideas with Art.*"

Saving Your Web Pages

When you save a Web page that you create, you actually save several different files. Word saves each element of the Web page (graphic images, bullets, lines, and so on) separately using the pathname you specified while using the Web Page Wizard. Keeping all the files for a Web page together becomes important when it's time to publish the Web page; you'll need to make sure then that you publish all the files.

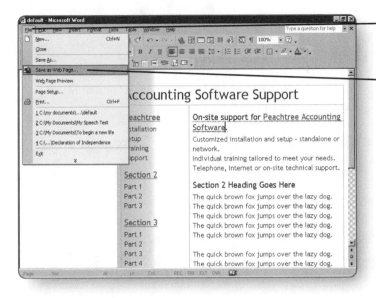

1. **Click** on **File**. The File menu will appear.

2. **Click** on **Save As Web Page**. The Save As dialog box will open.

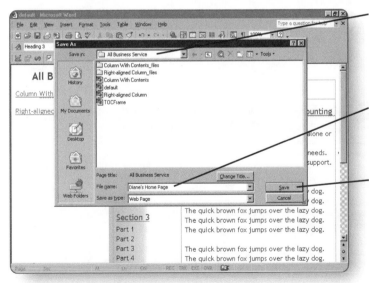

Notice that the default folder Word suggests is the one you identified in the Web Page Wizard.

You can leave the name "Default.htm" or you can change it to something you'll recognize.

3. **Click** on **Save**. The current page and all pages associated with the Web page will be saved.

Viewing the Document in Internet Explorer

Now that the document has been saved as HTML, it's time to see what it looks like in Internet Explorer.

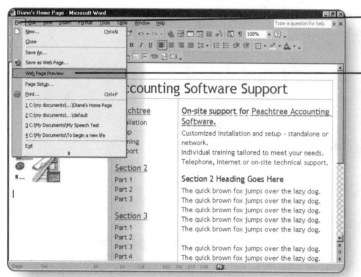

1. **Click** on **File**. The File menu will appear.

2. **Click** on **Web Page Preview**. The Internet Explorer window will display and you'll see the document as viewed through Internet Explorer.

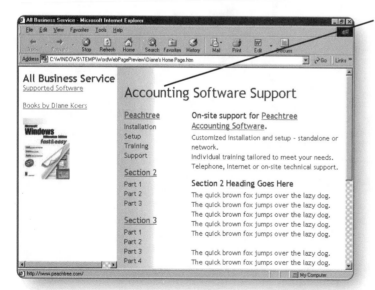

This is a Word document as viewed in Internet Explorer.

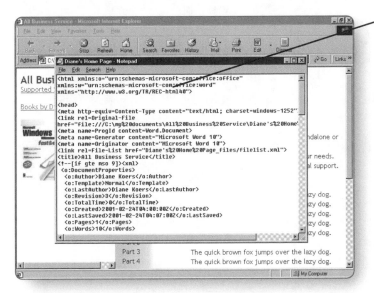

To view the HTML source code, from the Internet Explorer window, click on View Source. A window will open with all the HTML tags. Aren't you glad you have Office to do all this work for you!

Publishing Web Documents

You've created your Web documents; now the issue becomes how to make your Web pages accessible to your company's intranet or on the World Wide Web.

You'll need to save your Web pages and their related files (the graphics, lines, bullets, and so on) to a *Web folder*, which is a shortcut to a Web server. The Web server must support Web folders.

The steps required to save your files to a Web server vary between servers, so you'll need to check with your system administrator or Internet Service Provider.

26

Speaking with Word

Microsoft Office XP now supports speech recognition technology. With speech recognition, you can dictate directly into a microphone and Microsoft Word will either type the information you've dictated into a document or follow your menu commands.

Since speech recognition is still a relatively new technology, you probably won't find it 100 percent accurate in understanding your words, however, the one included with Microsoft Word beats the competition hands down! With proper training, you should expect about a 95 percent accuracy rate, meaning that Word should correctly identify 95 out of every 100 words you dictate.

The only drawback is that you won't like speech recognition on an older, slower computer. Your computer should have at least 128MB of RAM memory (more memory increases speech recognition performance) and be at least a Pentium II with 400MHz to effectively handle speech recognition. You'll also need a microphone, preferably a headset type unit. In this chapter, you'll learn how to:

- Install the speech recognition components
- Train speech recognition to your voice
- Record and correct dictation

Installing Speech

By default, the speech function is not installed with Microsoft Office. The first time you access speech, you'll be prompted to install it.

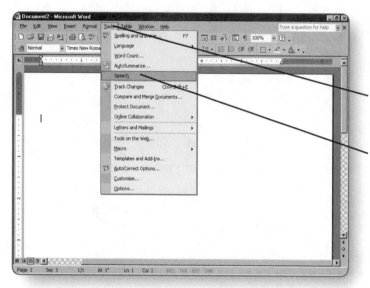

1. Open Microsoft Word. Word and its menu will appear onscreen.

2. Click on **Tools**. The Tools menu will appear.

3. Click on **Speech**. A message will display.

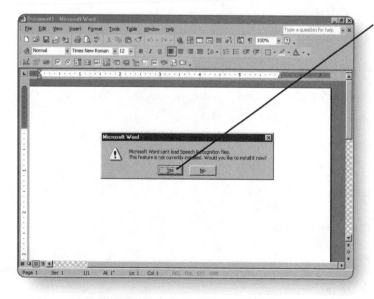

4. Click on **Yes**. The Welcome to Speech Recognition dialog box will open.

Setting Up Your Microphone

To increase accuracy, you'll need to set up your microphone and teach Speech Recognition about your speech patterns.

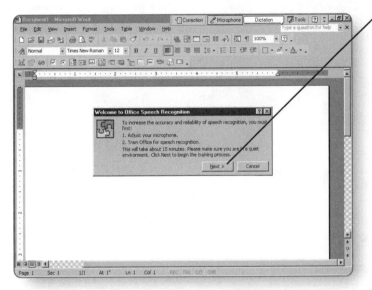

1. **Click** on **Next**. The Microphone Wizard will launch.

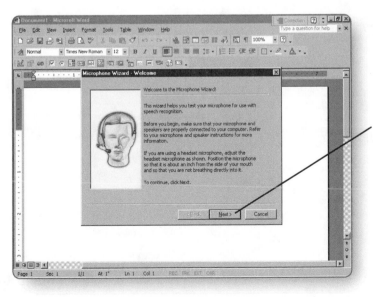

Position your microphone headset on your head or if you're using a handheld microphone, hold it in a position for you to speak into it.

2. **Click** on **Next**. You'll be asked to adjust your microphone volume.

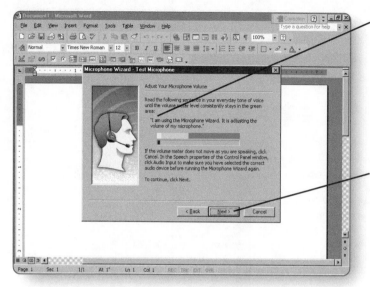

3. **Repeat** the **sentence** displayed on your screen. The volume meter will monitor your volume. Repeat the sentence as necessary to keep your volume in the green area of the volume meter.

4. **Click** on **Next**. The Test Positioning box will appear.

If you are using a headset microphone, you'll need to test the microphone position.

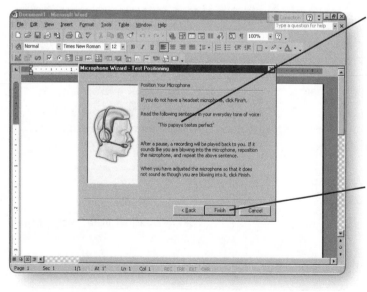

5. **Say** the **sentence** displayed on the screen. The recording will be played back to you.

If it sounds like you're blowing back into the microphone, move the headset microphone slightly and try the sentence again.

6. **Click** on **Finish**. The Default Speech Profile box will appear.

Training Speech Recognition

The speech recognition wizard will next need to collect samples of your voice. The training steps are the most important steps to making speech recognition work effectively.

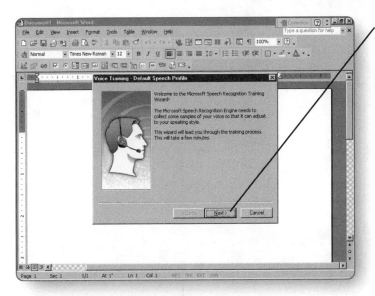

1. Click on **Next**. The next screen of the Default Speech Profile box will appear.

To accurately recognize your voice, Speech Recognition must determine your age and gender.

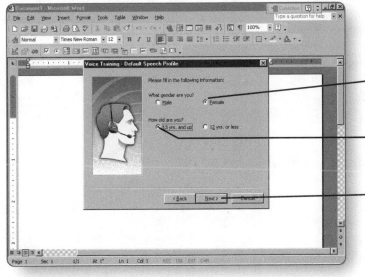

2. Click on a **gender**. The option will be selected.

3. Click on an **age bracket**. The option will be selected.

4. Click on **Next**. The next screen of the Default Speech Profile box will appear.

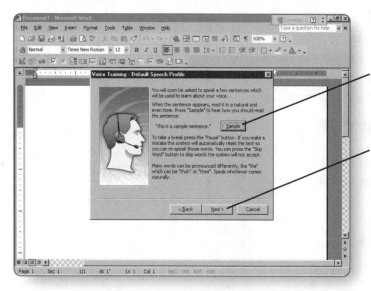

The sample speech illustrates how you should speak.

5. Click on the **Sample button.** You will hear sample text from your computer speakers.

6. Click on **Next.** The next screen of the Default Speech Profile box will appear.

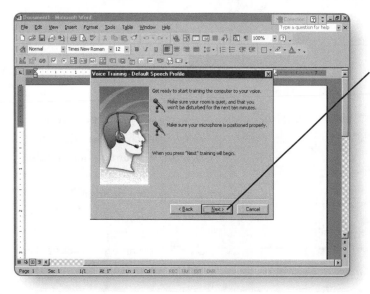

You're ready to begin speech recognition training.

7. Click on **Next.** The first paragraph of text will appear, ready for you to read.

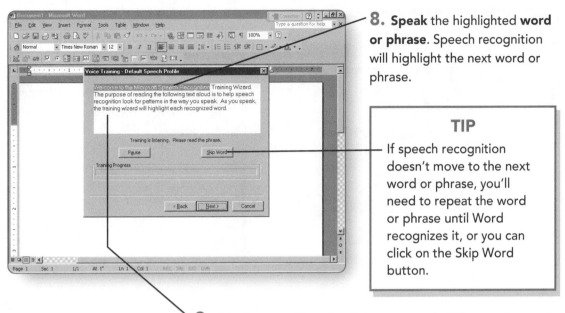

8. Speak the highlighted **word or phrase**. Speech recognition will highlight the next word or phrase.

TIP

If speech recognition doesn't move to the next word or phrase, you'll need to repeat the word or phrase until Word recognizes it, or you can click on the Skip Word button.

9. Continue reading aloud the paragraph. When you've read the entire paragraph, the next paragraph will display on the screen.

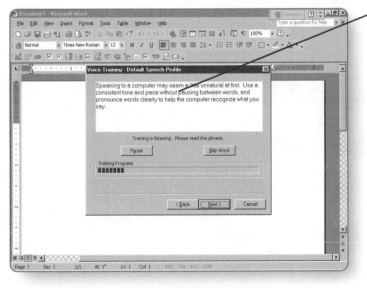

10. Read the **next paragraph**. Speech recognition will display several different paragraphs for you to read.

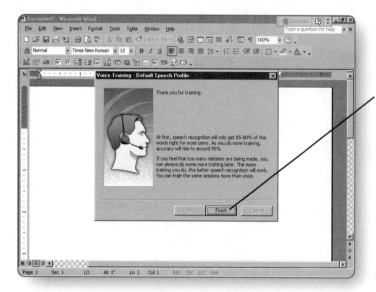

When you've completed all the reading, speech recognition will collect and save the data.

11. Click on **Finish**. A Welcome to Speech recognition video will appear.

The video will run automatically and explain the basics of working with speech recognition.

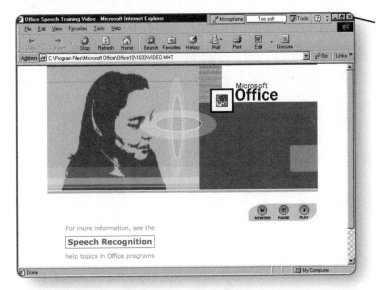

12. Click on the **Close box**. The video window will close and the Microsoft Word application will reappear.

Understanding the Language Bar

Speech recognition includes its own toolbar, called the *Language Bar*. The Language Bar lays on top of the Word title bar, making it easily visible.

Moving the Language Bar

If the Language Bar is in an inconvenient location, you can easily move it to a better one.

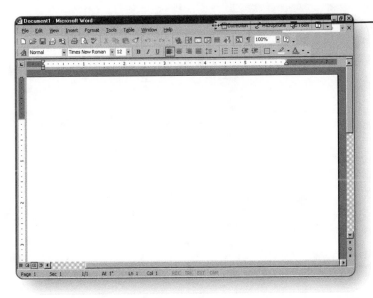

1. Position the **mouse** along the left edge of the Language Bar. The mouse pointer will turn into a four-headed arrow.

2. Drag the **Language Bar** to a new location. The Language Bar will move as you drag the mouse.

3. Release the **mouse button**. The Language Bar will remain in the new position.

Hiding the Language Bar

If you don't need to use the speech recognition at the moment, you can minimize the Language Bar to hide it.

1. **Click** on the **Minimize button**. It's the top arrow on the right side of the Language Bar. The Language Bar will disappear from your screen.

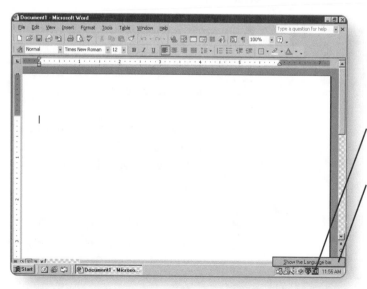

The Language Bar doesn't minimize like other applications. Instead, it locates itself in the System Tray and is represented by a small blue icon.

2. **Click** on the **Language Bar icon**. A menu will appear.

3. **Click** on **Show the Language Bar**. The Language Bar will reappear at its previous location.

Speaking Into Word

While speech recognition is available for all the Office XP applications, you'll probably use it most in Word.

Before you can dictate, you will need to make sure the microphone is activated.

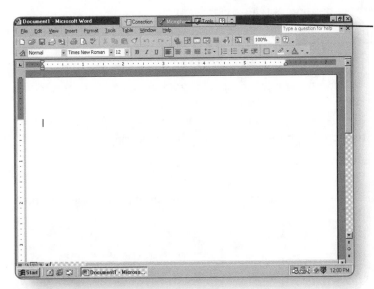

1. Click the **Microphone button**. The Language Bar will expand to show a Dictation button and a Voice Command button.

> ### TIP
> Try to keep the microphone in the same position. Moving it around can cause speech recognition to misunderstand your voice.

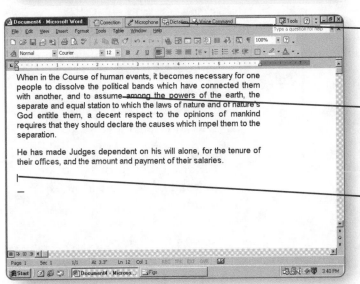

2. Click on the **Dictation button**. Speech recognition will activate Dictation mode.

For the purpose of illustration, the text in this figure shows the text I will read into the microphone.

3. Click in the **document** where you want the dictation to begin. The blinking insertion point will appear.

4. Speak into the **microphone**. The results will print on the screen, beginning with a blue highlight, then appearing as words.

Dictate into the microphone, speaking in a fairly normal consistent tone, pronouncing your words clearly, but not separating each syllable in a word. Because a phrase is easier for the computer to interpret than a single word, speak without pausing between words.

NOTE

The computer may not display your words on the screen immediately. Continue speaking and pause at the end of each sentence. The computer will display the recognized text on the screen after it finishes processing your voice.

The table below lists commands you can use during dictation.

Say	To
New line	Start text on the next line.
New paragraph	Start a new paragraph.
Tab	Press the TAB key once.
Enter	Press the ENTER key once.
Spelling mode	Spell out the next word. For example, say this before you spell out a company name or a person's name. Pause after spelling out the word to revert to normal dictation mode.
Forcenum	Enter a number or symbol instead of spelling it out. For example, say this to enter "7" instead of "seven." Pause after saying the number or symbol to revert to normal dictation mode.

In addition to the commands listed previously, you can also say most punctuation marks. Examples include:

Say	To Get
Comma	,
Question Mark	?
Exclamation Point	!
Colon	:
Semicolon	;
Ellipsis	...
Open Parend	(
Close Parend	)
Open Bracket	[
Close Bracket	]
Slash	/
Backslash	\
Dollar Sign	$
Number Sign	#
Ampersand	&

TIP

If you want the document to include words such as period, tab, semicolon, and so forth, you'll have to type them manually since speech recognition interprets them as punctuation marks or commands.

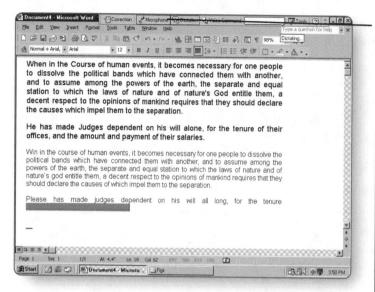

5. **Click** the **Microphone button** again. The microphone will turn off and the Dictation button will disappear from the Language Bar.

NOTE

If your headset has a Mute button that enables you to turn your microphone on or off, the headset's Mute button overrides the button on the Language bar.

Making Corrections

Speech recognition is not designed for completely hands-free operation. There are going to be items you'll need to correct by using your keyboard and mouse.

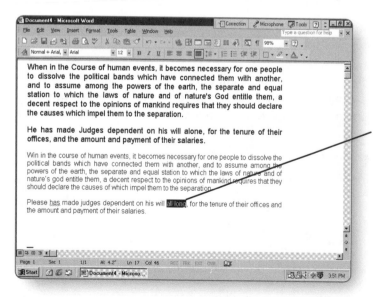

Correcting Manually

Make corrections to dictated text in the same manner as if you typed it yourself.

1. **Select** any **incorrect text**. The text will be highlighted.

2. **Type** a **correction**. The incorrect text will be replaced with the corrected text.

Selecting Correction Words

If speech recognition misunderstood you, you may be able to select the correct words from a supplied list.

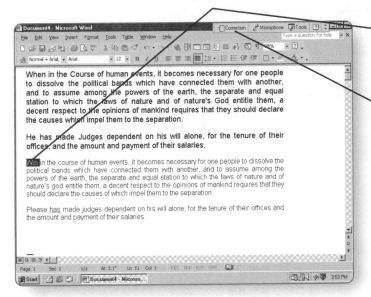

1. Select the **incorrect word or phrase**. The text will be highlighted.

2. Click on the **Correction button**. Speech recognition will repeat the word through your computer speakers.

NOTE

If the current word was not dictated, but manually typed, the Correction button will be unavailable.

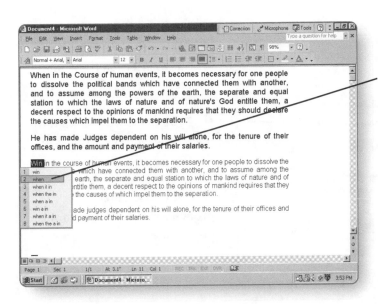

A list of alternative words will appear.

3. Click on a **correction**. The correction will replace the incorrect word.

Creating Special Words

Perhaps you have an unusual name, or a technical term that speech recognition doesn't recognize. You can train speech recognition to understand specific words.

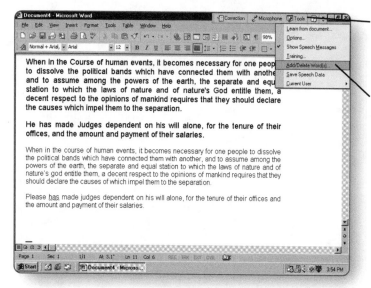

1. **Click** on the **Tools button** on the Language Bar. A menu will appear.

2. **Click** on **Add/Delete Word(s).** The Add/Delete Word(s) dialog box will open.

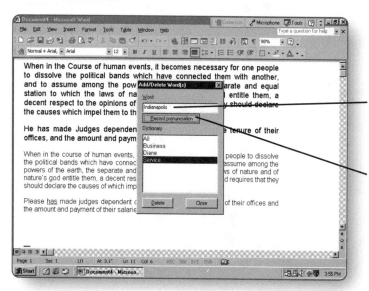

3. **Click** in the Word: **text box.** A blinking insertion point will appear.

4. **Type** the **word** you want to teach. The word will appear in the text box.

5. **Click** on **Record pronunciation.** The option will be activated.

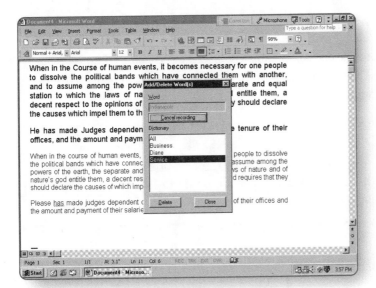

6. **Say** the **word you typed**. Speech recognition learns the word and adds it to the word list.

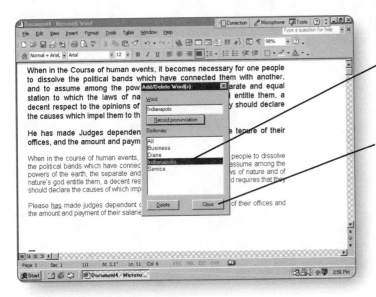

TIP

Click on the word to hear the computer pronunciation of the word.

7. Click on **Close**. The Add/Delete Word(s) dialog box will close.

Dictating Menu Commands

Speech recognition also can understand voice commands such as File Save or Edit Undo. It can even make selections from a dialog box.

NOTE

If the command you want requires you to select the text first, you'll need to select the text before you issue the voice command.

---

1. Click the **Microphone button**. The Language Bar will expand to show a Dictation button and a Voice Command button.

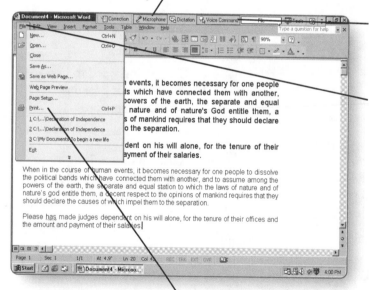

2. Click on the **Voice Command button**. The Voice Command mode will become activated.

3. Say a **menu command**. For this example, the command File was spoken so the File menu will open.

TIP

With Voice Command you can also format selected text by saying the word bold, italic, or underline.

---

4. Say the **next menu command**. For this example, the command Print was spoken, so the Print dialog box will open.

5. **Issue** a **command** into the dialog box by dictating the commands as you see them on the screen. For example, from the Print dialog box, to print only the current page, say Current Page.

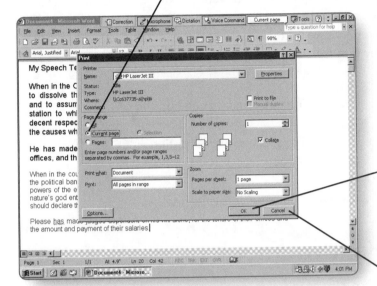

NOTE

Some portions of a dialog box will not respond to voice commands. You must use your keyboard or mouse to select them.

6a. **Say OK**. Word will accept the choices and execute the command.

OR

6b. **Say Cancel**. Word will close the dialog box without any action being taken.

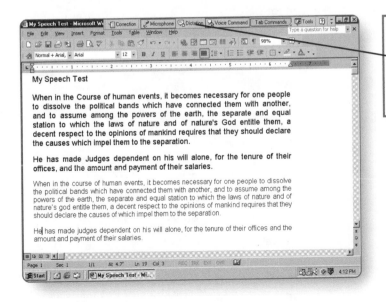

TIP

To return to Dictation mode, click on the Dictation button.

Working with the Keyboard Commands

Speech recognition includes several keyboard commands to assist you with your dictation. These keystrokes include using the Windows button on your keyboard along with a standard key that results in a speech recognition action.

- +V—Turns the microphone on and off.

- +T—Toggles between Dictation mode and Voice Command mode.

- +C—Activates Correction mode.

Handwriting

Office XP also includes the ability to read your handwriting when using a special tablet attached to your computer. Handwriting recognition and tablets are beyond the scope of this book and cannot be covered.

Part VII—Using Word Technology (25–26)

1. What is the format of a Web page called? *See Chapter 25 "Using Word to Create Web Pages"*

2. What purpose do frames provide on a Web page? *See "Using the Web Page Wizard" in Chapter 25*

3. What are themes? *See "Using Word Themes" in Chapter 25*

4. What happens to scrolling text if a user's Web browser doesn't support scrolling text? *See "Adding Scrolling Text" in Chapter 25*

5. Do Web pages load slower if they have a background sound included? *See "Including a Background Sound" in Chapter 25*

6. What can you do with speech recognition? *See Chapter 26 "Speaking with Word"*

7. What is the name of the toolbar included with speech recognition? *See "Understanding the Language Bar" in Chapter 26*

8. What Office XP applications support speech recognition? *See "Speaking Into Word" in Chapter 26*

9. When dictating text, what command do you issue to tell Word to generate a number instead of spelling the number? *See "Speaking Into Word" in Chapter 26*

10. What toolbar button do you click on to tell Word you want to issue menu commands? *See "Dictating Menu Commands" in Chapter 26*

PART VIII

Appendixes

Appendix A
   Installing Microsoft Office XP **381**

Appendix B
   Using Keyboard Shortcuts **397**

Installing Microsoft Office XP

When installing Microsoft Office, you can elect to install the entire Office suite, or you can install only desired components, such as Microsoft Word. Installing Office XP is practically automatic. In this appendix, you'll learn how to:

- Install Office XP on your computer
- Choose which Office components you want to install
- Detect and Repair problems
- Add and remove Office XP components
- Uninstall Office XP

Understanding System Requirements

The following is a list of minimum requirements to install and run Microsoft Office XP.

- Microsoft Windows 98, Windows 98 Second Edition, Windows Me, Windows NT® 4.0 with Service Pack 6 or greater, or Windows 2000. On systems running Windows NT 4.0 with Service Pack 6, the version of Internet Explorer must be upgraded to at least 4.01 with Service Pack 1.

- RAM requirements depend upon the operating system used. 64MB to 128MB is suggested.

- Hard disk space requirements will vary depending on configuration. If you have Windows 2000, Office will require 115MB of available hard disk space for the default configuration of Office Professional with FrontPage. If you don't have Windows 2000, Windows Me, or Office 2000 SR1, Office will require an extra 50MB of hard disk space for the Office System Pack. Custom installation choices may require more or less hard disk space.

- A CD-ROM drive is required for installation.

- A super VGA monitor (800x600) or higher-resolution with 256 colors or more.

- Microsoft Mouse, Microsoft® IntelliMouse®, or compatible pointing device.

- Pentium 133MHz or higher processor.

- A multimedia computer is required for sound and other multimedia effects. A hardware accelerated video card or MMX processor will provide improved graphical rendering performance. Pentium II 400MHz or higher processor, 128 or more MB of RAM, and a close-talk microphone and audio output device are required for speech recognition.

Installing Office XP

Before installing Microsoft Office, be sure to close any open applications and temporarily disable any antivirus programs running on your computer.

Installing Office XP is very quick and easy and will require very little decision on your part. In most cases, you can simply follow the instructions onscreen.

1. **Insert** the Office **Setup CD** into your computer's CD-ROM drive. The Office Setup Wizard will begin and the User Information box will open.

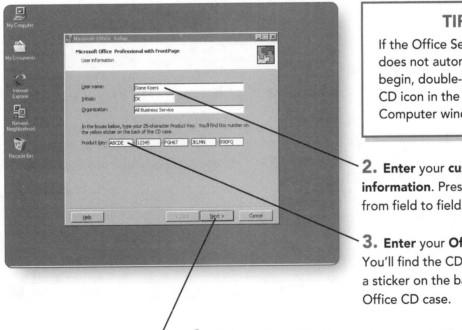

TIP

If the Office Setup Wizard does not automatically begin, double-click on the CD icon in the My Computer window.

2. **Enter** your **customer information**. Press Tab to move from field to field.

3. **Enter** your **Office CD Key**. You'll find the CD key number on a sticker on the back of the Office CD case.

4. **Click** on **Next**. The License Agreement will display.

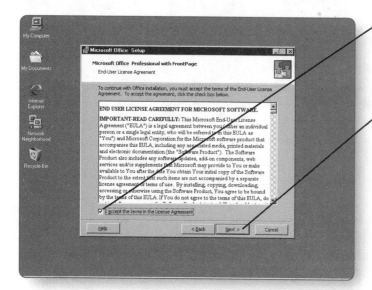

5. After reading the agreement, **click** on **I accept the terms in the License Agreement**. The option will be selected.

6. Click on **Next**. The next installation screen will display.

Installing with Default Settings

The fastest method to install is to use the Install Now utility, which will install the most commonly used features of Office, including Word, Excel, PowerPoint, Access, Front Page, and Outlook Express.

1a. **Click** on **Install Now**. The option will be selected.

OR

1b. **Click** on **Complete** if you want to install Office and all components on your system. The option will be selected.

OR

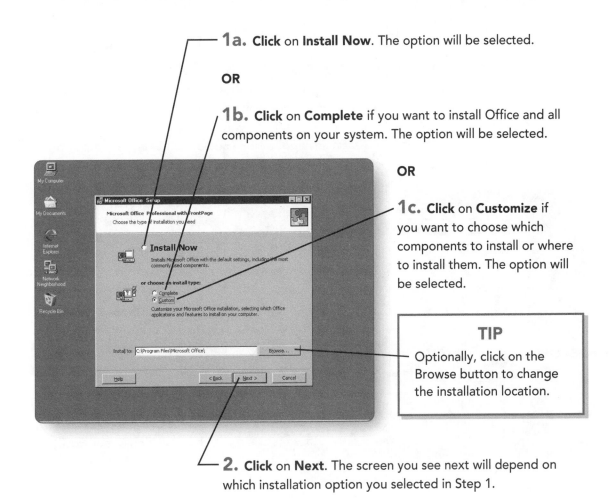

1c. **Click** on **Customize** if you want to choose which components to install or where to install them. The option will be selected.

TIP

Optionally, click on the Browse button to change the installation location.

2. **Click** on **Next**. The screen you see next will depend on which installation option you selected in Step 1.

Installing Office Components

If you are not going to be using all the components of Office XP, you can customize the installation process and elect to only install the portions you want to use.

1. **Click** on any **application** you do **NOT** want to install. The check mark will be removed from the option.

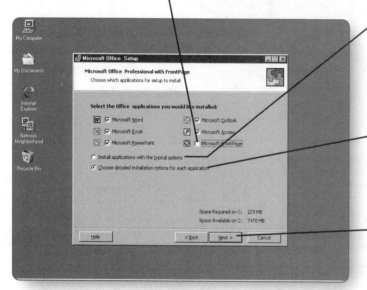

2a. **Click** on **Install applications with the typical options**. The option will be selected.

OR

2b. **Click** on **Choose detailed installation options for each application**. The option will be selected.

3. **Click** on **Next**. The screen you see next will depend on which installation option you selected in Step 2.

If you selected Step 2b previously, you'll now get the option of which components you want to install.

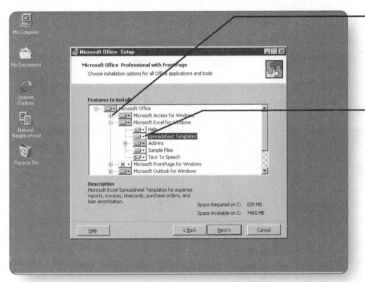

4. **Click** on a **plus sign** (+) to expand a list of features. The features listed under the category will appear.

5. **Click** on the **down arrow** (↓) to the right of the hard drive icon. A menu of available installation options for the feature will appear.

6. **Click** on the **button** next to the individual option and choose from the following settings:

- **Run from My Computer**. The component will be fully installed so you won't need the Office CD to run the application.

- **Run all from My Computer**. The selected component and all the components listed under it will be fully installed.

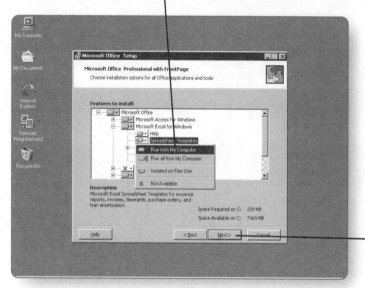

- **Install on First Use**. The first time you try to use the component, you will be prompted to insert the Office CD to complete the installation. This is a good choice for those components you're not sure you will need.

- **Not Available**. The component will not be installed at all.

7. **Click** on **Next**. The Begin installation screen will display.

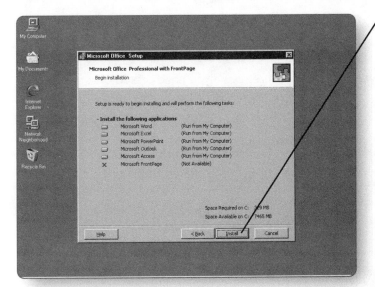

8. Click on **Install**. The installation process will begin.

NOTE

Be patient. This process could take several minutes to complete.

When installation is complete, a dialog box will open.

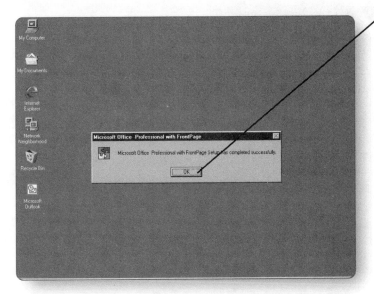

9. Click on **OK**. The installation will be complete.

When the installation is complete, you may be prompted to restart your system. Even if Office doesn't prompt you to restart, it is recommended that you restart your computer after any software installation.

Working in Maintenance Mode

Maintenance Mode is part of the Setup program. After you've initially installed Office, when you need to add or remove features, repair your Office installation, or remove the Office XP applications, you'll work in Maintenance Mode.

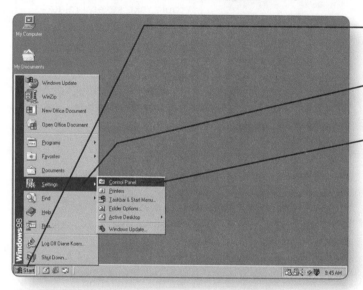

1. **Click** on **Start**. The Start menu will appear.

2. **Click** on **Settings**. The Settings submenu will appear.

3. **Click** on **Control Panel**. The Control Panel window will open.

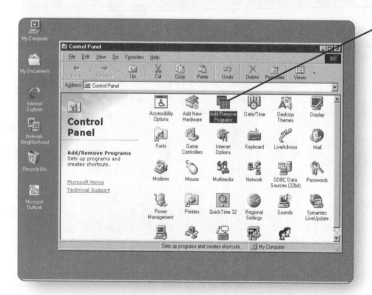

4. **Double-click** on **Add/Remove Programs**. The Add/Remove Programs Properties dialog box will open.

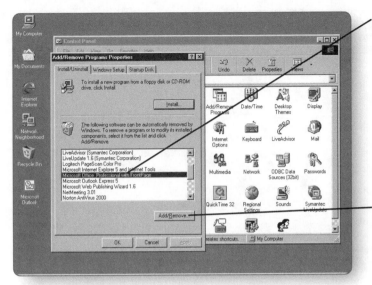

5. Click on **Microsoft Office Professional with FrontPage**. Depending on the variety of Office you have, the name you see may vary from the one shown, but the name will still contain the words Microsoft Office. The option will be selected.

6. Click on **Add/Remove**. The Office Installer will begin in Maintenance Mode.

Repairing or Reinstalling Office

If an Office application is behaving strangely, or refuses to work, most likely a needed file has become corrupted. Since you have no way of knowing which file is corrupted, you can't manually fix the problem yourself. Office, however, includes options to repair Office or completely reinstall it. Both options are available from the Repair Office button in Maintenance Mode.

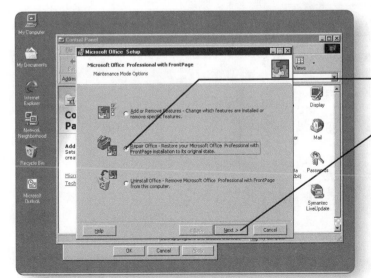

1. Click on **Repair Office**. The option will be selected.

2. Click on **Next**. An option will appear asking you what type of repair is needed.

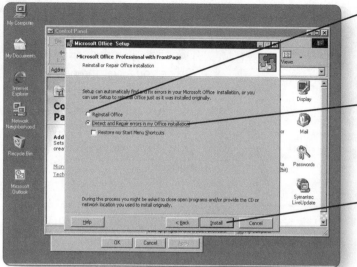

3a. **Click** on **Reinstall Office**. The option will be selected.

OR

3b. **Click** on **Detect and Repair errors in my Office installation**. The option will be selected.

4. **Click** on **Install**. The reinstall/repair process will begin. Office will attempt to fix any application errors it may find or will repeat the last installation.

When completed, a dialog box will open.

5. **Click** on **OK**. The dialog box will close.

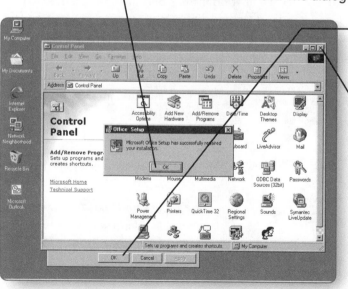

6. **Click** on **OK**. The Add/Remove Programs dialog box will close.

7. **Click** on the **Close box**. The Control Panel window will close.

Adding or Removing Components

Add or remove components also uses the Office Installer Maintenance mode.

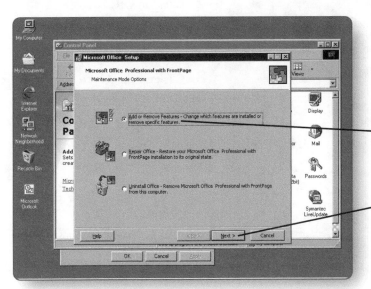

1. **Follow Steps 1-6** in "Working In Maintenance Mode" earlier in this chapter. The Office Installer will begin in Maintenance mode.

2. **Click** on **Add or Remove Features**. The Update Features window will open.

3. **Click** on **Next**. You'll be asked which features you want to add or remove.

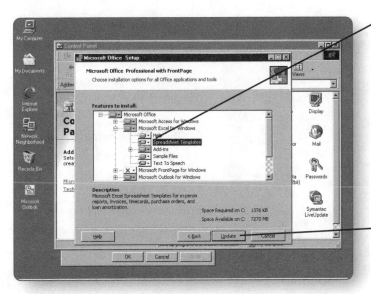

4. **Select** the **components** you want to add or remove. Selecting components to add or remove from the installation is similar to installing them.

See the previous section "Installing Office Components" for instructions on installing specific features.

5. **Click** on **Update**. The Office Installer will update Office to your selections.

When completed, a dialog box will open.

6. Click on **OK**. The dialog box will close.

7. Click on **OK**. The Add/Remove Programs dialog box will close.

8. Click on the **Close box**. The Control Panel window will close.

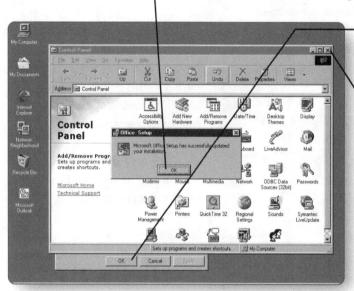

Uninstalling Microsoft Office

Again, you'll use the Windows Control Panel to remove the installation of Microsoft Office or any of its components.

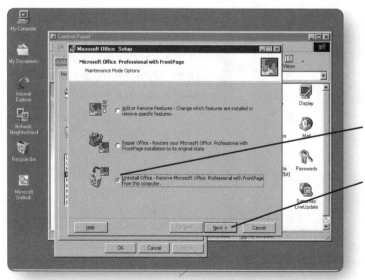

1. Follow Steps 1–6 in "Working In Maintenance Mode" earlier in this chapter. The Office Installer will begin in Maintenance mode.

2. Click on **Uninstall Office**. The option will be selected.

3. Click on **Next**. A confirmation box will open.

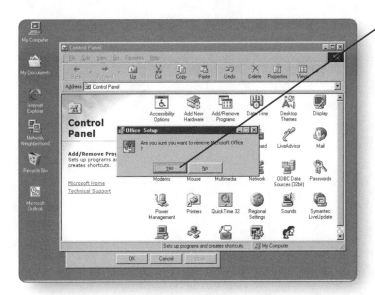

4. Click on **Yes**. The installer will begin removing the Office program and its components from your system.

When completed, a dialog box will open.

5. Click on **OK**. The dialog box will close.

6. Click on **OK**. The Add/Remove Programs dialog box will close.

7. Click on the **Close box**. The Control Panel window will close.

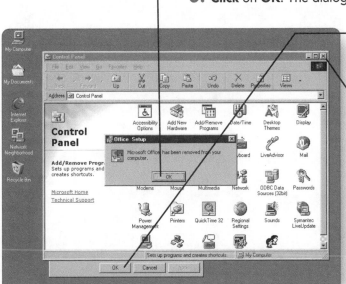

TIP

You may be prompted to restart your system. It is recommended you restart your computer after any software uninstallation.

B

Using Keyboard Shortcuts

You may have noticed the keyboard shortcuts listed on the right side of several of the menus. You can use these shortcuts to execute commands without using the mouse to activate menus. You many want to memorize these keyboard shortcuts. Not only will they speed your productivity, but they will also help decrease wrist strain caused by excessive mouse usage. In this appendix, you'll learn how to:

- Get up to speed with frequently used keyboard shortcuts
- Use keyboard combinations to edit text
- Use the speech shortcut keys

Learning the Basic Shortcuts

Trying to memorize all these keyboard shortcuts isn't as hard as you may think. Windows applications all share the same keyboard combinations to execute common commands. Once you get accustomed to using some of these keyboard shortcuts in Word, try them out on some of the other Office programs.

Getting Help

You don't need to wade through menus to get some help using the program. Try these useful keyboard shortcuts.

To execute this command	Do this
Use Help	Press the F1 key
Use the What's This? Button	Press Shift+F1

Working with Documents

The following table shows you a few of the more common keyboard shortcuts that you may want to use when working with documents.

To execute this command	Do this
Create a new document	Press Ctrl+N
Open a different document	Press Ctrl+O
Switch between open documents	Press Ctrl+F6
Save a document	Press Ctrl+S
Print a document	Press Ctrl+P
Close a document	Press Ctrl+W

Working with Text

The easiest keyboard shortcuts to learn are those that manipulate text. Try your hand at selecting, editing, and formatting text using some of the commonly used text combinations.

Selecting Text

Before you can perform any editing and formatting task on the text in your document, you need to select the text. This table shows you how to use keyboard combinations to select text. Before you begin, you need to move the cursor to the beginning of the text that you want to select.

To execute this command	**Do this**
Highlight the character to the right of the cursor	Press Shift+Right Arrow
Highlight the character to the left	Press Shift+Left Arrow
Highlight an entire word	Press Ctrl+Shift+Right Arrow
Highlight an entire line	Press Shift+End
Highlight a paragraph	Press Ctrl+Shift+Down Arrow
Select an entire page	Press Ctrl+A
Go to a specific page	Press Ctrl+G

Editing Text

Once you have selected the text to which you want to make the editing changes, apply one of the combinations in the following table.

To execute this command	Do this
Delete the character to the left of the cursor	Press Backspace
Delete the character to the right	Press Delete
Delete the word to the left of the cursor	Press Ctrl+Backspace
Delete the word to the right	Press Ctrl+Delete
Delete selected text	Press Ctrl+X
Make a copy of selected text	Press Ctrl+C
Paste the copied text	Press Ctrl+V
Spell check a document	Press the F7 key
Find text in a document	Press Ctrl+F
Replace text in a document	Press Ctrl+H
Undo an action	Press Ctrl+Z
Redo an action	Press Ctrl+Y

Formatting Text

To make your text look good, you may want to change the font, font style, or one of the many standardized paragraph styles.

To execute this command	Do this
Change the font	Press Ctrl+Shift+F
Change the size of the font	Press Ctrl+Shift+P
Make selected text bold	Press Ctrl+B
Make selected text italic	Press Ctrl+I
Make selected text underlined	Press Ctrl+U
Make selected text double underlined	Press Ctrl+Shift+D
Remove character formatting	Press Ctrl+Spacebar
Single space a paragraph	Press Ctrl+1
Double space a paragraph	Press Ctrl+2
Set 1.5 line spacing	Press Ctrl+5
Center a paragraph	Press Ctrl+E
Left align a paragraph	Press Ctrl+L
Right align a paragraph	Press Ctrl+R
Justify a paragraph	Press Ctrl+J
Left indent a paragraph	Press Ctrl+M
Right indent a paragraph	Press Ctrl+Shift+M
Remove paragraph formatting	Press Ctrl+Q

Speech Commands

In Chapter 26 "Speaking with Word," you learned how to dictate text and commands into Word. Here are a few commands to help when working with speech. These keyboard shortcuts work with the Windows key, located on the bottom row of your keyboard and feature a flying Windows logo.

To execute this command	Do this
Turn the microphone on and off	+ V
Toggle between Dictation mode and Voice Command mode	+ T
Activates Correction mode	+ C

Glossary

Alignment. The arrangement of text or an object in relation to a document's margins or the edges of a cell in a table. Alignment can be left, right, centered, or justified.

Applet. A small software program provided with Word for Windows that enables you to perform additional operations, such as WordArt, for enhanced text effects.

AutoCorrect. A feature of Word that automatically corrects common spelling mistakes (such as "teh" for "the").

AutoFormat. A Word feature used with tables. AutoFormat enables you to apply predefined sets of formatting to a table's text, rows, and columns.

AutoText. A feature of Word that enables you to save a set of text and insert it in your document by typing a word or phrase.

Bold. A style applied to text to make the font lines thicker.

Border. A visible line surrounding text or objects.

Break. An instruction embedded into a Word document that indicates a change, such as a Page Break, to start a new page.

Bullet. A symbol that precedes an item in a list. Bullets can be any shape found in a typeface, but most commonly are solid black circles.

Cell. The area in which a row and column in a table intersect.

Chart. Also called a Graph. A visual representation of numerical data.

Clip Art. A ready-made drawing that can be inserted in a Word document.

Clip Gallery. A collection of clip art, pictures, and sound files that comes with Microsoft Word.

Collect and Paste. A feature of Word that enables you to copy several selections to the Windows clipboard and paste them in a new location all at once.

Data form. A place where data, such as data used in a mail merge operation, is stored in individual records.

Data source. In a Word mail merge, the information that is used to replace field codes with personalized information, such as names and addresses.

Desktop. The main area of Windows where you can open and manage files and programs.

Dialog box. A window that appears during some procedures in Word that enables you to make settings by entering text, selecting things from lists, or checking boxes or buttons.

Drag and drop. A method of moving text or objects by clicking on an object with a mouse, dragging it to a new location, and releasing the mouse button to drop it into its new location.

Field. In a form letter, a field is a placeholder for corresponding data.

Fill. To place a color or line pattern in the interior of an object, such as a square or cell of a table.

Font. A design set of letters, symbols, and numbers.

Footer. Text entered in a footer placeholder, which is then automatically placed at the bottom of each document page.

Format. To add settings for font, font style, color, and line style to text or an object.

Format painter. A feature of Word that enables you to easily copy all formatting that's applied to one set of text to any other.

Go To. A feature of Word that enables you to enter a variety of criteria, such as page number or specific text, so that Word can place that location in your document onscreen.

Gradient. A shading effect that moves from lighter to darker in such a way that it suggests a light source shining on the object containing the gradient.

Graph. Also called Chart. A graph is a visual representation of numerical data.

Gridlines. The lines dividing rows and columns in a table.

Handle. Small squares that appear when you select an object that enable you to resize it.

Header. Text entered in a header placeholder, which is then automatically placed at the top of each document page.

Highlight. A feature that places colored highlighting onscreen for selected text.

Icon. A graphic representation used on toolbars to represent the various functions performed when those buttons are pressed with a mouse.

Indent. To set text away from a margin by a specific distance, as at the beginning of a paragraph.

Italic. A font style that applies a slanted effect to text.

Justify. One type of alignment that spreads letters on a line so that they are spaced out between the left and right margins.

Landscape. Orientation of a document so that, when printed, text runs from left to right along the longer edge of a piece of paper.

Language Bar. The toolbar used to work with the Office speech recognition feature.

Legend. In a chart, a feature that defines the relationship of the graphic symbols to the data elements for the reader.

Line style. Effects using width, arrows, and dashes that can be applied to a line.

Mail merge. A procedure in which you use a form document, insert placeholders for types of data (called fields), and merge that document with specific data to produce personalized mailings.

Margin. A border that runs around the outside of a document page, in which nothing will print.

Object. Any graphic, drawing, or other multimedia file placed within a Word document that can be selected and formatted.

Office Assistant. A feature of Word 2000 that enables you to enter questions in natural English language sentences.

Orientation. A setting that designates whether a document will print with text running along the long or short side of a piece of paper.

Outline. A hierarchy of lines of text that suggests major and minor ideas.

Page break. An instruction that can be embedded into a Word document to instruct Word to move to a new page at that point.

Page Setup. The collection of settings that relate to how the pages of your document are set up, including margins, orientation, and the size of paper on which each page will print.

Paste. To place text or an object on the Windows clipboard in a document.

Pattern. An arrangement of dots or lines that can be used to fill the center of an object.

Portrait. An orientation that places text from left to right along the shorter side of a piece of paper.

Print Layout. A view in Word that is commonly used for arranging objects on a page and drawing.

Print Preview. A Word feature that enables you to see a preview of how your printed document will look onscreen before you print it.

Protect. To make settings so that only someone with the correct password can modify a Word document.

Redo. To restore an action you have undone using the Undo command.

Right aligned. Text that is lined up with the right side of a tab setting or document margin, as with a row of numbers in a column.

Rotate. To move an object along a 360 degree path.

Ruler. An on-screen feature provided to help you place text and objects accurately on a page.

Scroll bar. A mechanism used with a mouse for navigating around a document horizontally or vertically.

Selection bar. An invisible bar along the left side of a document. When you place your mouse cursor in the bar, it can be used to select a single line or multiple lines of text.

Shading. A color that fills an object.

Shadow. A drawing effect that appears to place a shadow alongside an object.

Smart Tags. Small icons that appear throughout your document as you perform various tasks or enter certain types of text. Smart Tags are used to perform actions in Word that would normally require you to open other programs.

Sort. To arrange data alphanumerically in either ascending (A-Z) or descending (Z-A) order.

Speech Recognition. The feature of Word that recognizes and translates voice patterns to screen text.

Spelling checker. A feature of Word that checks the spelling of words in your document against a dictionary and flags possible errors for correction.

Status Bar. An area at the bottom of Word for Windows that provides information about the document, such as what page, line, and column your cursor is currently resting in.

Style. A predefined set of formats that you can apply to text all at once.

Symbol. A typeface that uses graphics such as circles, percentage signs, or smiling faces in place of letters and numbers.

Tab. A setting that can be placed along the width of a line of text that enables you to quickly jump your cursor to that setting.

Table. A collection of columns and rows, forming cells at their intersection, to organize sets of data.

Task Panes. A feature of Word that opens an additional window on the right side of the screen to assist you with various tasks.

Template. A predefined collection of formatting and style settings on which you can base a new document.

Text box. A floating text object that is created using the Word drawing toolbar; text can be entered into this object, which can be moved and resized, just like graphic objects.

Text wrap. This feature forces newly entered text to wrap to the next line when the insertion point reaches the right margin.

Tool tip. A Word Help feature that displays the name of a tool in a small box when you move your cursor over the tool.

Undo. To reverse the last action performed.

Uppercase. A capital letter.

View. In software, various displays of documents or information that enable you to perform different tasks or see different perspectives on information; for example, the Outline view in Word.

Wizard. A feature that walks you through certain procedures, producing something, such as a table, letter, or chart, based on answers you give to questions and selections made in Wizard dialog boxes.

Word count. A tally of the number of words in a document.

WordArt. An applet included with Word used for adding special effects to text, such as curving the text.

Wrap. *See* **Text Wrap**.

Zoom. To modify view settings so that what you are seeing on your screen is a percentage (larger or smaller) of a document page's actual size.

Index

* (asterisk), 33, 126
\ (backslash), 33
... (ellipsis), 8
¶ (paragraph symbol), 73
? (question mark), 33
/ (slash), 33
3-D button, 164
3-D palette, 164
3-dimensional effects, 164–165

A

Activation Wizard, 4
Add Field dialog box, 257
Add Template Page button, 341
Add to Contacts command, 71
Add to Document button, 269
Add/Delete Word(s) dialog box, 372–373
Add/Remove programs dialog box, 390–391, 394, 395
aligning
  AutoShapes, 163
  objects, 403
  paragraphs, 96
  table cells, 178–180
  with tabs, 92–93
  text, 92–93, 96–97, 403, 405
alignment buttons, 96
Animate command, 24–25

animation, 24–25, 106–107
Animations list box, 107
applets, 403
Application Close button, 48
Arrange All command, 52
Arrow keys, 18
arrows, 7, 18, 176
art. See clip art; images; WordArt
Assistant query window, 22
asterisk (*), 33, 126
Attach Template dialog box, 307
AutoComplete feature, 232–233
AutoCorrect dialog box, 126–127, 228–237
AutoCorrect feature, 228–232
  adding entries, 229
  deleting entries, 230
  described, 403
  symbols and, 122
  turning on/off, 228–229
  while typing, 231–232
AutoCorrect Options command, 126
AutoCorrect tab, 228–229
AutoFit feature. See Table AutoFit feature
AutoFormat As You Type tab, 127, 231
AutoFormat feature
  described, 403
  lists, 124–127
  table cells, 181–182

AutoFormat feature *(continued)*
  turning off, 126–127
AutoRecover feature, 34–35
AutoShapes button, 160
AutoShapes feature, 160–165
AutoSum button, 182, 183
AutoSum feature, 182–183
AutoText feature, 232–237
  adding entries, 233–235
  AutoComplete and, 232–233
  deleting entries, 236–237
  described, 403
  inserting entries with menu, 235–236
AutoText tab, 234, 236–237

B

Background Sound dialog box, 350–351
backslash (\), 33
Backspace key, 58, 85
bar charts, 206–207
Blank Document option, 37
bold text, 102, 403
borders, 190–191, 211, 403
Break command, 84
Break dialog box, 84
brightness, images, 143–144
Browse Themes button, 343
browsers. *See* Web browsers
bulleted lists, 127–130, 133
Bulleted tab, 129
bullets, 403
Bullets and Numbering dialog box, 129–131
Bullets button, 127, 128, 133
buttons. *See also specific buttons*
  alignment buttons, 96
  on toolbars, 8

C

cells, table
  aligning, 178–180
    AutoFormat feature, 181–182
    AutoSum feature, 182–183
    borders for, 190–191, 211
    described, 403
    editing text, 175, 212
    entering text, 175
    erasing partitions, 189
    formatting contents of, 178–182
    merging, 189
    totaling numbers in, 182–183
center tabs, 92
centering text, 96
Change Case command, 59
Change Case dialog box, 59–60
Change Text Direction button, 189
characters. *See also* fonts; text
  deleting, 58
  drop caps, 116–119
  special, 33, 115–122
Chart menu, 202, 207
Chart Options dialog box, 202
Chart toolbar, 198
Chart Type dialog box, 207–208
charts, 195–213
  adding title, 202
  bar charts, 206–207
  bar shapes, 206–207
  changing chart type, 207–208
  colors, 204–205
  column charts, 196–199, 207
  creating from tables, 196–199
  creating manually, 210–213
  deleting, 210
  described, 403
  editing, 201–208, 209
  fonts in, 203
  formatting text, 203
  hiding datasheets, 201
  line charts, 207
  Microsoft Graph Chart, 197, 211

patterns, 204–205
pie charts, 207
resizing, 199–200
Check grammar option, 249
Choose Assistant command, 25
Choose Profile dialog box, 280
Clear All button, 68
Clear Formatting option, 112
Click and Type feature, 14–15
clip art, 137–148. *See also* images; WordArt
    cropping, 145–146
    deleting, 148
    described, 137, 403
    inserting in documents, 138–140
    moving, 142–143
    resizing, 141–142
    searching for, 139
    wrapping text around, 146–148
Clip Gallery, 403
clipboard. *See* Office Clipboard
Clipboard task pane, 64, 67–68, 69
Clipboard toolbar, 68
Clippit. *See* Office Assistant
Close button, 12, 23, 30, 37, 68
Close command, 37
Collect and Paste feature, 403
color
    AutoShapes, 163
    charts, 204–205
    fonts, 103
    highlighting text, 104
Color Palette box, 103
column charts, 196–199, 207
Columns button, 216, 217, 222
Columns dialog box, 218–221
columns, document, 215–223
    adjusting width, 218–219
    changing number of, 217–218
    changing space between, 219–220
    creating, 216

deleting, 187
gutter widths, 219–220
inserting, 186
Print Layout view and, 86
removing, 222
vertical lines between, 220–221, 222
columns, table
    adjusting width, 176–178
    creating, 174
    entering, 171, 172
    selecting, 179
    size of, 172, 175
commands. *See also specific commands*
    dictating menu commands, 374–375
    dictation commands, 368
    keyboard shortcuts for, 398–402
    menu commands, 374–375
contact information, 71–72
contrast, images, 143–144
Control Panel, 390–395
Convert Notes dialog box, 328–329
Copy button, 64, 324
Copy command, 64
copying text, 64–65
Correction button, 371
Correction mode, 376, 402
Create New tab, 197, 211
Crop button, 145, 146
cropping images, 145–146
Customize Address List dialog box, 257–258
Cut and Paste feature, 62–63
Cut button, 62, 326
Cut command, 62
cutting text, 62

D
data
    in charts, 209
    editing, 209, 273
    in mail-merge documents, 255–263

data *(continued)*
  in mail-merge envelopes, 272–273, 274
  in records, 273
  sorting, 406
  in tables, 175
data forms, 403
data source, 404
datasheets
  creating charts, 210–213
  creating charts from tables, 197–198
  editing chart data, 209
  hiding, 201
dates, header/footer, 315–316
decimal tabs, 92
Delete key
  deleting art, 148
  deleting charts, 210
  deleting note reference marks, 327
  deleting table cells, 213
  deleting text, 56, 58, 59
deleting
  art, 148
  AutoCorrect entries, 230
  AutoText entries, 236–237
  charts, 210
  endnotes, 327
  footnotes, 327
  note reference marks, 327
  page breaks, 85
  styles, 297–298
  table cells, 213
  table columns, 187
  table rows, 187
  tabs, 94
  text, 56, 58–59
desktop, 404
Detect and Repair option, 392
dialog boxes
  Add Field, 257
  Add/Delete Word(s), 372–373

Add/Remove programs, 390–391, 394, 395
Attach Template, 307
AutoCorrect, 126–127, 228–237
Background Sound, 350–351
Break, 84
Bullets and Numbering, 129–131
Change Case, 59–60
Chart Options, 202
Chart Type, 207–208
Choose Profile, 280
Columns, 218–221
Convert Notes, 328–329
Customize Address List, 257–258
described, 404
Drop Cap, 116–119
Edit WordArt Text, 150–154
Envelope Options, 271
Envelopes and Labels, 268–269
Fill Effects, 204–205
Find and Replace, 19, 237–241
Font, 105–107, 113–114
Footnote and Endnote, 321–322, 328–329
Format, 203
Format Data Series, 204–206
Greeting Line, 261–262
Insert Address Block, 260–261, 274, 282–283
Insert Hyperlink, 351–352
Insert Merge Field, 262–263
Insert Picture, 140–141
Insert Table, 170–171
Labels Options, 278–279
Mail Merge Recipients, 259, 272–273, 281
Merge to Printer, 264, 276
New Address List, 256–258
New Style, 295–296
Object, 196–197, 210–211
Office Assistant, 25–28
Open, 38–39
Options, 35, 290–291
Page Setup, 78–83, 317

Print, 45–47, 264–265, 276–277
Save Address List, 258–259
Save As. *See* Save As dialog box
Scrolling Text, 347–349
Select Data Source, 272
Spelling and Grammar, 246–249
Symbol, 120–122
Table AutoFormat, 181
Table Properties, 191–192
Templates. *See* Templates dialog box
Templates and Add-ins, 306–308
Thesaurus, 250–251
Word Count, 242
WordArt Gallery, 150
dictation. *See* speech recognition technology
Dictation button, 367, 375
dictation commands, 368
Dictation mode, 376, 402
dictionaries, 244, 246, 247
document screen, 6
Document Template option, 305
documents. *See also* pages
    activating, 52
    adding WordArt to, 150–152
    closing, 37–38
    columns, 215–223
    creating with task pane, 36–37
    creating with toolbar, 36
    deselecting text, 58
    displaying statistics for, 242
    editing, 53, 55–73, 400
    e-mailing, 40–41
    endnotes, 319–330
    fonts. *See* fonts
    footers, 313–318
    footnotes, 319–330
    grammar checking, 244, 245–249
    headers, 313–318
    inserting clip art, 138–140
    inserting images, 140–141

line spacing, 95
mail-merge, 253–265
margins, 78–80, 96
moving between, 52–53
naming/renaming, 32, 34
navigating in, 14–19
numbering pages, 315–316
opening, 38–40
orientation, 81
page breaks, 83–85, 403, 405
paper size, 47, 82–83
previewing, 41–44
printing, 41–47
recently used, 40
recovering, 34–35
resaving, 34
saving, 32–33, 38, 48
saving as templates, 304–306
saving as Web pages, 336–338
scaling for printing, 46–47
searching in, 237–241
selecting text, 57–58, 399
setting paper size, 82–83
spell checking, 244, 246–249, 406
viewing in Normal view, 87
viewing in Print Layout view, 86
viewing multiple, 52–53
viewing styles in, 290–291
word count in, 242, 407
Zoom feature, 88–89, 407
Down Arrow key, 176
Drag and Drop feature
    described, 404
    moving art, 142–143
    moving tables, 192–194
    moving text, 66–67
Draw button, 191
Draw Table button, 174
Draw Table feature, 172–175
drawing, 160–163. *See also* images; WordArt

Drawing toolbar, 159–165
  3-dimensional effects, 164–165
  adding text to objects, 162–163
  AutoShapes, 160–165
  creating shadows, 163–164
  described, 159
  displaying, 160
Drop Cap dialog box, 116–119
drop caps, 116–119

E

Edit menu, 19
Edit Text button, 152
Edit WordArt Text dialog box, 150–154
editing
  charts, 201–209
  documents, 53, 55–73, 400
  keyboard shortcuts for, 400
  records, 273
  table cells, 175
  templates, 308–312
  text, 53, 55–73, 400
  Web pages, 346–352
  WordArt, 152–154
Effects boxes, 106
ellipsis (...), 8
e-mail button, 40
e-mailing documents, 40–41
endnotes, 319–330
  converting to footnotes, 328–330
  copying, 324–326
  creating, 320–324
  deleting, 327
  moving, 326–327
Enter key, 13, 125
Enter Page Number text box, 19
Envelope Options dialog box, 271
envelopes
  arranging data on, 274
  completing merge process, 275–277
    creating merged envelopes, 270–277
    generating single envelope, 268–269
    opening data file for, 272–273
    printing, 276–277
Envelopes and Labels dialog box, 268–269
Eraser button, 188
Exit command, 48

F

fields. *See also* records
    described, 255, 404
    mail-merge documents, 257–263
    navigating between, 256
File menu, 32, 37
files. *See* documents
Fill Effects dialog box, 204–205
fills, 404
Find and Replace dialog box, 19, 237–241
Find and Replace feature, 237–241. *see also* searching
Find command, 237–239
Find Next button, 238, 240
folders
    My Documents folder, 33
    navigating between, 39
    Templates folder, 304, 305
    Web folder, 355
Font Color button, 103
Font dialog box, 105–107, 113–114
Font drop-down list, 100–101, 153
Font Options button, 296
Font Size drop-down box, 101–102, 153
Font tab, 106, 113, 203
fonts, 99–114. *See also* text
    adding animation to, 106–107
    AutoShapes, 163
    bold, 102, 403
    changing default, 113–114
    charts, 203
    choosing type, 100–101, 296

color, 103
default text, 112–114, 292
described, 404
drop caps, 116–119
highlighting, 104
italic, 102, 404
restoring default, 112
size of, 101–102, 296
special characters, 120–122
special effects, 105–106
symbols, 120–122
underline, 102
in WordArt, 153
footers, 313–318, 404
Footnote and Endnote dialog box, 321–322, 328–329
footnotes, 319–330
converting to endnotes, 328–330
copying, 324–326
creating, 320–324
deleting, 327
moving, 326–327
form letters, 253–265
Format Data Series dialog box, 204–206
Format dialog box, 203
Format menu, 6–7, 59, 105, 106
Format Painter button, 108, 109
Format Painter tool, 108–109, 404
formatting
chart text, 203
clearing, 112
clipboard and, 69–70
copying, 108–109
described, 404
lists, 127–133
revealing, 298–299
Smart Tags and, 69–70
table cell contents, 178–182
text, 111, 401
while typing, 231–232

Formatting toolbar, 290
frames, 341
Frames toolbar, 345

G

Gallery tab, 25–26
General Templates option, 339
Go To command, 18–19, 404
gradient, 404
grammar checking, 244, 245–249
graphics. See clip art; images; WordArt
graphs, 404
Greeting Line dialog box, 261–262
gridlines, chart, 404
gutter widths, column, 219–220

H

handles, 157, 404
handwriting recognition, 376
Header and Footer toolbar, 314–318
headers, 313–318, 404
headings, table, 191–192
Help features, 21–30
keyboard shortcuts, 398
Microsoft Web site, 30
Office Assistant, 22–28, 405
searching for help topics, 22–23, 30
What's This? command, 28–29
Help menu, 28, 30
Highlight button, 104
highlights, 104, 404
HTML source code, 355
HTML tags, 336, 355
hyperlinks
turning off, 232
in Web pages, 351–352

I

I-beam, 15
icons, 404

images. *See also* clip art; WordArt
3-dimensional effects, 164–165
adding text to, 162–163
AutoShapes, 160–165
brightness, 143–144
contrast, 143–144
cropping, 145–146
in documents, 140–141
moving, 142–143
resizing, 141–142
shadows, 163–164, 406
tip box for, 139
in Web pages, 338, 352
wrapping text around, 146–148
indents, 404
Insert Address Block dialog box, 260–261, 274, 282–283
Insert button, 121, 141
Insert Clip Art task pane, 138–140
Insert Date button, 315
Insert Hyperlink dialog box, 351–352
Insert menu, 120, 235
Insert Merge Field dialog box, 262–263
insert mode, 56
Insert Page Number button, 316
Insert Picture dialog box, 140–141
Insert Table button, 172
Insert Table dialog box, 170–171
insertion point, 6, 13–16, 56
Install button, 392
Install Now utility, 384–385
installing
Microsoft Office XP, 381–395
speech function, 358
Internet Explorer, 354–355
italic text, 102, 404

J

justifying text, 96, 404

K

Keep Source Formatting option, 70
Keep Text Only option, 70
keyboard navigation, 18, 42
keyboard shortcuts, 397–402
basic shortcuts, 398
editing text, 400
executing commands, 398–402
formatting text, 401
help shortcuts, 398
navigation keys, 18, 42
selecting text, 399
speech commands, 376, 402
working with documents, 398

L

labels, 277–284
Labels Options dialog box, 278–279
Landscape option, 81, 405
Landscape orientation, 405
Language Bar, 365–366, 405
Layout tab, 317
legends, chart, 405
Less Brightness button, 144
Less Contrast button, 144
License Agreement, 383–384
line charts, 207
Line Spacing button, 95
Line Style text box, 190
lines
around table cells, 190–191
between columns, 220–221, 222
selecting, 58
spacing, 95, 296
styles, 405
links. *See* hyperlinks
lists, 123–133
AutoFormat feature, 124–127
automatic numbering and, 125

bulleted, 127–130, 133
changing styles, 129
creating with AutoFormat, 124–126
formatting, 127–133
multilevel, 130–133
numbered, 125, 127–133
outlines, 130–133
removing formatting, 133

M

magnifying glass, 42
mail merge, 405
Mail Merge Recipients dialog box, 259, 272–273, 281
Mail Merge task pane, 254–265, 270–284
Mail Merge Wizard, 254–255, 270, 277
mail-merge documents, 253–265
    adding data fields, 257–259
    creating merged envelopes, 270–277
    data source, 253, 255–256
    main document, 253, 254–255
    merge fields, 253, 260–263
    previewing mail merge, 263–265
    selecting recipients, 259–260
Maintenance Mode, Office XP, 390–395
margins, 78–80, 96
Margins tab, 79, 80, 81
Match Destination Formatting option, 70
menu bar, 5
menus. *See also specific menus*
    dictating menu commands, 354–355
    personalized, 6–8
Merge to Printer dialog box, 264, 276
merged documents. *See* mail-merge documents
merged envelopes, 270–277
merged mailing labels, 277–284
microphone
    adjusting volume, 359–360
    headset microphone, 360

keyboard shortcuts for, 376, 402
    Mute button on, 370
    position of, 359, 360, 367
    setting up, 359–360
    speaking into, 367, 368
    turning off, 370, 376, 402
    turning on, 367, 376, 402
Microphone button, 367, 370, 374
Microphone Wizard, 359–360
Microsoft Graph, 197
Microsoft Graph Chart, 197, 211
Microsoft Office XP
    adding components, 393–394
    default settings, 384–385
    installing, 383–389
    installing components, 386–389
    Maintenance Mode, 390–395
    reinstalling, 391–392
    removing components, 393–394
    repairing, 391–392
    system requirements, 382
    uninstalling, 394–395
Microsoft Outlook, 69, 71–72, 280–281
Microsoft Web site, 30
Microsoft Word
    exiting, 48
    getting started with, 3–19
    speech recognition technology, 357–376
    starting, 4
    system requirements, 382
    tools for. *See* tools
    Word screen, 5–6
Microsoft Word command, 4
Microsoft Word Help button, 27
More Brightness button, 144
More Contrast button, 144
Multiple Pages button, 43
Mute button, 370
My Documents folder, 33

N

Name option, 45
navigating
    between fields, 256
navigation
    Click and Type feature, 14–15
    between folders, 39
    Go To command, 18–19
    keyboard shortcuts, 18, 42
    on screen, 14–19
    scroll bars, 16–17
    in tables, 176
New Address List dialog box, 256–258
New Blank Document button, 36
New button, 302
New Document task pane
    templates, 302–303, 308–309, 311–312
    Web pages, 338–339
New Style dialog box, 295–296
newspaper columns. *See* columns, document
Next Record button, 264
Normal view, 87
note reference mark, 324–326, 327
Number of copies option, 45
numbered lists, 125, 127–133
Numbered tab, 130
Numbering button, 127, 128, 133
numbering pages, 315–316
numbers, AutoSum tool for, 182–183

O

Object dialog box, 196–197, 210–211
objects
    3-dimensional effects, 164–165
    adding text to, 162–163
    aligning, 403
    described, 405
objects, AutoShape, 159–165
objects, WordArt

    editing, 152–154
    inserting in documents, 150–152
    moving, 155–156
    reshaping, 154–155
    rotating, 157
Office Assistant, 22–28, 405
Office Assistant dialog box, 25–28
Office CD key, 383
Office Clipboard, 67–68
    clearing, 68
    closing, 68
    copying text, 64
    described, 62, 67
    formatted text and, 69–70
    moving text, 62
    opening, 67
    using Smart Tags with, 69–70
Office on the Web command, 30
Office Setup Wizard, 383–389
One Page button, 44
Open button, 39
Open dialog box, 38–39
Options dialog box, 35, 290–291
options, menu, 8
orientation, 405
outline numbered lists, 130–133
Outline Numbered tab, 131
outlines, 130–133, 405
Outlook. *See* Microsoft Outlook

P

Page break option, 84
page breaks, 83–85, 403, 405
Page Down key, 42, 107
Page range option, 45
Page Setup, 78–83, 317, 405
Page Setup button, 317
Page Setup dialog box, 78–83, 317
Page Up key, 42, 107

pages. *See also* documents; Web pages
  arranging text on, 91–97
  breaking, 83–85, 403, 405
  Go To command, 18–19
  previewing, 41–44
  printing range of, 45
  size, 47, 82–83
  working with, 77–89
panes, 10–12
  changing, 11
  Clipboard task pane, 64, 67–68, 69
  closing, 11–12
  creating documents with, 36–37
  described, 10, 406
  illustrated, 5
  Insert Clip Art task pane, 138–140
  Mail Merge task pane, 254–265, 270–284
  New Document task pane. *See* New
    Document task pane
  opening documents, 40
  redisplaying, 12
  Reveal Formatting task pane, 298–299
  Styles and Formatting task pane, 110–112,
    295–298
paper size, 47, 82–83
Paper tab, 82–83
Paragraph Options button, 296
paragraph symbol (¶), 73
paragraphs
  aligning, 96
  drop caps for, 116–119
  line spacing for, 95, 296
  selecting, 57
  styles, 289–299
Paste All button, 68
Paste button, 63, 65, 325, 327
pasting items, 63, 65, 405
patterns, 204–205, 405
Patterns tab, 204
personalized menus, 6–8

photographs. *See* images
Picture menu, 138, 140, 150
Picture toolbar, 143–147
pictures. *See* clip art; images
pie charts, 207
portrait orientation, 405
previewing
  documents, 41–44
  mail-merge documents, 263–265
  Web pages, 354
Print button, 44, 269
Print command, 45, 46
Print dialog box
  printing documents, 45–47
  printing envelopes, 276–277
  printing merged documents, 264–265
Print Layout view, 86, 138, 405
Print Preview button, 42
Print Preview feature, 41–44, 405
printing
  documents, 41–47
  envelopes, 276–277
  merged documents, 264–265
publishing Web pages, 355

Q

question mark (?), 33

R

Record pronunciation option, 372
records, 255, 264, 273. *See also* fields
Redo button, 61
Redo command, 61
Redo feature, 61, 405
redoing actions, 61, 405
Reinstall Office option, 392
Remove Page button, 342
Remove Split command, 5
Repair Office option, 391–392
Replace All button, 240

Replace button, 240

Replace command, 239–241

resaving documents, 34

Reset Picture button, 146

Reveal Formatting feature, 298–299

Reveal Formatting task pane, 298–299

review questions

    Part I, Creating Your First Document, 74

    Part II, Making Your Documents Look Good, 134

    Part III, Adding Visual Interest, 166

    Part IV, Using Tables, Charts, and Columns, 166

    Part V, Using the Word Tools, 285

    Part VI, Working with Long Documents, 331

    Part VII, Using Word Technology, 377

Rotate handle, 157

rotating items, 157, 405

rows, table

    adding to end of table, 184

    creating, 174

    deleting, 187

    entering, 171, 172

    headings for, 191–192

    inserting between existing rows, 185

    selecting, 179

    size of, 172, 175

ruler, 92–94, 406

S

Sample button, 362

Save Address List dialog box, 258–259

Save As dialog box

    documents, 32–33

    templates, 304–305, 309–310

    Web pages, 336–337, 353

Save As Web Page command, 336

Save button, 34

Save in drop-down list box, 33

Save tab, 35

saving

    AutoRecover feature, 34–35

    documents, 32–34, 38, 48

    documents as templates, 304–306

    documents as Web pages, 336–338

    Web pages, 352–353

scaling documents, 46–47

screen navigation, 14–19

scroll bars, 6, 16–17, 406

scroll box, 16–17

Scrolling Text dialog box, 347–349

scrolling text, Web pages, 347–349

searching. *See also* Find and Replace feature

    for clip art, 139

    for help topics, 22–23, 30

    for text, 237–241

Select All command, 57

Select Data Source dialog box, 272

selection bar, 406

Send a Copy button, 41

shading, 406

Shadow button, 163

shadow palette, 163

shadows, 163–164, 406

Shape tab, 206

shapes

    3-dimensional effects, 164–165

    AutoShapes feature, 160–165

    bar shapes, 206–207

    WordArt Shape button, 154

shortcuts. *See* keyboard shortcuts

Show at Startup option, 12

Show/Hide¶ button, 72–73

slash (/), 33

Smart Tag icon, 63, 70, 71

Smart Tags, 69–72

    adding contact information from, 71–72

    automatic numbering and, 125

    described, 69, 406

    using with clipboard, 69–70

using with Outlook, 69, 71–72

sorting data, 406

Sound button, 350–351

sound, in Web pages, 350–351

special characters, 33, 115–122. *See also* symbols

Special Characters tab, 121–122

special effects, 105–106

speech recognition technology, 357–376

creating special words, 372–373

described, 406

dictating menu commands, 374–375

dictation commands, 368

installing speech function, 358

keyboard commands and, 376

keyboard shortcuts, 402

Language Bar, 365–366

making corrections, 370–371

microphone. *See* microphone

speaking into Word, 367–375

system requirements, 382

training process, 361–365

spell checking, 244, 246–249, 406

Spelling and Grammar button, 246

Spelling and Grammar dialog box, 246–249

Split command, 50

Standard toolbar, 172

Start button, 4

statistics, document, 242

status bar, 6, 406

style area, 290–291

Style drop-down list, 294

Style text box, 292

styles

creating, 293–296

deleting, 297–298

described, 406

lines, 405

lists, 127–133

paragraphs, 289–299

viewing in document, 290–291

working with, 292

Styles and Formatting task pane, 110–112, 295–298

Symbol dialog box, 120–122

Symbol tab, 120

symbols. *See also* special characters

described, 406

displaying nonprinting, 72–73

inserting, 120–122

system requirements, 382

T

Tab button, 92

Table AutoFit feature, 178

Table AutoFormat button, 181

Table AutoFormat dialog box, 181

table grid, 172

Table menu, 170–171, 178

Table Properties dialog box, 191–192

tables, 169–194

borders, 190–191

cells. *See* cells, table

changing text direction, 189

columns. *See* columns, table

creating charts from, 196–199

creating with Draw Table feature, 172–175

creating with Table menu, 170–171

creating with toolbar, 172

described, 406

entering text, 175

formatting, 178–182

headings, 191–192

moving, 192–194

navigating in, 176

rows. *See* rows, table

totaling numbers in, 182–183

Tables and Borders button, 173

Tables and Borders toolbar, 173

tabs, 92–94, 406

Task Pane command, 12
task panes, 10–12
    changing, 11
    Clipboard task pane, 64, 67–68, 69
    closing, 11–12
    creating documents with, 36–37
    described, 10, 406
    illustrated, 5
    Insert Clip Art task pane, 138–140
    Mail Merge task pane, 254–265, 270–284
    New Document task pane. *See* New
        Document task pane
    opening documents, 40
    redisplaying, 12
    Reveal Formatting task pane, 298–299
    Styles and Formatting task pane, 110–112,
        295–298
templates, 301–312
    applying, 306–308
    described, 301, 406
    editing, 308–312
    saving documents as, 304–306
    using, 302–303
    for Web pages, 339, 341–342
Templates and Add-ins dialog box, 306–308
Templates dialog box
    creating Web pages, 339
    custom templates, 306
    deleting templates, 311
    editing templates, 308–309
    using templates, 302–303
Templates folder, 304, 305
text. *See also* characters; fonts
    adding animation to, 106–107
    adding to objects, 162–163
    aligning, 96–97, 403, 405
    applying formatting to, 111
    arranging on page, 91–97
    centering, 96
    changing case, 59–60

    in charts, 203
    clearing formatting from, 112
    copying, 64–65
    cutting, 62
    default fonts, 112, 292
    deleting, 56, 58–59
    deselecting, 58
    Drag and Drop feature, 66–67
    drop caps, 116–119
    editing, 53, 55–73, 400
    entering, 13–14
    entering in tables, 175
    entering in Web pages, 346
    formatting, 203, 401
    highlighting, 104, 404
    I-beam, 15
    identifying characteristics, 111
    inserting, 56
    insertion point, 6, 13–16, 56
    justifying, 96, 404
    keyboard shortcuts, 399–402
    moving, 62–63, 66–67
    Office clipboard, 67–68
    pasting, 63, 65
    Redo feature, 61
    scrolling text in Web pages, 347–349
    searching for, 237–241
    selecting, 57–58, 399
    special characters, 120–122
    symbols, 120–122
    Undo feature, 60, 61
    wrapping, 13–14, 406
    wrapping around art, 146–148
text boxes, 162–163, 406
Text Effects tab, 107
Text Wrapping button, 147, 155
themes, 343–345
Thesaurus, 250–251
time, header/footer, 315–316
title bar, 5, 53

Titles tab, 202

Tool tips, 406

toolbars

buttons on, 8

Chart toolbar, 198

Clipboard toolbar, 68

creating documents with, 36

creating tables with, 172

displaying, 10

Drawing toolbar. *See* Drawing toolbar

Formatting toolbar, 290

Frames toolbar, 345

Header and Footer toolbar, 314–318

hiding, 10

illustrated, 5

moving, 9

Picture toolbar, 143–147

printing from, 44

restoring, 9

Tables and Borders toolbar, 173

using, 8–10

viewing additional, 10

Web Tools toolbar, 347, 350

Word toolbar, 102

tools, 227–284

AutoComplete feature, 232–233

AutoCorrect feature. *See* AutoCorrect
feature

AutoFormat feature. *See* AutoFormat feature

AutoRecover feature, 34–35

AutoShapes feature, 160–165

AutoSum feature, 182–183

AutoText feature. *See* AutoText feature

document statistics, 242

envelope creation, 268–277

Find and Replace feature, 237–241

grammar checker, 244, 245–249

label creation, 277–284

mail-merge feature, 253–265

spell checker, 244, 246–249, 406

Table AutoFit feature, 178

Thesaurus, 250–251

Word Count command, 242

Tools button, 372

Tools menu, 35, 126

U

underlined text, 102

Undo button, 60, 61, 67, 182

Undo command, 60

Undo feature, 60, 61, 406

undoing actions, 60, 61, 67, 182, 406

Uninstall Office option, 394

Up Arrow key, 176

Update button, 393

Update Features window, 393

User Information box, 383

V

View menu, 87

View tab, 291

views

described, 406

Normal view, 87

Print Layout view, 86, 138, 405

Web Layout view, 87, 138, 338

Voice Command button, 367, 374

Voice Command mode, 376, 402

voice recognition. *See* speech recognition
technology

W

Web browsers

Internet Explorer, 354–355

saving Web pages, 337

viewing source code with, 355

viewing Web pages in, 354–355

Web folder, 355

Web Layout view, 87, 138, 338

Web Page Preview command, 354

Web Page Wizard, 338–343, 344
Web pages, 335–355
    background sound, 350–351
    creating, 338–345
    creating with Web Page Wizard, 338–343
    editing, 346–352
    entering text in, 346
    frames, 341
    hyperlinks in, 351–352
    images in, 338, 352
    location for, 340
    publishing, 355
    rearranging pages, 343
    removing, 342
    saving, 352–353
    saving documents as, 336–338
    scrolling text in, 347–349
    templates for, 339, 341–342
    themes, 343–345
    viewing in browser, 354–355
    viewing source code, 355
    Web Layout view, 87
Web Pages tab, 339
Web server, 355
Web sites
    Microsoft, 30
    naming, 340
Web Tools toolbar, 347, 350
What's This? command, 28–29
white space, 77
Window menu, 50, 51, 52
windows
    arranging, 50–51
    moving between documents, 52–53
    removing splits, 51
    restoring to maximized size, 53

    splitting, 50–51
    viewing multiple documents, 52–53
    working with, 49–53
Windows Clipboard. *See* Office Clipboard
Windows Maximize feature, 53
wizards
    Activation Wizard, 4
    described, 407
    Mail Merge Wizard, 254–255, 270, 277
    Microphone Wizard, 359–360
    Office Setup Wizard, 383–389
    Web Page Wizard, 338–343, 344
Word. *See* Microsoft Word
word count, 242, 407
Word Count command, 242
Word Count dialog box, 242
Word screen, 5–6
Word templates. *See* templates
Word themes, 343–345
Word toolbar, 102
word wrap feature, 13–14
WordArt, 149–157. *See also* clip art; images
    adding to documents, 150–152
    changing font attributes, 153
    described, 149, 407
    editing, 152–154
    moving objects, 155–156
    reshaping objects, 154–155
    rotating objects, 157
WordArt Gallery dialog box, 150
WordArt Shape button, 154
wrapping text, 13–14, 146–148, 406

Z
Zoom feature, 88–89, 407